Mental

Dr Steve Ellen is a professor of psychiatry at the University of Melbourne and the Director of Psychosocial Oncology at the Peter MacCallum Cancer Centre. He is a broadcaster on 3RRR, a weekly regular on ABC Melbourne and has written for medical journals, textbooks and print media.

Catherine Deveny is a writer, commentator and comedian. She is the author of eight books, including *Use Your Words*, *The Happiness Show*, *Free to a Good Home*, *Say When* and *It's Not My Fault They Print Them*.

Mental

Become your own
mental health expert

Dr Steve Ellen and
Catherine Deveny

HEAD
ZEUS

An Anima Book

First published in Australia and New Zealand in 2018 by Black Inc
This Anima edition first published in the UK in 2018 by Head of Zeus Ltd
This paperback edition published in 2019 by Head of Zeus Ltd

9 7 5 3 1 2 4 6 8

A catalogue record for this book is available from
the British Library.

ISBN (PB): 9781789540673
ISBN (E): 9781789540659

Printed and bound in Great Britain by
CPI Group (UK) Ltd, Croydon CR0 4YY

Head of Zeus Ltd
First Floor East
5–8 Hardwick Street
London EC1R 4RG

WWW.HEADOFZEUS.COM

Contents

PART III THE TREATMENTS

Introduction

Perhaps we should begin by introducing ourselves.

I'm Steve, a psychiatrist who has been working as a clinician for the past twenty-eight years. I've worked mainly in general hospitals helping people with medical and surgical problems – this includes pretty much everything: overdoses; depression; anxiety; eating disorders; schizophrenia; coping with trauma and illnesses, including cancer, HIV/AIDS and transplants; and anything else that might bring a person to a hospital. I also do a little research and teaching, and am a professor at the University of Melbourne. About fifteen years ago I developed an interest in health communication and since then have worked in radio, print and TV. I also suffered depression for about a year, and this helped inspire the writing of this book.

And I'm Dev, a writer, comedian, social commentator and public speaker. I've experienced lots of mental health problems and treatments – and developed a strong sense of what does and doesn't work for me. I'm grateful for the help I've received, but also concerned that getting the right help is not as easy as many people think. Also, I believe the things you do yourself and the help you get from the people you love are probably more important than all the drugs and therapy in the world. Figuring out the right formula is the real challenge.

We're both really passionate about mental health. We know what it's like to suffer from mental health issues, and how hard it is to find good, clear advice. So we wanted to put everything you need to know into one book. We were keen to make it a cracking read but also a valuable reference.

Mental is for people living with a mental illness, people with loved ones who might have a mental illness, and the curious – amateur shrinks. It's also a guide for people who come into contact with the mentally ill but feel underprepared – lawyers, the media, teachers, carers, whoever.

We hope to increase understanding, reduce stigma, and provide an accessible and readable book that covers the length and breadth of the field. Our aim is to explain mental illness in a way that is easy to understand for the intelligent layperson. No prior knowledge is required. We've tried to give both a birds-eye view *and* a peek under the bonnet. We've included the latest medical information, but we've also provided reflections on the cultural and political context of mental health care.

By reading *Mental*, we hope you'll learn about mental health, you'll think about yourself and others, you'll know what to do if life goes wrong, and you'll be inspired to seek out more information. We want this to be the beginning of a conversation, not the end. We've researched the information well, but not exhaustively. And we've tried to give you quality perspectives and opinion in a field where disagreement and dissent is the norm – without boring you senseless with endless debate.

More than anything, *Mental* is not a replacement for face-to-face help. You cannot treat yourself just with this book. But it will give you the latest knowledge and understanding in a field that is endlessly fascinating and constantly evolving.

We hope you enjoy reading *Mental* as much as we enjoyed writing it.

Steve Ellen
Catherine Deveny (Dev)

PART I
THE BIG PICTURE

What Is
Mental Illness?

How do we define mental illness? Well, there's a short answer and a long answer.

The short answer is that a mental illness is any problem with your emotions, behaviour or thinking that affects the way you function to a degree that worries you. One definition of mental health is: 'A mental illness is a health problem that significantly affects how a person feels, thinks, behaves, and interacts with other people.'

If that's enough for you, skip the rest of this chapter and have a cuppa instead. If not, read on!

The long definition of mental illness – and definitions of all the disorders that fall under its umbrella – is provided in large classification manuals, the most popular being ICD-10 – the *International Statistical Classification of Diseases and Related Health Problems, 10th Revision* – (soon to be 11th) in the UK and Europe and the DSM – the *Diagnostic and Statistical Manual of Mental Disorders* – in the USA and Australia. You'll hear of these often in the field of mental health.

Classification manuals get updated pretty regularly and there is always much debate around them. It is worthwhile knowing a little about how definitions and classification work, as they are the foundations upon which diagnosis and treatment lies.

Definitions in health care determine who gets help; who gets paid how much; and who gets all the benefits of sickness, such as time off work and sympathy. They assist CCGs – *Clinical Commissioning Groups* – in allocating resources. If you understand how these definitions work, psychiatry will make a lot more sense.

Diagnosis

Diagnosis can set you free; it can be liberating. It can provide clarity, it can be a relief – an 'aha' moment – not just for you, but for everyone around you too. Dev discovered she was dyslexic when she was thirty-eight – it was a missing part of her puzzle. She says: 'Finding out I was dyslexic was a triumph for the eight-year-old me who was constantly told she wasn't trying hard enough to learn her times tables or remember how to spell.'

But there's a downside to diagnosis too: it can be limiting. Having a label can make others prejudiced towards you. They may treat you unfairly or discriminate against you. It can also lower your expectations of *yourself* if you take it as an excuse not to live up to your full potential.

People with disabilities carry the soft
burden of low expectations.

Graeme Innes

Finally, when diagnosis is used in an accusatory fashion, it can be used to stereotype people. For instance, someone might say: 'You don't want to travel with someone who is bipolar – they'll be unreliable and unpredictable.'

However, in most cases, diagnosis is beneficial overall – it offers the potential for insight into your situation and helps you and the people around you have realistic expectations.

Classification

There are two main texts used to classify mental illnesses – the ICD-10, as mentioned above, and the DSM. The ICD-10 classifies every illness, but the DSM is just about mental illnesses. Both are used by mental health clinicians, but the ICD-10 is more commonly used in the UK.

Both manuals are mind-numbingly dull to read, but they are often referred to as medical 'bibles', simply because everything in healthcare starts with them.

The definitions of mental illnesses in these classification manuals contribute to the decisions about what health practitioners think should be treated. By implication, they say: 'These are illnesses and you should get help for them!' With physical problems – for example, a broken arm – it's pretty obvious something is wrong. Everyone will agree you should go to the doctor to have it treated. But when your problem is something that's harder to see, like anxiety, do you go to a doctor or do you seek help elsewhere first?

Health professionals take these definitions and design

treatment pathways for the various conditions. In the UK, NICE – the *National Institute for Health and Care Excellence* – established in 2002, provides evidence-based guidance and quality standards to support the identification, treatment and management of mental health conditions in both adults and children. 'If you have a mental illness (say, anxiety), as defined by the definition in these manuals and guidelines, this treatment should ensure you improve by a significant degree in a reasonable time frame.'

The insurance industry uses both NICE and classification manuals to assign payments and determine what treatments they will cover officially. They say: 'If you have anxiety as defined by this definition, you are entitled to a certain amount of treatment privately, under your policy.'

This means that people with vested interests can use classification to push agendas. For example, the private health industry and drug companies love broad and inclusive definitions, because they mean more people get diagnosed and they make more money – disease mongering has become a serious concern. But there are also many skilled, brilliant and passionate health professionals who push for broad definitions so more people get help. On the other hand, organisations that pay for health care (like insurers) often argue for narrower and stricter definitions to limit costs.

It's not a perfect system, but the reality is that definitions set the agenda for what gets treated and what gets funded.

What counts as a mental illness?

In psychiatry, we mostly use the term 'disorder' rather than 'illness' or 'disease'. The term 'illness' is too vague – no one agrees on what it means! And 'disease' implies there is some underlying pathology – a disruption in the structure or function of the body. Since we don't really know why we have mental illnesses, and since for most problems no pathology has been clearly found, we avoid using the word disease.

No matter how you define mental illness, there are two key problems: how do we define normal behaviour and how bad does a problem need to be to be called a disorder?

Everyone has their own sense of what is normal. There is no universal yardstick. We are all crazy in our own way. We view life through a lens that has been constructed from our own past experiences. This includes our personality, our culture, our beliefs (especially religious beliefs) and the era we live in.

Until 1973, the DSM included homosexuality as a disorder. This was a judgement; society regarded homosexuality as abnormal. Multiple things happened to change this view. Gay activists began protesting. More and more people came 'out of the closet', suggesting homosexuality wasn't as unusual as initially thought. Research backed this up. In 1973, homosexuality was officially removed from the DSM. Treatments like conversion therapies are now more or less extinct in medicine, although some religious groups still think it's possible to 'pray away the gay'.

Hoarding disorder, on the other hand, is a recent addition to the DSM. Hoarding went from being an insult to becoming a formal diagnosis. People who have a conscious, ongoing urge to accumulate possessions, as well as corresponding feelings of anxiety whenever those possessions get thrown away, can now be diagnosed and treated. Until 2013, when the latest edition of the DSM came out, hoarding was an experimental category for further research. Times change; diagnoses change.

One of the most recent disorders to be included in the DSM is gambling disorder. That doesn't mean everyone who gambles has a disorder. In order to be diagnosed with it, someone must have had at least four key symptoms of persistent and recurrent gambling behaviour, associated with impairment or distress, over a period of at least twelve months.

With symptoms we all experience at some stage in our lives, such as sadness or anxiety, the problem becomes one of degrees – how much is too much? These are human experiences and they all occur on a continuum – there is no clear cut-off between a normal amount and an abnormal amount of worry or sadness, and there never will be.

Psychiatry often gets criticised for being vague and subjective, but the problem of defining normality exists for all health issues. When does high blood pressure get defined as hypertension? When does a fast-growing cell get defined as cancer? At what blood sugar level should diabetes be diagnosed?

To get around the problem of normal versus abnormal in psychiatry, a few simple steps are employed. First, we take a group of symptoms that seem to cluster together to form a syndrome. For example, in depression we have lowered mood, lack of enjoyment in everyday activities, weight loss, altered sleep, agitation, fatigue, guilty ruminations, poor concentration and suicidal thoughts. Then we set a cut-off point – for depression, we say you must have five of the listed nine symptoms. Then we refer to a minimum timeframe – for depression, it is a minimum of two weeks of these symptoms. Finally, we say the symptoms must either cause significant distress or impair the person's functioning in some way – for example, interfere with their work, relationships or education.

Symptoms + a timeframe + distress or impairment = *a disorder*

But there is wriggle room. In clinical practice, the disorders are not meant to be used rigidly. If someone is assessed as being on the edge of a disorder, clinical judgement is required.

There are many occasions in clinical practice where a person's problems don't fit snugly into a category and judgement and experience are required to make a diagnosis and form a treatment plan. Classification systems provide a basis but are not sophisticated or flexible enough to take in all aspects of human experience.

Categories of disorders

The current version of the DSM (it's up to the fifth edition: DSM-5) lists twenty major categories of psychiatric disorder and about 300 separate disorders. The major categories are:

- neuro-developmental disorders, such as intellectual disability, autism and learning disorders
- schizophrenia and psychotic disorders
- bipolar disorder

- depressive disorders, including seasonal affective disorder and grief
- anxiety disorders, including panic disorders and phobias
- obsessive-compulsive disorder
- trauma and stress-related disorders
- dissociative disorders, such as dissociative identity disorder, which used to be called multiple personality disorder
- somatic disorders, which includes a broad group of problems that present with prominent physical symptoms but are thought to have a primarily psychological basis
- feeding and eating disorders, such as anorexia
- bed wetting
- sleep–wake disorders, such as insomnia and narcolepsy
- sexual dysfunctions, such as problems with arousal
- gender dysphoria
- disruptive, impulse-control and conduct disorders
- substance-related and addictive disorders
- neurocognitive disorders, such as dementia and delirium
- personality disorders
- paraphilic disorders, such as fetishes that cause the person distress or impairment
- medication-induced disorders (disorders that result from the side effects of medication).

It's interesting to ponder what the ICD and DSM categories will look like in fifty years' time. If history is anything to go by, there are bound to be some categories on this list that have been removed, and other common behaviours or ideas today that are considered disorders in the future – maybe misogyny, maybe racism, maybe even religion!

The diagnostic hierarchy

The ICD and DSM often get criticised for being a cookbook approach to human suffering. With approximately 300 disorders described in the DSM, psychiatry can simply look like a giant list of recipes, where symptoms are ingredients and you work backwards to decide which recipe fits the meal in front of you.

It is not meant to work like this – there are huge overlaps between the various disorders and there will always be grey zones where a person could be diagnosed with several disorders. So there need to be some guiding principles for determining which primary disorder to diagnose.

A famous problem-solving principle known as 'Occam's razor' is often applied to medical diagnostic decisions: among competing hypotheses, the one with the least assumptions should be selected. In other words, choose the simplest answer to a problem. In medicine, this means choose the one diagnosis that explains the most symptoms.

The diagnostic hierarchy helps doctors select the diagnosis that explains the most symptoms. It's a guide that is embedded into the classification systems. It is a hierarchy of the key psychiatric disorders, whereby the disorder highest in the hierarchy takes diagnostic precedence over those disorders below it in the hierarchy.

Organic disorders (Key symptoms: memory impairment, decreased conscious state)

↓

> **Psychotic disorders** (Key symptoms: delusions, hallucinations, thought disorder)
>
> ↓
>
> **Mood disorders** (Key symptoms: depression or mania)
>
> ↓
>
> **Anxiety disorders** (Key symptom: anxiety)
>
> ↓
>
> **Behaviour disorders** (Key symptoms: sleep, appetite or behavioural change)

Let's look at some examples. If a patient has an organic disorder such as dementia or delirium, they will have memory impairment or a decreased conscious state. They may also have symptoms from all the other disorders below in the hierarchy: for example, hallucinations, depression, anxiety and behavioural change – this is completely expected in organic disorders.

If a patient has a psychotic disorder such as schizophrenia, then they must have either hallucinations, delusions or thought disorder, as well as anything below it in the hierarchy (such as depression or anxiety), but they should *not* have any symptoms of an organic disorder – their memory and conscious state should be normal.

Similarly, if a patient has a mood disorder – for example, depression – they may have anxiety and behavioural symptoms, but they should not have psychotic symptoms or organic symptoms.

Right down the bottom of the hierarchy, if a patient has a behaviour disorder such as anorexia or insomnia, or the various childhood behaviour disorders, they should not have organic, psychotic, mood or anxiety symptoms. If they did have any of those symptoms, a disorder further up the hierarchy should be considered first.

While it is a very useful tool, there are many exceptions to the principles of the diagnostic hierarchy. Just like the criteria for each disorder, the diagnostic hierarchy (which Dev calls the 'crazy ladder') is not meant to be used rigidly. If a person has prominent depression over a long period and only mild and occasional psychotic symptoms, you would not automatically diagnose a psychotic disorder first; you would consider the circumstances and use clinical judgement.

Finally, some people have more than one disorder – called co-morbidity. A common example of co-morbidity is having both depression and anxiety. For example, if a person had an anxiety disorder such as panic disorder for two years, and then develops depression, we would probably diagnose both disorders. If, however, they had panic attacks and depressive symptoms for roughly the same amount of time, we would probably just diagnose depression (it's highest on the hierarchy) and not diagnose panic disorder unless after successfully treating the depression the panic attacks remained.

If this seems very confusing, don't be surprised. Even experienced clinicians take years to get the hang of the diagnostic hierarchy.

Classification is not the be all and end all. If you had a choice between someone simply using a classification system to make a diagnosis and an experienced clinician assessing you for a diagnosis, you'd choose the experienced clinician every time.

Diagnosis is as much an art as a science.

2

What Causes Mental Illness?

B ooks on the causes of mental health abound. But to be honest, not much is known with certainty and knowing the cause of a disorder is not as clinically helpful as you'd expect – even when we strongly suspect a particular cause, such as brain pathology or past events – we usually can't do much to change it, we can only deal with the consequences. Psychiatrists in training spend huge amounts of time learning the various aetiological theories (causes) of mental illness, but once they start to practise in the field, this knowledge tends to fade into the background. Learning to communicate effectively, understand people's plights and problems and know the best treatments to offer take priority.

The majority of treatments come from trials of what works – not from theories about causation. For example, most drugs are found more by chance than deliberate effort, and then trialled in people for various conditions. In psychiatry, most of the time we don't know how the drugs work. They give us clues to causation because we study the biological effects of the drugs.

But these are only clues – we don't understand brain biology well enough to know all the effects of the drugs. ECT (electro-convulsive therapy) is another example – we know it treats depression, but have very little idea how it does so – and it has barely advanced our knowledge of causation at all.

That's not to say understanding what causes mental illness isn't important – some of the best treatments and greatest advances come from solid scientific research into what makes humans tick and what causes them to fall off the rails.

For *Mental*, we decided to be pragmatic in explaining the theories of causation in mental illness and confine it to just one chapter – this one! We decided to give you a flavour of how we understand mental illness, rather than try to list all the possible causes of each mental illness. Discussing the causes of every illness would take too long and bore you unnecessarily. We hope this book is just the beginning of your search for understanding, and that it inspires more personal research and exploration.

In order to discuss causes, we've started with some general information about how we understand cause and effect in mental health, and then we look in more depth at the example of depression to see how this works in practice.

Different kinds of causes

There are so many ideas and theories about the origins of mental illness, it can be hard to find some structure and order in them. But famous US psychiatrist George Engel offered one possible structure when he introduced the biopsychosocial model as a way to help understand how biology, psychology and social factors interact to produce illness. It's by far the most accepted model in mental health.

Engel's model was introduced to counteract the biomedical model, which attributes all disease to biological factors. The biomedical model is also sometimes called the disease model – the idea that illness results from biology gone wrong.

In the biopsychosocial model, factors can be roughly considered to be either biological, psychological or social. Some factors might easily fit into more than one category. Biological factors include medical illnesses, drugs, chemical changes in the body and hereditary factors. Psychological factors include our childhood experiences, life experiences such as abuse or trauma, and the way we experience losses. Social factors include our relationships, our stressors and how we are connected in society (isolation is a big contributor to mental health problems).

When you search for the causes (or aetiology) of any particular mental illness, you will often find them divided into biological, psychological and social causes. The following table is a brief example of how this might be done for a few different disorders. Each factor has an evidence base, but it may or may not turn out to be true (all theories of causes in mental health are in their infancy), and may or may not be at play in any given individual. The table opposite gives some examples only – there are many other theories that have not been included.

Each factor has some research behind it that establishes the degree of scientific certainty with which the theory is held. This is called the 'evidence base'. Some factors have a strong evidence

	Biological	Psychological	Social
Depression	• Genetics • Brain chemistry • Physical illness • Aging • Gender	• Losses • Trauma • Personality style	• Isolation • Social disadvantage • Lack of meaningful relationships • Abuse • Life events
Anxiety	• Brain chemistry • Genetics • Physical illness • Drugs – stimulants (caffeine, amphetamines etc.)	• Personality traits • Coping skills • Cognitive style (thinking patterns) • Unconscious mechanisms • Stress	• Abuse • Early parenting styles • Social disadvantage
Schizophrenia	• Genetics • Abnormal brain anatomy or chemistry • Fetal problems – low weight, infections, lack of oxygen, and more • Abuse of drugs • Infections and immune problems		• Social adversity • City living • Unsupportive, dysfunctional relationships

	Biological	Psychological	Social
Eating disorders	• Genetics • Nutritional deficiencies • Hormonal abnormalities	• Negative body image • Poor self-esteem • Personality traits such as perfectionism	• Childhood abuse • Societal emphasis on weight and body image • Dysfunctional family relationships • Athletic-oriented sports • Stressful life changes • Peer pressure • Cultural norms

base, from years of research all around the world. Research into other factors is in its infancy and is not much more than a good educated guess.

Over the years, different theories come in and out of vogue, depending on what research is occurring and how different experts interpret the evidence. There has been an explosion of biological research in the last few decades, largely because new tools (such as genetic techniques and brain imaging) have improved so much. That doesn't mean the other theories are wrong; it just means we re-evaluate how we understand mental illness according to the science of our time.

Who knows? Tomorrow someone might discover something that throws every previous theory on its head. We can only hope!

What causes depression?

Depression is a great example to drill down into. It's well studied, and there are many competing theories about what causes it.

At the end of the day, the unfortunate truth is that we simply do not understand as much as we'd like about the causes of depression. We have lots of theories, but none are even close to satisfactory at this point in the history of medical science. You can bet that by the time your kids grow up, the theories will be completely different to the ones of today.

Nevertheless, here are a few current ideas.

Biological causes

Brain chemistry

Changes in brain chemistry have long been linked to depression. As far back as the 1960s, scientists noticed that depressed people had lower levels of certain chemicals in their brains, especially neurotransmitters and the neuroreceptors they interact with. In a nutshell, neurones (nerve cells) release chemicals (neurotransmitters) to trigger other neurones, which have neuroreceptors on their surface. It's a bit like a lock and key – one cell releases keys that unlock and trigger other cells.

Many people will tell you that depression is due to chemical changes in your brain. They might tell you that depression is due to a lack of serotonin or noradrenaline activity. This is not the complete truth. What is true is that in depressed people, on average, there are lower amounts of serotonin and noradrenaline. This is part of the biology of depression – but it isn't necessarily the *cause* of depression. One of the really common mistakes we make when talking about depression is to mix up the *biology* of the disorder with the *cause*.

There are literally thousands of tiny steps in the biology of depression, and we probably understand about a third of them – if that. For instance, if you find yourself depressed after a particular incident, such as an assault or losing your job, your serotonin levels will probably go down. Similarly, if your depression happens out of the blue for no apparent reason, you may have lower levels of serotonin. But you might be depressed and have no changes in serotonin levels at all. Serotonin is a small part of the biology of depression, but is not itself the cause.

The reason this distinction is important is because these chemical changes get used as an excuse by some groups to encourage people to take antidepressant medications, and this is just plain wrong. You may choose to take antidepressants, but that choice should be made according to your treatment preferences and the severity of your symptoms – not according to a presumed cause that we cannot know for sure is the true cause in any one individual.

Genetics

We know genetic factors play a part in depression, but we do not yet know how important they are. Some research suggests the overall loading of genetics in depression is about 40 per cent (so about 60 per cent is due to life experiences). We know that for some types of depression the risk may be particularly high: for example, in bipolar-type depression there is a particularly strong genetic relationship – the current estimates (and they are only estimates) suggest that if you have an identical twin brother or sister with bipolar disorder your chance of having it is around 50 per cent; if one parent or sibling has it, your chance is 10 per cent; and if two parents have it, 40 per cent. This is a lot higher than the average chance for any of us having it, which is about 1.5 per cent.

For normal (non-bipolar) depression, the figures are less clear. It appears that if you have a parent or sibling with clinical depression, the risk of you having it is two or three times greater.

So far no one has been able to identify a specific gene associated with depression.

A large-scale study in 2016 compared the genetic maps of over 75,000 people with depression to over 230,000 without depression – they found fifteen regions in the genome that seemed to be associated with depression. How these genes work and interact with life experience to cause depression is unknown. But the more of them you have, the higher your risk.

Studies like this one are important, because they give further clues about what to study to understand depression. Once we understand these genes better, we'll know more about the biology of depression, which in turn may lead to better treatments.

It's also important to know that just because you have genes that predispose you to depression, it does not mean you will get depressed. There is an important concept to know: epigenetics. In the past, your genes were seen as your destiny. But the latest evidence suggests this is not even close to being the case – your destiny is the result of your genes interacting with your environment (epigenetics). So how you express your genes depends on what happens in your life.

In summary, all of those figures above are pretty useless, at least until we understand what does and doesn't turn your genetic risk into a reality – and we are not at that point yet. So if your genes suggest a high risk of depression, you should not assume you will get it. If anything, you should just take it to mean that you need to be careful – take your mental health seriously, have a plan in place in case you do feel overly sad, and talk to your doctor – but whatever you do, don't start to think it means you will get depressed – the science simply does not support that conclusion.

Physical illness

Being sick increases your chances of depression significantly. This is especially true for any illness that is chronic, causes pain, involves the brain or may lead to death. We can't say exactly why this is so. Perhaps it's the biological disturbance caused by illness, perhaps the side effects of treatment, perhaps the psychological stress of illness – or, most likely, a combination of all those factors.

Gender

Women are roughly twice as likely to get depression as men. No one really knows why. Men are twice as likely to have other problems, such as drug and alcohol addictions, so maybe women just express their distress differently to men? Maybe they are more emotionally articulate? Maybe there is less social pressure on women to deny their depression, so it's just more heavily reported in women? Or is it a phenomenon related to being a woman – maybe genetic, or maybe due to societal attitudes and the experiences of women in patriarchal societies? We don't know, but the numbers are real. Twice as many women report depression, but the suicide rate is known to be higher in men.

Age

The risk of depression increases with age. There are peaks and troughs along the way, but overall the older we get the higher the risk. While we've included this in the biology section because age results in so many biological changes, you could equally refer to age as a factor in the psychology or social section.

Psychological causes

Psychological factors are important in depression – that's a tautology. Depression is classed as a psychological disorder, so of course psychological factors figure prominently. But what we mean is that certain types of events – especially losses and trauma – are more likely to lead to depression.

Losses include the loss of a relationship, status, money – and much more. Relationships are the most significant losses, particularly the loss of a close relative – a child, parent or partner. If you experience such losses at a young age, it seems to be even more damaging. And the more losses you have, the greater the risk of depression.

Trauma has a similar effect to losses. After any major trauma, about 15 per cent of people get a psychological problem within a year; of this number, roughly half get depressed and half get post-traumatic stress disorder. Traumas are defined as life-threatening events robberies, assaults, car accidents or war. Some traumas have higher psychological risks than others – those where support afterwards is lacking, those that are repetitive, and those in which there is less of a sense of personal control are the riskiest. Also, the risk seems to be additive – meaning each trauma you experience adds to your risk of developing depression or PTSD.

Personality is also an important factor. Certain personality types are more or less prone to depression. People who are anxious, shy, self-critical or particularly sensitive to rejection tend to suffer more from depression.

Social factors

Social and psychological factors overlap. Social factors are our relationships, our employment status, our financial status, our housing circumstances and so on. To most people it is pretty obvious that the quality of our life circumstances would affect whether we get depressed or not. Despite this, researchers struggle to understand exactly what mechanisms are involved, and how social factors interact with our personalities and genetic make-up.

The biggest social factors contributing to depression are isolation, a lack of meaningful relationships, social disadvantage and abuse. All of these increase the risk of depression.

The significance of abuse as a contributing factor has been brought to light only in the last few decades. Until the 1980s, abuse was thought to be relatively uncommon, and when it did occur, especially to children, it was not thought to be a major problem. Children were thought to be very resilient. But in the '80s, studies emerged suggesting abuse, especially sexual abuse (but also physical and emotional abuse), was far more common than originally thought. Adult men and women started to share their stories, previously kept secret, and the effects of abuse on their lives. Researchers started to look at it more carefully. To everyone's horror, abuse has turned out to be common, widespread and perpetrated by a range of different groups. It became clear that it is a major cause of depression. As the studies progressed, abuse has also turned out to be a major cause of many other psychiatric problems as well – addictions, personality problems and schizophrenia – and it has been found to be a key contributor to suicide.

Another significant social issue that may contribute to depression is stress caused by life events. Life events include things such as marriage, divorce, the birth of a child, a significant change in financial or employment circumstances – all of these trigger different emotional states. Some events are affected by our behaviour and some are independent (for example, you may have a car crash because you are a risk-taker and you speed, or it may be totally random because someone else crashed into you). All sorts of life events can trigger depression, especially events involving threat, loss, humiliation or defeat. After big life events, your risk of depression increases approximately fivefold in the following year.

Can you ever pick the exact cause in an individual?

Most of our knowledge about the causes of depression comes from studying large groups of people. Whether we can use this to help us understand a particular individual is debatable. We can brainstorm which events and experiences and brain chemicals might be causing depression in a particular person, but it's all from group studies – we can't say anything much with certainty. We can just talk about overall risks and probabilities.

We can't measure the level of serotonin in your brain and say anything meaningful about whether you are depressed or not. We can't assess the trauma you suffered and know whether you will get depressed or not: some people do, some people don't.

It's fair to say that after all the decades of research so far on the causes of depression, we still don't understand why some people get depressed, others get anxious and others again remain well. The researchers keep saying we are on the verge of a breakthrough, but we really don't even understand the basics of why humans have emotions, let alone why we have extremes of emotions.

So if you see a professional for depression, they may hypothesise about the causes, but it will just be an educated guess. Of course, it's human nature for people to want answers from their clinicians and it's understandable that clinicians want to provide answers. But, if you are depressed, the truth is no one can say why. Clinicians sometimes claim they do know, but they are misrepresenting their intuition as fact.

While it is important for us to search for answers and meaning, we need to accept that in the field of mental health we are still in the scientific dark ages. Therefore, by all means, let's talk and theorise and search for answers, but remember to keep an open mind. We just don't know enough yet.

What we do know is a little bit about how to manipulate emotions – how to ease depression or mania or anxiety. And as a first step, perhaps knowing a bit about how to *fix* a problem is more important than knowing exactly what caused it. Maybe that will come in the future.

3

Getting Help

Of course life is not meant to be all spring sunshine and balmy nights. We all have down times – including times when we are stressed, depressed, anxious, eating badly, sleeping poorly, feeling tired, arguing with partners and not enjoying work.

But the bad times shouldn't outweigh the good times. If they are, it might be time to seek help.

How affected do you need to be to get help?

Most people have struggled with this question at some stage. Recognising you have a problem can be confronting. It is often family and friends who are the first to notice something is not right, and at first their advice to get help can seem interfering or intrusive (and sometimes it really is!).

A good place to start is to ask yourself a series of questions about your general outlook on life:

- Am I happy with myself?
- Am I enjoying life?

- Are the things that usually make me happy no longer fun?
- Are my relationships satisfying?
- Is my work suffering?
- Is my physical health being affected by my mental health?

Consider how you are physically:

- Am I sleeping well and feeling reasonably refreshed in the morning?
- Has my weight changed considerably recently?
- Am I using alcohol or drugs to deal with stress?
- Can I concentrate?

It's also wise to do a little reading of some reputable mental health sites on the internet. You can even look up your symptoms and get a sense of what might be going on for you.

You might be wondering how much 'bad' is normal. If you need a rule of thumb, the bad times shouldn't last more than a month at a time. Also ask yourself these questions:

- Are your bad feelings ruining your everyday life?
- Can you laugh, can you socialise and can you work?
- Look at a photo of yourself from a year ago – do you feel like you're the same person?

If, after considering your answers, you are still unsure, then talk to someone you trust to get a second opinion. Ask a friend – someone who you feel understands you. Or ask your general practitioner (GP). A GP is especially good, as they'll be independent and will know the right questions to ask. While friends know you best, they can also be excessively swayed by their own experiences. And let's face it, they're not trained. Be warned:

there is a possibility that friends or family may respond in a way that reflects *their* problems and needs. They're not impartial; they're in a relationship with you.

Can you be so unwell you don't realise it?

The problem with the above advice is it implies you are well enough to be your own judge. But sometimes mental health problems sneak up on you and you don't realise until it's too late.

Here are some red flags that indicate you need to see a GP:
- thoughts of suicide
- inability to work
- not being able to stop worrying
- feeling like you can't turn your brain off
- feeling like there is no way out of your problems
- being scared to leave the house
- feeling like everyone has turned on you
- having lost more than 5 kilograms of weight unexpectedly
- sleeping poorly for more than a couple of weeks
- crying frequently.

Using drugs or alcohol to feel better or in a manner that suggests problems (failed attempts to cut back, others getting annoyed at your use, feeling guilty about your use, taking more to avoid the symptoms of withdrawal).

If you have any of these, book in to see your general practitioner as soon as possible.

Why start with your GP?

GPs are usually the best starting point. They have about five to eight years of training in all aspects of health, can detect physical problems (that may impact on psychological symptoms), have usually done at least two months of psychiatry in their undergraduate training (and often more as a graduate) and are aware of all the different places you can be referred for specialist support.

A GP will ask about your symptoms and help you figure out what problem you are dealing with. The good ones will be aware of the local options available for mental health treatment. Some GPs even have a mental health clinician that visits their practice.

The catch is that some GPs are bad with mental health. Some are prejudiced against this area of health care and openly say they hate it and avoid mental health problems. Others have poor people skills and miss psychiatric problems. On the other hand, there are many GPs who love mental health, are naturally gifted at it and do extra training to support their interest. 'So how do I know if my GP is good at mental health?' we hear you ask. Simple: use your words. Ask them, 'Are you good at mental health?' If the answer is no, ask them whether a colleague in the practice would be a better fit.

The other risk to consider with doctors of all types is they sometimes over-medicalise. For example, they take a problem (such as shyness, grief or boisterous kids) and give it a medical diagnosis (social anxiety disorder, depression or attention deficit disorder). They take a purely medical approach – like give medications. Sometimes they might be right, but mostly they are oversimplifying things in a misguided attempt at helping.

The key is not to be put off by a bad experience when trying to get mental health care (or any health care for that matter). Find a GP who is a good fit; someone you trust – a good GP is worth their weight in gold.

Mainstream or alternative approach?

Keep an open mind: both mainstream and alternative approaches to mental health can be beneficial. But many people will dismiss an entire range of possible solutions. Either they don't want to listen to 'hippy, dope-smoking alternative health nuts' or they wouldn't be caught dead taking advice from 'suit-wearing, corporatised bureaucrats with stethoscopes'. However, most people fall somewhere in between. They usually start with the approach that most closely reflects their beliefs, but their search for help needn't stop there.

All treatments, whether they are mainstream or alternative, have an evidence base to justify their use. Mainstream treatments are simply those with an evidence base that meets basic standards of science (essentially, that a study into its effectiveness has been published in a peer-reviewed journal, uses statistics to measure the treatment effect, takes measures to avoid bias from the researchers, and has been reproduced by independent researchers in a different lab). There is often evidence that alternative treatments are effective, but the evidence base might not meet scientific standards.

To make matters even more complicated, there is good evidence that the more you believe in something, the more a treatment approach aligns with your philosophies and belief systems, the more likely it is to work. Perhaps this is because you *want* it to work more so you make it work. You're more motivated, you try harder, and you find it easier to make the changes suggested in that treatment.

Choosing an alternative treatment that you trust over a mainstream treatment you don't trust could therefore be wise, even from a scientific viewpoint. Confusing, isn't it!

Then there are the placebo and nocebo effects to consider.

Placebo is Latin for 'I will please'. The placebo effect refers to the well-established observation that up to a third of people improve on a drug or treatment that they are told will help them but is in fact inert, meaning it has no effect! The reasons are unclear, despite lots of research, but it seems to relate to the belief that you are making an effort to get well – this does something to the body that is healing.

In contrast, *nocebo* means 'I will harm' in Latin. In the nocebo effect, an inert drug or treatment, which the patient believes will be effective, results in side effects or worsening of the symptoms. It is not as well proven or common as the placebo effect, but it does occur, and is similarly difficult to explain.

The point is that doing something you believe in seems to help – even if science cannot yet explain it.

As science marches on, more and more alternative therapies are undergoing the rigorous and expensive evaluations required to meet the standards of mainstream medicine. Evidence of the effectiveness of therapies such as yoga, hypnosis, nutritional supplements and exercise programs is being gathered and they are moving into the mainstream.

The downside to the alternative health market is that it's poorly regulated. Mainstream medicine has lots of regulations to protect you – treatments must be safe, the scientific evidence must be extensive, and the benefits claimed must be realistic and honestly stated. Some alternative health treatments have no such protections, so outlandish claims can be made and safety is not guaranteed. It's a lucrative industry, so as well as attracting good people, it also attracts charlatans who like to hide in the shadows of poor regulation.

Whichever approach you take, keep these tips in mind:

1. Avoid excessively expensive treatments; they are often a clue to a scam.

2. Avoid 'gurus' who claim unique abilities. People who claim special powers are usually lying.

3. Testimonials or reports from happy customers are useless. They are often fake. If real, they are selectively chosen (meaning the bad ones don't get published). One size doesn't fit all – that person who wrote the testimonial may be significantly different to you.

4. Most importantly, set a deadline – if the treatment isn't starting to work within about three months, try something else.

Which sort of clinician will you see?

There is no right or wrong answer to this question. There is no one profession that is the best. Experience and communication skills can be more important than the type of training they have undergone. We've known people with very little training who were naturally gifted communicators or who have Jedi-level empathy combined with decades in the business – and they trump the most educated of clinicians.

The most important thing of all is that you *like* and *trust* the person you are seeing.

Psychologists

A psychologist is an expert in human behaviour and emotions. They study the brain, memory and development, and apply this to understanding how people think, behave and feel. Psychological treatments include talk therapies, behaviour therapies and group therapies. Psychologists are professionals, meaning they have codes of ethics and professional standards of behaviour, with close regulation.

The pathways to becoming a psychologist vary from country to country, but usually six years of training is required as a minimum. This includes a three-year undergraduate degree (for instance, a bachelor of arts majoring in psychology), a postgraduate honours year, and finally a two- or three-year practical or research program with supervision.

Psychologists can specialise in a range of areas, including different forms of psychotherapy (such as cognitive behaviour therapy, mindfulness therapies, psychoanalytic therapies), neuropsychology, health psychology, forensic psychology, sports psychology and organisational psychology.

Some psychologists also have the title of 'doctor', meaning

they have completed a research degree (a Doctor of Philosophy, or PhD). They are not medical doctors. Psychologists in most countries cannot prescribe medications, order physical tests or perform physical examinations.

If you're after talk-based therapy, a psychologist is your best bet. In contrast to psychiatrists, who spend years of their training learning about drugs and medical conditions, all of the training and clinical practice for psychologists is focused on talking therapies.

Psychiatrists

A psychiatrist is a medical doctor who has specialised in mental health. This means they understand both physical and mental illnesses. It also means they can prescribe medications, deliver various therapies and treatments, and address social concerns such as relationships, housing and employment.

Training to be a psychiatrist begins with four to six years of general medical training. They then have to work for a year or two as a general doctor before entering specialty training, which takes another four to six years. The average psychiatrist therefore has about twelve years of formal training, plus some on-the-job experience.

There is enormous overlap in the disorders that psychologists and psychiatrists treat, but in general psychiatrists treat people on the more severe end of the spectrum (schizophrenia, bipolar disorder, addictions), whereas psychologists focus more on common, everyday problems such as anxiety, depression and stressful life events such as divorce. This isn't a firm rule though: there are many psychologists who specialise in seeing people with severe depression or schizophrenia, and many psychiatrists treating people experiencing more common struggles of daily living.

Counsellors or therapists

These are vague terms that mean different things to different people. A counsellor, usually of graduate level, is trained in giving help around a particular problem – such as marriage, employment or finances. A psychotherapist (therapist for short), usually of postgraduate level, is trained in a specific psychological therapy that can be applied to a defined set of problems. BACP – *British Association of Counselling and Psychotherapy* – requires one year equivalent full-time training plus 100 supervised clinical hours.

The limitation of counsellors is that they may only be trained in treating one problem. The limitation of therapists is that they may be trained to treat every problem using only one technique.

Also, these are not regulated terms – meaning anyone can refer to themselves as a therapist or counsellor. But a practitioner can only call themselves a psychologist or psychiatrist if they meet certain government-dictated regulations.

If you are interested in seeing a therapist or counsellor, make sure you ask about their qualifications (the good ones usually have a website with all of their qualifications listed).

Many social workers also train in therapy or counselling. They often have as many years of training as a psychologist, and may also have years of clinical experience. A health care clinician's title alone is therefore not the best guide.

Shrinks

The term *shrink* was originally a slang term for 'psychiatrist'. It began as *head shrinker* and came from the rather mean comparison between psychiatrists and historical tribes whose custom it was to shrink the heads of slain enemies. In *Mental*, we've use the term shrink to mean any clinician (psychiatrist, psychologist, therapist, counsellor, etc.) that works in mental health. There is no decent collective term for all types of mental health clinician (and reading 'mental health clinician' over and over would do your head in), so we use *shrink* or *clinician*.

Seeing the right shrink

To see a mental health professional, you will usually need a referral from your GP as you would to see any other specialist (secondary care). Within the NHS most referrals will go to the mental health team. If the GP or mental health team member feels you need to see a psychiatrist specifically, they will arrange it for you. If you wish to see a psychiatrist privately, your GP may be willing to recommend someone or you may wish to contact local private hospitals or search online for local clinicians. If you are referred to a psychiatrist, it will most likely be one who specialises in an area of psychiatry that relates to your problem.

Private psychologists, psychiatrists, counsellors and thera-pists are available in most inner-city areas, but tend to be less available in rural areas. The waiting times are usually less than for NHS services, and they can usually see you more often. The cost depends on the type of clinician, and how much they choose to charge. Professional organisations set 'recommended fees' but clinicians are not obliged to comply. Unfortunately, there is very little correlation between how much a clinician charges and their quality. Quite frankly, it's a maze! But the good news is your GP can help you negotiate the maze and find the right shrink for you.

NHS services are basically free of charge. They include hospitals, clinics (sometimes called 'outpatients'), and various free services partly funded by the NHS in conjunction with community organisations. NHS services usually have longer waiting times and you don't get to choose your clinician. Also, the clinicians are more likely to change (they often rotate through jobs), meaning you might have to change shrinks during your treatment. Make sure you do your own research into the NHS services in your area.

Many NHS services run on a shoestring budget, and are beset with the usual politics and crankiness that go with government jobs. Some services struggle to maintain their staff due to constant funding cuts and changes in government. On the other hand, they often have a greater range of clinicians than private clinics, and offer extras such as home visits, crisis teams and case management.

Do you need to like your shrink?

When you see someone for a mental health problem, you need to like them, trust them and feel comfortable in their company. The magic ingredient is rapport – and that can't be manufactured.

Choosing a shrink is not like choosing a surgeon – where skill is more important than rapport. It's nice to feel comfortable with a surgeon, but it's not a deal breaker. As long as they have a steady hand, a sharp knife and come recommended by a trusted doctor, you're good to go. But with a shrink, rapport is a deal breaker.

Be wary of personal recommendations. Don't ignore them, but don't put too much weight on them either.

If you've put together a shortlist of private shrinks, ring each one and ask to speak to them (not all will talk on the phone, but it's worth a try). Ask three key questions:

- Do you deal with my sort of problem?
- What is the waiting time for an appointment?
- What is the cost?

Remember, most clinicians are busy and cannot spend long on the phone, so don't go into too much detail at this stage – they will also be evaluating you as a potential patient, so don't push your luck on the phone. Simply find out quickly if they sound nice, can see you within a reasonable time (usually about two to four weeks) and what out-of-pocket expenses are involved. On the other hand, some practitioners like to use the first phone call as a mini-assessment (or triage) to see if you are likely to fit well together. So just in case, be prepared to talk – find a quiet, private place to make that first phone call.

Next, you need to make a choice and take a leap of faith. Once you go along and visit them, give them a chance. Don't judge a book by its cover and don't jump to conclusions. You often need about two or three visits to decide if someone is right for you. By then, the clinician should have answered two questions:

- What do they think is wrong with you?
- What treatment do they recommend?

And you should have answered your key questions:

- Do I trust them?
- Do they seem genuine?

At this point you may want to return to your GP to discuss their diagnosis and treatment plan. It's often time well spent checking with another professional as to whether the clinician you have chosen is on the right track. For a problem that is likely to require long-term treatment it is especially wise to seek a second opinion.

A little warning – it's very common to get worse before you get better when you first start therapy. So don't give up if at first you feel worse; that's normal. Do change therapists if there is no rapport between you or you feel you are not being listened to – but not based on symptoms alone. When you're going to plant a new garden, you dig up the old one first. You're pulling things apart in order to put them back together, and the start can be the hardest part.

Clues your shrink is a dud

The world is not perfect –some clinicians are substandard, but there are some warning signs that give them away. Watch out for anyone who:

- is too fast – if they make a diagnosis in under 30 minutes they haven't done the job properly – they are cutting corners.

- claims excessive certainty. There is very little that is certain in psychiatry. Clinicians who are certain are usually just blind to alternatives.

- has a guru mentality. Some clinicians think they have special powers of understanding and reason. This usually just reflects arrogance. These clinicians can be tempting – they offer false hope, they make you think you are a special case and they make out they will give you special care no one else can offer. It's an illusion – it mostly ends in disappointment. When you are in distress, you need sensible, honest people helping you.

- is very expensive. Unlike the rest of the capitalist world, where there is a reasonably clear relationship between cost and quality, in health care this relationship does not hold up. However, there is a reasonably clear relationship between integrity and clinical skill. Good clinicians are mostly intelligent and honest and do the job for a combination of reasons – they like helping people, they like building their skills and they value their reputation. They want to make a fair living, but they are rarely greedy – they will charge a fair price. Dodgy clinicians are often greedy and are doing the job for financial gain. Charging above market price is a warning sign. Your GP may give you a rough guide to market price.

Remember, you might not find the right person behind the first door you knock on. You might have to try a few before you get lucky. This is not unusual. It's an unfortunate feature of the business – different patients respond to different clinicians in different ways.

Just because you think the first psychologist or psychiatrist you see is not a good fit doesn't mean the whole profession is flawed. It just means you haven't found the right person for you yet. Keep trying, do more research, try a different clinical group (psychologist, psychiatrist, therapist). Go back to your GP and tell them why it didn't work out and ask them for other options. Don't give up.

Most mental health problems take a while to fix, so putting effort into finding the right clinician can save you lots of time, money and energy in the long run.

How do you encourage someone else to get help?

This is a very common question. At some point in their life, everyone is faced with a relative, friend or work colleague who appears to need help. But assisting someone with something as personal as a mental health problem is delicate. You walk the fine line between being constructive and being intrusive. You have to balance your own opinions with their views. There are many traps. Tread carefully; friendships can easily be damaged. Before taking any steps, pause and think ahead.

Here are some questions to ask yourself.

What has led you to think this person has a problem?

This question may seem obvious, but it is vital. Boundaries are important – sometimes it's hard to know where you stop and the other person begins. It's very easy to mix up your own life with those close to you.

For instance, just because you sought help in a certain situation, doesn't necessarily mean the other person needs help. A typical example is grief – you might have found the death of a parent difficult and you may have needed help processing it. When your close friend then loses a parent, you might mix up your experience with theirs and encourage them repeatedly to get help. Always try to be objective. They may not need help.

Often it's a good idea to talk to other people about the person you are worried about to see if they share your view of the situation.

Is their problem affecting you?

If the answer is yes, tread carefully. The mental health of our loved ones often has an impact on us. As a consequence, we can confuse our needs with theirs. Try to remove your own needs from the equation. Any attempt to get help for someone else should be solely focused on that person. Deal with your own issues separately. Go see a shrink yourself. When it comes to helping your friend, try to have their needs uppermost in your mind.

The practical stuff

Now for some practical tips.

Begin by asking your friend if they are okay. As surprising as it sounds, this is hard. There is often a temptation to tell them they are not well and give evidence to support your belief. Instead, try questions such as 'Are you feeling alright lately?' Or say: 'You don't seem yourself. Is it my imagination, or are you going through a tough time?'

Then sit quietly and listen. Avoid the temptation to interrupt. Let them talk at their pace. But if they say they don't want to talk, don't force the issue; it is rarely helpful. Just say something like: 'No worries, I hope you don't mind me asking, I was just a little worried. If you change your mind and want to chat just let me know.' Then wait – many people think about it and take up the opportunity at a later time.

Once you've established that help is wanted, figure out how much you should do and how much you should leave to them. The best outcome is for each of us to fix our own problems, but that's not always possible. Say something like: 'What can I do to help?' If appropriate, add: 'I'd like to help, but I don't want to intrude. You tell me how best I can help.'

Some mental health problems totally debilitate the sufferer. People suffering severe depression have no motivation, their concentration and planning are impaired, they feel hopeless and worthless and so they don't believe anything will help. Sometimes they are also suicidal. In this situation, you have to take the lead. You have to be intrusive. You might even go behind their back if you think their life is at risk. Services such as Samaritans or SANEline are really helpful for getting the opinion of an expert.

In other situations, you cannot force a person to get help. Addictive problems such as drugs and gambling are often in this category (but not always), as are problems with trauma – the person has to feel ready to face their demons. Gentle encouragement helps, but not if it strays into intrusiveness.

One of the hardest parts of getting help is finding out about the service options. If you want to be helpful and practical, do some research for your friend. Use the internet or speak to a professional and make a simple list of treatment options that your friend can assess and contemplate. Include various options, because you won't know the full extent of their problem or the treatment options that they'll feel comfortable with. Give a few websites that deal with their likely problem, and a good GP, and any other professionals you can find. It's simple, and could get them on the right path.

4

Seeing a Shrink for the First Time

Going to a shrink for the first time can be daunting. We've both done it. We wondered what they'd see – maybe stuff we were afraid to let out?

Steve wondered if his shrink would see his darkest fears – maybe he was not such a good person, maybe unkind traits outweighed kind traits? She might say, 'Steve, you're a shit person.'

Dev, on the other hand, was not nervous at all. As a writer, she has been very public about her private life. She didn't care who knew she was going to therapy, but her shrink said he'd only treat her on the proviso it remained private and she didn't write about it while the therapy was happening. In retrospect, Dev feels her shrink's decision to set up therapy as a private and safe place for her was a very wise decision.

Most people wonder how much they'll be prepared to share with a therapist. Most people know they won't share everything; how much they share will depend on how much they trust the shrink. But most people also know that to gain the most benefit from the process, they have to be as open as possible. So don't worry: you don't have to tell your shrink everything. They might want you to, but unless you want to tell them, you don't have to. Also, trust builds over time, and then more private material can emerge. Therapy can still be effective when you share limited information.

You'll also find you can't help second-guessing your shrink in the early phases. You'll be assessing them while they assess you. Second-guessing is normal – it's hard to avoid being 'meta-cognitive' about the whole thing – it can feel like looking at a rollercoaster from above while also enjoying the ride. Make yourself feel part of the process. Ask lots of questions. It might help you open up. Of course, not everyone is the same – some don't want to know the process – some feel safety in trusting others. Each of us is different.

Shrinks know that patients are often wary, especially in the initial phase. They know that it will take time to hear the full story of your life and to build trust. They know you are self-conscious. They know that you'll tell the basic facts to begin with, and that over time, if things are going well, more details will emerge.

Good shrinks are skilled at knowing when you are covering up. Or knowing when there is more to a story than you're saying. Good shrinks develop a strong intuition for knowing when you are bothered, anxious or protecting yourself. And they are also good at knowing when you are ready to open up. They don't force you. They let it unfold at your pace. Sometimes they might gently direct you somewhere to give you the chance to explore, but they push you only as far as they think is safe and useful.

Information can reveal itself at strange times. For example, it is very common, not just in psychiatry but in all clinical encounters, for patients to reveal a key bit of information just as they are standing at the door ready to leave.

What happens in the first appointment?

When you first see a clinician, they do an assessment – gather information, figure out what is wrong – and then make a treatment plan. Sometimes the assessment phase is quick – taking just one session – but it can also be spread over a number of one-hour sessions. For example, a standard assessment for a single problem such as depression usually takes about an hour. More information will emerge in the treatment phase, but it's usually possible to cover the basic information in the first session.

The assessment interview serves two purposes – to find out your problems and to build a trusting relationship. These goals are being balanced the whole time.

The therapist will usually start the interview by explaining what will occur. This is a pretty typical introduction:

Hi, what name do you prefer to be called? Please feel free to call me Steve. As you know, I'm a psychiatrist. You've been referred by such-and-such. Today is essentially an assessment. I'm going to ask you to tell me in your own words why you've come along. Then I'm going to ask some questions to clarify various aspects of what you've told me. After that I'll find out a bit about your background to put everything in context – stuff like how you grew up, what you do for a living and your relationships.

If at any time the questions don't make sense or you're wondering why I'm asking things, just say so and I'll explain more. Feel free to tell me if there are things you don't want to talk about.

At the end I'll tell you what I think about what you've told me and if necessary we can talk about treatment options.

Let me make sure I have all your basic information right … [Then I ask name, age and occupation.]

So, to get the ball rolling, tell me about why you've come.

Every clinician does this in their own way and with their own style, but the whole time they are piecing together information. Once the person is talking, the information is being collected. Sometimes it comes out easily and with little direction (especially if the patient has seen previous clinicians and has told their story many times). Sometimes it requires lots of direction and questions.

Good clinicians use open questions such as 'Tell me about your family' rather than closed questions like 'How long did you live with your family?' Open questions elicit more information, but take longer. The balance depends on the patient and how easily they communicate their problems.

In medicine, this process is called 'taking a history', as distinct from 'doing an examination'. It's an old adage in medicine that 90 per cent of diagnosis comes from the history, about 9 per cent from the examination and about 1 per cent from the tests (although with all the fancy tests available these days the numbers might have changed – but history-taking is still king!).

The history sought in this first interview has several components.

Why are you here?

This is where the shrink finds out what *you* think is wrong. Most patients tell their clinician a little about the key problem, like 'I have panic attacks' and then give their ideas about how it came about. Good shrinks give you at least a few minutes, if not way longer, to talk and explain before they interrupt and ask clarifying questions.

Questions to tease out the problem

The first few questions gradually turn into a conversation about your problems. Shrinks like to tease out aspects of your problem. For example, if you say you have an eating disorder, they'll ask: 'For how long?' 'How did it start?' 'Have you told anyone?' 'What do you eat in a day?' 'What is your weight?' 'Do you binge?' 'Do you vomit?' The list of possible questions is endless, but in the first interview they'll be limited, as the clinician will know you'll tell them more once trust (often called rapport) develops.

Systems review

Your shrink will ask a series of questions to cover other problems you might have forgotten to mention or thought were not relevant – called a 'systems review'. It's like a general check-up – a bit like when you go to the doctor for a flu shot and they also check your blood pressure.

They will ask about all sorts of potential problems – both psychological and physical. For example, if you came along because of depression, after all the details about your depression have been covered, they'd ask about other stuff: 'Have you ever suffered anxiety?' 'What about eating problems?' 'Have you ever suffered a manic episode?' 'Do you have any general health problems?' Nearly all health problems interact with each other, so they need a full picture.

In psychiatry the systems review explores the key domains of mental health: mood, psychosis, cognitive function, anxiety, behaviour, and drug or alcohol use. We normally check for suicidal ideas or plans as well.

Sometimes patients think this is a waste of time and get a little frustrated. But a thorough assessment is important for treatment planning and to get the diagnosis right.

Past history

Past history means any illnesses and treatments you've had in the past. The best predictor of the future is the past, so this information is vital. Past problems give clues to the nature and causes of your present problems, and also tell us about what treatments work for you.

Family history

In the family history stage of the interview, your shrink will ask a little about your family, where you fit in, and the quality of family relationships. Then, they will ask you about the mental health of your family.

Many psychological disorders have some genetic component

or, if not genetic, are linked in some way to your upbringing. This includes your extended family – for example, the more relatives you have with schizophrenia, the higher your chance of having schizophrenia (but even with a family full of mental illness you are still more likely *not* to have problems).

Personal history

This is a big part of the first few interviews. This is basically your life story. It is where your shrink finds out about your life so far. The emphasis of the personal history section depends on your problems, but includes to various degrees: your mother's pregnancy, birth, infancy, primary schooling, secondary schooling, university, relationships, jobs and what your life consists of right now. Shrinks check for problems at various points in your life – criminal matters, drug use, major traumas and anything else that seems important. There are hundreds of clues they look for – some tiny. For example, if your mother had the flu during the second three months of your pregnancy, you have a very small increased chance of developing schizophrenia. Everything adds up to the unique jigsaw that is you!

Personality

All shrinks try to assess personality, but it is very difficult. They tend to ask about how you see yourself, how others see you, and about your formative relationships. They form opinions slowly, after they hear about how you responded to various situations. They also slowly see how you react to various situations in the consulting room.

Personality is difficult to define, and assessments are

ultimately in the eye of the beholder – and we all assess personality through the lens of our own personality, so our opinions are inherently flawed. Nevertheless, we do our best to form an opinion. Good shrinks keep an open mind and recognise the limitations of their assessment.

Mental state examination (MSE)

This is the shrink's equivalent to the physical examination from your general doctor. Everything up until now is based on what you tell your shrink – it's subjective: your opinion! The MSE is the shrink's attempt at an objective evaluation. The whole time you are in the room they are observing you for the MSE, which they usually write down after the consultation (although some people keep notes as they go). Some parts of the MSE require specific questions but others can be observed from your behaviour alone.

The MSE is divided into various categories – and while they are all linked to each other, we try to separate them out into various elements, as each gives information about various disorders.

- **Appearance and behaviour** – how you look and behave during the interview. For example, are you agitated, suggesting depression? Are you dressed inappropriately, suggesting mania?
- **Speech** – your rate, tone and volume. For example, depressed people tend to be softly spoken and speak slowly with a flat tone. Manic people speak fast and loud, and rush to get everything out.
- **Affect** – what we observe about your emotional state at

the time of the interview. We look at the quality (happy, sad, anxious, angry, frustrated, etc.), the intensity of emotions, and the range – how quickly you move from one emotional state to another. We also note whether the emotional state matches the content of the interview – do you look sad when talking about sad things?

- **Thought** – Your thought process is as important as your thought content. We assess various aspects of thinking. 'Stream' describes how quickly your thoughts emerge. 'Form of thinking' describes the logical aspects – are the thoughts linked clearly? Sometimes a patient's ideas make little sense, or the links between ideas are tenuous, or thoughts are well linked but don't lead to conclusions.

Finally, we look at the thought content. This is what you are actually talking about: sad themes, paranoid themes, relationships, a traumatic event. It's all about the topics that are important to you.

- **Perception** – Psychiatric disorders can lead to problems with perception. Hallucinations can occur in any of the five senses (sight, hearing, taste, smell and touch), but the most common is auditory hallucinations (hearing voices). Hallucinations often, but not always, suggest psychosis.

- **Cognition** – the process of acquiring knowledge and understanding. The brain is more complex than we understand (at least for now) but we know some of the basic functions. Testing your cognitive function requires a series of questions to tease out all elements of thinking, including your memory, attention and your

ability to solve problems and plan for the future. Some
of the tests are very easy, such as asking you to give
the date and say where you live (called 'orientation').
while others are much harder. Most cognitive tests
can be done in the consulting room with a pen and
paper, but if there are problems we will often use a
computer to do more advanced testing or even refer
patients to a neuropsychologist who spends an hour or
two testing in detail. Cognitive problems are commonest
in dementia, but can occur in other psychiatric disorders
as well.

- **Insight and judgement** – Here we observe what you
  think is wrong and whether you are making reasonable
  decisions. Sometimes this is easy – like a patient with
  schizophrenia who has a delusion that they are the
  president of their country; they lack insight. At other
  times it is trickier, like if the clinician thinks you have
  depression, but you don't believe it; which of you
  lacks insight?

Making a diagnosis

At the end of the history and mental state examination, the
shrink should have some idea of what is wrong. At this point
they home in on three things:
- diagnosis
- differential diagnosis – a list of alternative diagnostic
  possibilities

- formulation – why you present this way at this time.

If your problems fit into a neat category, then a diagnosis is made. For example, the clinician might write a diagnosis of depression, and write differential diagnoses of adjustment disorder (meaning you are struggling to cope with something but not quite depressed) and anxiety disorder (anxiety and depression are hard to distinguish at times).

As well as having an idea of your diagnosis, most shrinks develop and write a formulation. This is a statement that answers the question: Why is *this person*, presenting in *this way*, at *this time*? The formulation summarises your history and mental state examination, and then looks at what factors predispose you to these problems (such as childhood experience, or past trauma), what factors might have precipitated your problem (such as divorce or other stressors) and what factors are perpetuating your problem (like your personality or ongoing stressors like financial hardship). Under each of these areas (predisposing, precipitating, perpetuating) the formulation considers biological, psychological and social factors.

Here is an example of a formulation (although most are usually a lot longer):

Adele Nguyen is a 49-year-old woman presenting with a range of depressive symptoms following a serious car crash nine months ago. She rates her depression as severe and has never experienced symptoms like this before. She reports she sleeps only a few hours per night, worries constantly, and has thought suicide might be an alternative but has no plans and says she could never do it to her family. Mental state examination reveals slow speech and a depressed affect but no impairment in cognition. She is currently well supported by her partner and extended family. She remains on high doses of pain medications.

Adele is predisposed in part by a strong family history of depression. Her mother and two maternal aunts suffered depression for most of their lives, and one aunt died by suicide. Adele described seeing her mother depressed on many occasions, and said she was often unable to be a parent as Adele grew up. Adele also experienced a number of traumas in her formative years. Her best friend died in a car crash at age 16, and Adele was assaulted at a nightclub in her early twenties. She reports both of these incidents have stayed with her and memories have returned recently.

The precipitant to these symptoms was a car crash in which Adele broke her lower leg and suffered a dislocated shoulder. She had no head injuries. She spent ten days in hospital. The recovery has been good although there is ongoing pain in her shoulder.

Perpetuating factors include the financial stress of not returning to work yet, her fear that she may never return, and ongoing rehabilitation for her shoulder. She also worries her partner may leave – the accident has put a strain on their relationship, and she thinks her partner may just be waiting for her to recover to leave.

The most likely diagnosis is depression, the main differential diagnoses are post-traumatic stress disorder and medication (analgesic)-induced depression.

Investigations and tests

Most psychiatrists consider ordering tests to exclude medical causes of mental health problems. There are a multitude of possible tests, but the reality is that undiagnosed medical causes of mental illness are rare, and so they usually come back from the lab with 'normal' stamped across the results sheet.

The commonest are blood tests looking for general signs of disease or specific organ function tests (kidney, liver, thyroid). We sometimes look for specific infections that can cause mental health problems (HIV, syphilis).

Occasionally we ask for brain imaging to exclude neurological disease (while neurological diseases are rare, when they occur, psychiatric symptoms are common). There are a few options: an MRI (magnetic resonance imaging) looks in fine detail at brain structure, and is especially good for detecting tumours; a CT (computerised tomography) is quicker and cheaper and shows almost as much structural detail as an MRI; finally, there is functional imaging, like PET (positron emission tomography), which can show how well the brain is functioning, useful for suspected dementia.

The other tests sometimes ordered are neuropsychological tests. These are questions and puzzles designed to test all aspects of brain function. They test everything from your memory to your ability to reason and even your IQ. Most are done on computers, a bit like video games. They take about an hour and are usually used to diagnose dementia or look for acquired brain damage.

Management plan

The final task of the assessment process is the management plan. This is essentially a list of treatments the clinician recommends. You can accept or reject each option, or go away and do some research of your own, or seek a second opinion.

We each have our own ideas about what will make us better. Some patients prefer talk therapy, others medications. Some like to trust the clinician completely; others like to research themselves. Some are in a hurry; others want to take it slowly. The clinician's job is not only to recommend treatments, but to help tease out your preferences. The dizzying number of options can seem endless.

The goal is to find a treatment plan you both agree on. The key is to find common ground. Clinicians who have a 'one size fits all' approach to treatment only get it right if you just happen, by chance, to be amenable to their version of treatment. The plan usually includes short-term and long-term suggestions, as well as a number of options. The plan also highlights risks (like the risk of self-harm or suicide) and documents the approach to those risks.

Some clinicians like to make a rough grid to look at immediate versus longer-term considerations, and divide them according to the rough distinction of biological, psychological and social treatments. Here is an example:

Ben Dylan. Probable diagnosis: post-traumatic stress disorder (moderate severity, not working, marital breakdown, drinking moderate amounts of alcohol)

	Biological	Psychological	Social
Immediate	• Cut back alcohol • Exercise program	• Cognitive behaviour therapy, either individual or in a local group • Consider relaxation options – yoga?	• Marital counselling (urgent)
Intermediate	• Trial of anti-depressants	• Alcohol group support if necessary (Alcoholics anonymous?)	• Suggest financial counselling
Long-term			• Employment rehabilitation program

Despite this plan looking simple, each of the suggestions will take between two and twelve weeks to complete. During that time the clinician will collect more information, update their diagnosis, and adjust the management plan according to how the patient responds to each step.

Are the notes written down and can you see them?

Yes. In the old days the doctor often kept the plan in their head, but that's no longer acceptable. Complaints bodies, courts and various other regulations state quite clearly that notes must be kept. The notes act as a memory aid for the clinician and also as a record of what has happened in case problems arise. The notes are written either during the session or straight afterwards.

It is now very common for patients to request to see their notes. Most countries have laws supporting this right – including the UK. It may be required that you fill out a form to request your notes, but more and more the barriers are being removed. There is debate about the pros and cons of full access to notes for patients, but we support it because it makes patients active participants in their treatment process and removes any ambiguity about what is and isn't recommended. Of course it would also mean doctors would have to change their writing style – less jargon, minimal acronyms and abbreviations. This will take time and training.

Also, the tricky issue of writing scary possible diagnoses that the clinician wants to keep in mind but not yet share with the patient needs to be sorted out. For example, a doctor might be wondering whether you have HIV but not want to mention it until they have ruled out other possible causes of your problems; they don't want to alarm you unnecessarily.

Different clinicians, different styles

Not every shrink works in the same way! The description above is the basic plan. Some shrinks do it in a different order, or spread it out, or have a particular way that they've developed. Some are business-like and efficient others are slower and more pensive. Similarly, everyone keeps his or her notes slightly differently. This doesn't mean anyone is wrong or incompetent or better! The system is diverse.

5

Our Stories

We both agreed it was important to describe our personal experiences with mental illness as part of this book. Dev was super keen, Steve was super reluctant, but we both agreed that sharing our personal stories was important. Despite all our knowledge and experience, we each put weight on different things, and determined different paths to take to recovery.

The information in this book is only half of the equation – the other half is your individual beliefs, your gut feelings, your circumstances and your choices. By writing about our own experiences of mental illness, we hope it will show how we matched our knowledge with our own lives to reach our own conclusions. Neither of us think that our conclusions should be your conclusions. Neither of us believe we have the right answers. We simply wanted to tell our own experiences of mental illness and how we responded.

Steve's story

I've been depressed. The whole shebang – sad every day, crying at night, dreadful concentration, crappy sleepless nights, anger and rage, endless replaying of the same thoughts in my head, fear it would never end and sometimes thinking I'd rather not go on.

In retrospect, it had been building for a while, but despite this I didn't expect it. I was taken completely by surprise.

Can a shrink be blind to their own emotions? Can a shrink get depressed? I'm sure we all know the answer to this – yes. In fact, many people think it's almost a prerequisite: that shrinks become shrinks to sort out their own problems. Knowledge about health problems isn't like immunisation. It doesn't always protect you. It's a double-edged sword – you know the symptoms, you know the services, you can fast-track help, but your judgement is skewed, you misdiagnose yourself, you underestimate the amount of help you'll need, and you are scared your colleagues will find out that you are unwell.

I didn't tell a soul – not my colleagues, not my best friends, not my family. At least not until I was over the worst, and even then hardly anyone and I probably left some important people out.

I'm only writing this now because Dev told me I should come clean – and intellectually, I agree. It's ironic that these days footballers talk about their depression and mental illnesses openly in the media, but doctors still hide theirs away, while arguing that we need to reduce stigma. If we can't talk about our own experiences with mental illness, who can?

So I know we need to be honest. But I'm still nervous about it.

Why? Partly because I'm not sure I'm distant enough from the experience to present the truth clearly and partly because I like to keep my emotions to myself. Also, I hate pity – I dread the thought of someone sadly hugging me. If you know me and you're tempted: thanks, but please – no!

Part of it is also anxiety about being judged. Judgement is stupid but real. Some people think: if shrinks can't help themselves, how can they possibly help others? Intuitively this makes sense: 'His treatments clearly don't work – he's depressed himself'. It's like seeing a bald hair doctor. But in reality, what we do in a consulting room is a process, based on medical research and training. It's worth saying again: knowing stuff doesn't give you immunity.

The trigger for my depression was a relationship break-up. I was in love and I got dumped. Not cruelly, not unexpectedly and not out of the blue. We'd been on and off a few times. It was tiring.

While it had been coming for a while, the final blow shook me. I'd gone away to help sort out my feelings and felt like I'd figured out a path forward to resolve our differences. I came back, almost excited, to sort the mess out. But it was too late. She'd moved on.

The relationship was over. Suddenly I was alone and the choice wasn't mine. All the clichés kicked in – I'd lost my best friend, my confidante, my lover, the person I thought about before I fell asleep, the person I most wanted to touch, the person I most like to watch laugh.

This is how it felt. At first, I guess it was fairly typical grief – break-up stuff: anger, recriminations, longing, mood swings, ruminations, conversations in my head about how to retrieve the situation. I didn't worry about these feelings at all. I'd been through a divorce and other break-ups and I knew they would pass. It was just a waiting game.

But after about four weeks I was getting worse, not better. For the first time in my life I couldn't concentrate – this surprised me the most. Someone would text for a coffee, I'd say I would be there in 15 minutes, and then I'd forget! They'd call 20 minutes later and say, 'Where are you?' It was weird. And my sleeping was poor – I was waking up about 4 am in the morning and ruminating.

The ruminations were the worst of all for me – a repetitive, negative cycle of thoughts where you never come to a conclusion. They were not just about the relationship, but about anything that had happened the previous day. My brain felt like a broken record. It was as if I was thinking the same sentence over and over for hours. This really scared me – I just couldn't turn it off.

I was sad whenever I was alone. If people were around me, I could distract myself but I felt detached – like I was watching everything, not actually a part of it, but like a player in a movie. I couldn't laugh. Smiling was not a problem, but there was no laughter, and usually I laugh a lot. Sometimes when I cried, especially at night, it felt cathartic, it felt good – but not always. Sometimes it felt desperate.

I felt pathetic. Especially early on, before I realised I was depressed. I kept thinking, 'This is a relationship break-up. Get the fuck over it. It happens to everyone. Stop being so self-pitying, so narcissistic.' But I couldn't.

So what did I do? At about the two-month mark, I started to think about strategies to move on. By then I was beginning to worry – I knew this was the longest period of feeling down I'd ever had.

My first plan was to DIY (do it yourself), then wait and see. I wondered whether I could fix the relationship, whether I'd tried hard enough – but each time I made contact I felt worse, and it didn't seem possible. I exercised regularly. I'd always been a gym junkie, but I started going more often.

I also went back to smoking. Not as a treatment, but because I couldn't resist. I'd given up for eight years prior to the relationship, but smoked on and off during it. After we broke up, I quit again, but then decided early on that I didn't have the energy or willpower to stay off cigarettes. I also drank, but carefully. I limited myself to two beers per night to relax, but no more unless I was out with friends. And I got stoned about once every few weeks – I hadn't smoked marijuana since uni, but I found the odd joint gave me a night off from feeling sorry for myself. I was desperate; I was trying anything. I do not suggest others try these things! I'm just trying to tell the truth – this is what I did. I don't really know if these things helped.

I did go slightly into hyperdrive. I've always been an energetic person. My colleagues often joke that I was manic. I can't count the times people have said to me, 'Missed your lithium dose this morning, Steve?' But during this period of time I said 'yes' to every task or project put in front of me.

I thought about getting professional help, but decided it was still early days and I'd wait it out. Surprisingly, I think I was still functioning pretty well. When I was at work I felt my best. I did feel distracted, but despite my poor concentration nothing seemed to go wrong. I took a few extra steps to make sure they didn't – I starting writing copious 'to do' lists in my diary to compensate for my poor concentration, and I would check my diary every hour or so. I slightly cut back on face-to-face clinical work (seeing depressed people made me tearful, and I wasn't sure I could contain my tears). I was lucky my job as a psychiatrist in a public hospital had plenty of different sorts of tasks and lots of other clinicians to pick up the slack. No one seemed to notice. I worked harder on other tasks.

I started keeping a diary, noting in it a daily score out of ten of how depressed I felt to monitor myself. I found that writing the diary stopped my ruminations. If I put my thoughts on paper, they seemed to leave my head. Writing also felt good. Prior to this I'd been a very reluctant writer (when I co-wrote a textbook, *Psych-lite*, my co-author would lock me in a room until I'd reached various deadlines), but now writing felt like a creative pursuit, I wrote over 15,000 words in this time. I cringe when I read it now.

Funnily enough, around this time I bought a spot in Catherine Deveny's 'Gunnas Writing Masterclass' for my ex-girlfriend. It was a sad, over-the-top attempt at a birthday gift (surely designed to win her back) – she'd been a keen amateur writer. As soon as I'd paid for it online, I knew it was an excessive, pleading gift. So, given I was enjoying my diary writing, I decided to do it myself rather than give the extravagant gift (I sent her a novel I thought she'd like instead).

It was that writing course that led to this book. Swings and roundabouts!

By the four-month mark, I was no better. I decided it was time to get help. During my previous divorce, a relationship counsellor had suggested I'd benefit from individual therapy. I'd gone once but didn't think it was my thing. But she was right. I booked into a new therapist. I considered a psychiatrist, but couldn't think of anyone – it felt like I knew pretty much everyone in town. So I chose a non-medical therapist.

This was my turning point. It's hard to put the process of therapy into words, but here are a few brief, incomplete thoughts. It gave me an hour per week with someone who listened and cared. I gained new perspectives. I found there was more to my depression than the relationship break-up. I talked a lot about the death of my mother. I talked a lot about other relation-ships that had ended – even going back to my teenage years. I talked about difficulties with intimacy and trust. I talked about my divorce and the people I'd let down. I talked about non-relationship stuff – pressures, expectations. I mostly dreaded the sessions, but afterwards felt relieved, unburdened and lighter. My ruminations started to disappear.

My sadness slowly melted away. I started to laugh again.

I stayed in therapy for about a year. I probably should have stayed longer, but I ran out of steam. I'm sure there's still work to be done.

Of course, lots of other things happened during that year. I started dating again; projects I took on worked out. In a sense, it turned out to be one of the most productive times I'd ever experienced.

What else helped me? Definitely the support of my friends and family. I didn't know then, and still don't know now, whether they cottoned on to my depression at the time. But some people seemed to sense something was wrong and put in extra effort.

I received more invitations to dinner or to just hang out. More offers to include me in things. Lots of gestures of friendship. Friends and family really are the best life insurance.

Probably most of all it helped having a good relationship with my son. When I felt my lowest and really didn't want to go on, I always knew I wouldn't end my life as long as I had my son. And when I was with him, I felt close to okay. As long as that sense didn't go away, I knew, fundamentally, that I'd be fine in time.

In retrospect, I wonder why I became depressed. I still don't think I know. Probably a culmination of many things – especially poor relationship skills. I'm pretty sure the break-up was just the straw that broke the camel's back. I also think I am slightly prone to mood swings – not in the bipolar range, but not that far off either. My natural state is to be ever-so-slightly manic.

And finally, I know I struggle to recognise and acknowledge my own emotions. For me it feels like pulling teeth to express some particular emotions. And yes, I know that sounds weird for a shrink – but I don't think it is that rare. In fact, I often see this in my colleagues too.

Do I think experiencing depression helped me in any way? Yes. Doctors often say the experience of illness changes their perspective and makes them better doctors. I'd previously thought this was a little trite – but now I've joined that club. I think I now appreciate the experiences of others better. Also, one of the great pleasures in being a doctor is the joy of helping others. This seems to have doubled for me now. Having been helped so much and seen the benefits, I get a little more joy from helping.

I also think I've softened a little towards other people. I've always tried not to be too judgemental, but I've not always suc-ceeded. I think I'm a little more forgiving now. I've felt lost and in need of help. I think I accept it better in others now.

I understand my behaviour in relationships better (thanks to therapy) but I still I have a long way to go in this domain! I open up more, and am trying to be honest with myself. Time will tell if it makes a difference.

One thing that resulted was a newfound joy in writing. I'd always seen writing as a chore – something you did on demand at university to jump academic hurdles. Now I enjoy it. It feels like a whole new arena has opened up.

I do feel slightly vulnerable and worried it might happen again, but not overwhelmingly so, because I'm pretty sure I'd cope better a second time around. But I'm a little more cautious in some ways – I watch how much I take on, I make sure I get the balance right between doing things for others versus myself, and I cut myself a little more slack with my various ambitions – I try not to beat myself up over failings.

Sure, I'd rather I'd never suffered depression, but in a way I'm not sure I can explain, I'm glad it happened.

Dev asked me whether I considered medications. I did, but I didn't want to see another doctor because of the stigma of depression. I was worried about being judged and feared that they would talk to others. I also wasn't comfortable with the power imbalance – it was confronting imagining entering the doctor–patient relationship as a patient when I was used to speaking to other doctors as a colleague and peer. I could have self-prescribed, but I knew the risks of antidepressants were too great to do it alone – and of course it's illegal!

This points to a major problem I've seen over and over again: as doctors, we shout from the rooftops about reducing stigma, but our actions don't always match our words. We don't admit our problems, we don't share our illnesses, and in so doing we contribute to the very problem we claim to be fighting. I can't count the times I've organised interstate care for doctors with mental illnesses because they don't want their colleagues to know they're seeking treatment. It's the same for lawyers, high-profile media professionals and politicians.

It's really encouraging to see stigma reduction catching on in the general population, but there are pockets such as these professions where little has changed.

Every time we hide a problem, we give it power. We contribute to secrecy and make it harder for others in the same boat to get the help.

We need to change.

Dev's story

My experience with depression and anxiety has made me who I am, and I'm delighted with how things have turned out. In saying this, I am not glorifying suffering. But having depression, being dyslexic and growing up around others who were not neurologically or emotionally typical forced me to reach deeper, see clearer and look beyond social constructs and 'the way things are supposed to be'. It helped make me smarter, kinder and better at loving the right people in the right way.

I grew up surrounded by mental illness and it gave me a

unique and liberating perspective. The yawning chasm between the ideal of the perfect person, family, parents and home and my real-life experience of these things made me question all traditional constructs. Now, at 47 years of age, I have three sons and a partner I adore. The father of my sons and I separated, and after extremely hard work on both our parts we have a lovely relationship. I am a financially, creatively, intellectually and emotionally independent feminist and atheist. And I am not sure I would ever have arrived at this place of understanding, clarity, freedom and peace without the mismatch I experienced between how things were supposed to be and how they actually were. It took a bit of a tantrum about reality to get there, but as they say: hell is truth seen too late and the truth will set you free.

My first memory was from around the age of two. It was night and I was having my nappy changed on a bed with a view of the front yard. I remember my mum saying, 'Your father's gone to the pub and left his glasses at home.' I turned my head and saw Dad walking along the footpath away from the house. I still remember that moment vividly. I thought: 'Mum is sad and I want to make her happy and make things better.' My dad was many things – and an alcoholic was one of them.

That memory had often popped back into my head throughout my life, but I initially dismissed it as a dream because my father never wore glasses. But the emotion from the memory was so acute and clear. One day I mentioned it to Mum, saying the only reason I knew it wasn't real was because Dad never wore glasses. 'Oh yes he did,' Mum said, 'but he kept losing them. So he eventually stopped buying them.'

Mum insists I can't possibly remember something from such a young age. Luckily, I don't need for her to believe it to know it's true. This is not the only thing, nor in any way close to the most important thing, she's been reluctant to believe.

I have no memory of life without depression. Thinking about that early memory now I can see that my emotions as a two-year-old could be more accurately described as: 'I am sad because Mum is sad and I desperately want to make myself happy by making her happy and fixing the situation.'

Many times in my life (though no longer, thanks to therapy), I have felt as if there were an invisible tube between me and people I loved who suffered mental illness. I would feel their emotions pour into me through this tube. I was desperate to 'fix' them in order to stop the emotional backwash flowing into me.

They say one in five people suffer mental illness, but this has always struck me as odd and inaccurate, because growing up I was surrounded by people with mental illness and people affected by it. I did not know a single person who wasn't affected by it. There were a lot of people having nervous breakdowns too. (What happened to nervous breakdowns and what the hell were they? What do we call them now?) [*Dev, it was a catch-all term to mean acute mental illness, usually depression or anxiety brought on by stress. Some people still use it. It's less confronting than 'mental illness'. I quite like it. – Steve*]

Mum has suffered mental illness my whole life, and perhaps her whole life too. She is not sure when she began to suffer depression, as for her it was so linked with low self-esteem it's difficult to discern one problem from the other. What I do know is that she suffered it her whole married life until the present day. That's over fifty years. I'm fairly certain my father, along with being an alcoholic and a whole bunch of other things, had a personality disorder. Narcissistic personality disorder is my bet. My cousin, great-grandmother and Dad's best friend died by suicide as an outcome of mental illness. In their cases, it was bipolar disorder.

I'll never know for sure if the depression and anxiety I have managed my whole life was a result of growing up around mental illness, but this is what I remember. My childhood was full of sadness, anger, poverty, resentment, disappointment and envy, all threaded together and punctuated with the odd happy moment. The happy moments were often the saddest. When things are bad, you can bolster yourself with the thought that happy times are around the corner. When things are happy, you know it won't last and fear what's coming next. You wonder when the next wave will come, how long it will last, how far you'll be dragged out to sea and how deep you'll be pulled under. Everyone seemed to be comparing their reality against the crazy expectations of what life, families, relationships and themselves were 'supposed to be'. Religion, sexism, racism, patriotism, classism, family, truth, fairness, social expectations, gender roles – the whole thing was a giant mental clusterfuck.

I was depressed as a child. We called it sad back then. I was also anxious; we called it worried back then. Because I was living in a chaotic environment with parents who were barely coping, I didn't say anything. It made me feel better to pray, do craft, help out at home and try to be good. In retrospect, I now realise these were self-soothing ways to deal with anxiety and depression – I still do many of them today. Things were pretty horrible, so it made sense to feel sad. I tried my best to cheer myself up and gee myself along.

At our place, we five kids never threw tantrums. The adults did. When people tell stories about their belligerent, recalcitrant teen, I say, 'Well, that's a sign of excellent parenting. You can't be a teenager properly and go through the emotional gymnastics necessary unless you have parents who are being actual adults.'

My teen years were particularly tough. Anyone who knew me would probably have described me as chatty and fun. The sad truth was I was depressed and anxious much of the time.

I was also boy-crazy. I think my preoccupation with love and romance was my response to not feeling loved, accepted or cared for; it was also a response to the lack of affection in my family and to my dysfunctional relationship with my father. The boy-craziness felt like a deep feeling of loss for not having a boyfriend. I thought having a boyfriend would stop the sadness and the worry, the anxiety and depression. Somehow feeling 'chosen' by someone would make me feel I was 'good enough' and 'special'. I know. Sad but true.

The idea of 'The One' – the belief that out there for everyone was the one perfect romantic partner and without The One we would be in a constant state of despair – permeated everything in my childhood. When we found the perfect crooked lid that would fit the flawed crooked jar we each were, suddenly we would be whole and no longer a useless, worthless empty vessel: that was the thinking. I heard about The One at church, saw the idea peddled in ads, heard about it in jokes, music, fairytales, books, television and films – to the background drone of people constantly denigrating their partners and relationships in general.

Finding The One was promoted as the only way to 'escape', other than winning the lottery. Education, self-realisation, creative satisfaction, an alternative lifestyle, travel – none of these were ever mentioned.

Being a young working-class Catholic girl, my sole worth was my virginity and my ability to be a slave, incubator and handmaiden of the patriarchy and the church.

It was confusing and oppressive.

I saw a really bad 'active listening' counsellor for a few weeks during Year 12, but it wasn't until I was at university that I had a good two years with a fairly competent psychologist. I went to a therapist to break the cycle of going out with guys who treated me poorly – a typical issue for a girl in her early twenties. It was fascinating to unravel parts of my chaotic childhood and my relationship with my flawed human parents to see where the patterns started and how they affected my current behaviour.

I remember having a light bulb moment in that therapy room. I was about twenty-two and discussing my constant worry about my parents and how responsible I felt for them.

My therapist said, 'Your parents are adults.'

The world stopped for a moment. My parents being adults and their role being to care for us – and not us for them – had never dawned on me! I had lived my whole life feeling it was my job to fix them, heal them and make them happy.

Things looked up from there. My experience in the therapy room that day was akin to a swift skeletal manipulation, with an audible crack and realignment. I went from feeling constantly worried and responsible for my parents to learning how to parent myself.

When I had children myself I found being a parent way easier than I ever expected. I put that down to the fact I was what they call a 'parentified' child – a child who has become a caregiver to their parents. I'm also lucky to have many innate abilities, characteristics and interests that make it easier to parent: I have low expectations; I'm a completionist, rather than a perfectionist; I enjoy people, cooking and organising; I am very independent and was keen to raise independent and resilient kids. I have never lived my life through my children. I didn't have kids because I needed a life. I had them because I had a life I wanted to share. My desire to parent was very much connected with it being a rite of passage. I wanted to experience getting pregnant, giving birth, watching a human grow and being a part of the great scientific experiment that is becoming a parent.

But you know how the old saying goes: 'How do you make God laugh? Tell him your plans.' When our youngest son was six, my relationship with their dad began to deteriorate. When you begin a relationship, you never for a moment think the tiny annoying things you hope will disappear or you'll both fix together will end up taking over everything.

The breakdown of the relationship with the boy's dad coincided with a huge raise in my public profile and I suffered a long and severe depression. The boy's dad (I *hate* calling him my ex) also had emotional issues, so both of us learnt a lot from supporting each other.

My GP picked up my depression. I hadn't twigged. I was

busy: raising three kids and every week writing two newspaper columns, running 50 kilometres and performing publicly. I looked better than I ever had, I was earning more, was very fit and super-productive. Yet, I had a persistent tummy upset. My stomach grumbled, I had bad breath, I was unable to eat and my mind was like a constant whirligig. The doctor quizzed me a little, I broke open and he suggested some therapy. I was all up for it.

My GP referred me to a psychotherapist, Joel;, and we began intensive weekly psychodynamic psychotherapy. Because there was a family history of bipolar, and because I presented quite manic and productive yet deeply depressed, both my GP and Joe thought there was a strong likelihood I was bipolar. They suggested I try taking lithium.

'No, thanks,' I said. 'Not for now.'

Why? Why did I refuse what could have been a magic pill that alleviated my crushing, unrelenting pain?

Two reasons. A friend who I trusted felt I wasn't bipolar. He reminded me that I was still able to file two columns a week and had been for years. Joel did think it was possible I was bipolar, but also made this observation: 'To cope with the depressed condition of your childhood you seem to have developed or uncovered a switch you activated into a busyness, a produc-tiveness, to cope. Kind of a springboard or ejector seat out of the gloom via creativity, helping out, filling your schedule up to distract and exhaust yourself so you could stave off depression and rumination.'

I am not anti-medication, but I don't believe it should be the first resort. In my perfect world, no one would have medication without therapy. During my depression I was in deep, constant pain, despair and dread and I understood going on to medication could be unsettling: there were no guarantees, and it could make me worse. I was barely hanging onto the precipice by my fingernails, so I was fearful medication could push me into an even worse place. The thought there could be an even worse place horrified me. I felt as if I were juggling two broken bottles, three knives, and a chainsaw – that was on fire. The thought of taking medication was like they'd be throwing a live baby in for me to juggle as well.

I also understood therapy worked best without any anesthetising: if possible no drugs, alcohol, gambling, reckless sex or medication. My understanding was that in order to locate the emotional wounds, you need to be as conscious as possible. To feel them acutely enough to grieve them, you need to be raw, unsedated and natural.

My understanding of what it would be like to take antidepressants in the best possible scenario was that my feelings would be 'letterboxed', the extremes at either end would be reduced or erased entirely.

Another reason I was reluctant to take medication was because of its reputation for killing creativity. Creativity and writing in particular were the only things that gave me any positive emotions. I felt a sense of power, agency, catharsis, satisfaction and peace when I wrote. So I made a decision to say no to medication. If I got to a point where I couldn't file a column, then I'd go to the GP and get a prescription. Until then, I would continue to slog through.

One morning, mid-winter, I woke up and it was dire. I got the

Weetabix ready for the kids on the kitchen table and wandered out the front in my nightie and had a cigarette. In the dark. It was freezing cold. 6.30 am. (While I was depressed, I smoked three or four cigarettes a day. I hated it. But I was compelled.) As I sat on my front porch watching the sun come up, I thought, 'I can't do it anymore. I am supposed to file a column today but I've got nothing. I'll get the kids off to school, go see the GP and go on the happy pills. I give up. This is too hard. I can't do it on my own any more.'

So I made an appointment with the GP for 11.30 am. I got the kids off to school and found myself at my laptop. I thought, 'Your appointment is at 11.30. You have two hours. See if there's anything there.'

So I wrote. I wrote the following piece. I filed the column, cancelled the appointment and never ended up taking the medication. I have had more positive feedback for this piece than anything I have ever written.

Just keep going: A tribute to everyday heroes

Every morning I sit on the front deck and drink my coffee, watching people propelling themselves through life. And I'm in awe of how people can keep going. What a wonder the human spirit is.

I watch office workers, jolted out of their slumber by the alarm clock, who have shovelled in their breakfast, thrown on their clothes and rushed to catch the train to a job they hate. I say good morning to elderly neighbours who gingerly walk around the block trying to get their creaky bones and foggy heads working after a night of constant pain and little sleep. I wave to the woman from down the road who has lost her mother after a long fight with cancer. She is shrouded in grief, yet she gets her kids up and dressed, the lunches made and has, against all odds, got the kids to school on time again. And I cheer my mate, overwhelmed by anxiety and depression, who runs every morning. He forces himself out of bed when what he wants is to pull the duvet over his head and disappear. Where's his medal? Where are all of their medals?

No one will ever know the extent of the battles some people among us are fighting and how tough they are finding life. How they find the courage, the bravery and the blind hope to push them through the day. When everything is such an effort, some people are only able to live in five-minute increments. Lurching from one coffee to the next. From one mood swing to the next. From one wave of pain to the next. These are people whose favourite part of the day is the moment before they fall asleep. Because they know they'll have a break from their pain. These people's boilers aren't working and all they are operating with is the pilot light. That's why these people are my heroes.

Winston Churchill said, 'When you find yourself in hell, just keep going.'

While many of us have the luxury of spending our time discussing house prices, Mary-Kate and Ashley's lattes being spiked with full-fat milk or 'Is it art? Is it porn?' so many around us are struggling. I saw a postcard last week that reminded me of how tough some people are doing it: 'Be kind — for everyone you meet is fighting a hard battle.'

You don't read much about pain in the newspaper. But it's all around us. It's all politics, sport, terror, business, celebrities, the economy and recipes. For many, gloom and doom is a welcome distraction from the lacerating pain of their broken heart, the weight of their depression or the terrifying and overwhelming pull of addiction.

We only have one life. The idea is to make the most of it. Some people have more options than others. For those with options, sometimes that in itself can be the weight.

Could change lead you to a better life? And if so, then what change? If only there were mortgage brokers for life who could run your stats through a computer program and furnish us all with the best life solution. 'Option five provides you with the highest level of satisfaction and the lowest level of dissatisfaction. So lose weight, sell your house, stay with your wife, become a dentist, stop eating cheese and buy a new mattress.'

Not everyone can keep going. Some people's pain is so profound that the only place they find peace is in death. Like many, I have been touched by suicide and, as difficult as it is to comprehend, deep in my heart I know my loved ones were just desperate to find peace.

Let's help others in pain find some sweet relief. Let's start a cheer squad for people overwhelmed by emotional pain, physical pain, exhaustion and insomnia. For parents up with babies night after night, people caring for the sick and disabled round the clock and for those whose lives have been ripped apart at the seams. Let's cheer them on from the sidelines: 'You bloody legend! You're a hero! Just. Keep. Going.'

There's a website called grouphug for anonymous online confessions. And amid all the pain I found this contribution:

There are two things that I have found to always be true in life, no matter what. 1. Every day the sun will rise. It is a different day with endless possibilities. 2. This too will pass. These words, engraved on an ancient Sultan's ring, made him solemn in happy times and happy during sad times. Remember these always.

You are amazing. You're doing a great job. Just. Keep. Going.

Things got better.

The boy's dad moved out. The world began to clear and settle.

A few weeks after he left, I was in the shower and gripped with a sense of anxiety, grief and dread. I remember clearly thinking, 'Everything will be fine when we're living separately.'

We *were* living separately. He'd left. Yet I was gripped with a feeling I associated with us being under the same roof.

It reminded me of something my therapist had told me about snoring. People are not generally woken by snoring. They wake up, hear the snoring and assume the snoring is what woke them. Chances are they have been sleeping next to the snoring for days, months or years with no problems.

Correlation does not mean causation. Don't assume your depression will disappear if you have the perfect house, job, body or partner. It may make things easier, but if you're blaming external factors for your low mood it's easy to not be proactive in your mental health self-care.

I'm not sure what helped me out of my deep depression. Therapy? Exercise? Change of living circumstances? Reading self-help books? Writing? Mostly time, I assume. And actively throwing whatever I could at it in an attempt to feel better.

My advice to others would be: do what you can, where you are, with what you have. When you don't know what to do, do anything. Feelings are not fact, emotions change, this is just how it is now. This goes for people suffering and their loved ones.

Psychotherapy is hard work, but the breakthroughs and insight it gave me has allowed me to live a big, happy, brave life full of mostly happy moments with the odd blip.

With therapy, I found it was grief that helped me process and move beyond the negative patterns. Even these days, when I experience the odd pang of grief I immediately have a positive association with growth, peace and clarity.

You realise the therapy is working when you laugh more, you spend less time ruminating, you are kinder to yourself and others, and you are no longer finding yourself in unhealthy situations. It's like giving up smoking and being able to have a packet of cigarettes on a coffee table and not being tempted in the least.

At the end of my therapy I remember being at a party talking to a guy who was a self-deprecating narcissist. He was doing the 'bird with a broken wing, no one understands me but you seem to' routine that I normally would have been sucked in by.

I remember feeling nothing and being amazed. I thought, 'Wow, once upon a time this is the kind of guy who I'd end up having some tortured relationship with – but now, nothing.' The strings that once would have been pulled seemed to have been cut and cauterised.

My partner also has little visits from the Black Dog and it's a privilege and a pleasure being allowed in his inner sanctum. He's a very private person and he trusts me. He is also super-smart and meta-cognitive, so we talk about each other's ups and downs freely, openly and frequently. It's helped me understand myself better as well.

I have a son who manages his depression very well. He will identify it and say, 'I'm depressed.' He doesn't go and get drunk, punch a wall, or blame it on stress at school or lack of a girlfriend.

He came down with a bout recently and I said, 'I can get you an appointment with a counsellor immediately, you can go see the doctor and he could refer you to a psychologist, or we could have a go treating it here. The things you have told me and I have seen that help are running, writing and baths. You could also take St John's wort and magnesium for a few weeks and see if that helps.' He found this advice a help.

What I have realised watching my son, partner and friends manage depression and experiencing my own is that the older you get, the better you get at predicting when it's coming, identifying when you're in it, and knowing things to do to prevent the frequency, duration and severity of bouts.

The reduction of stigma has been massive in getting people help so they can manage as best as possible. No more 'stiff upper lip', 'get over yourself', 'stop overthinking things'. People are more likely to voice their mental health issues and others are more likely to listen without judgement.

It is incredibly valuable to have someone close to you who is objective and who you can check in with and confide in. Someone who knows you, your wishes and what has worked in the past. They can remind you what you have told them helps, what they have observed has helped and that it's only temporary. You have been here before and come out the other side.

While Steve and I were writing this book, I told him about the holiday house we go to every winter. We'd just come back from our yearly trip. I had picked up my 15-year-old from the coach in a small town close by. As we drove towards the winter house, my son said, 'I can see the winter house already in my mind. I know exactly what it will be like. It's so familiar to me. Before I left home I remember consciously thinking, "Remember this, standing here in my home," because when I go to the winter house I forget home. And when I come home I forget the winter house. When I come home I feel as if I was never there, and when I am there I can't remember home. It's like all the winter house memories join up together and all the home memories join up together.'

Depression feels like that. Slipping between two worlds. When you are in one it feels as if you have been there forever.

It's hard to convince people to do preventative things when they are well to avoid depression. Really hard. Because the optimists think, 'Well, that's over and it will never happen again,' the pessimists think, 'What's the point in doing anything with no guarantee it will help. There's nothing I can do but suck it up.'

So here I am at 47. Very happy, satisfied and fulfilled, and although I understand what causes depression and anxiety I, like most, am very hard on myself when it hits. I blame external things for my depression and my own shortcomings. Until I surrender to it.

For many years, I thought everything would be fine if work was more stable, my relationship was less high maintenance, that person would stop being a dick, etc. Depression has a sneaky way of making you feel it's your fault no matter how informed you are about mental illness.

It's only now I have no financial worries, a dream career, lovely independent kids, am fit and healthy and have a very happy, uncomplicated relationship and I *still* suffer/manage depression that I truly understand it can happen to anyone at any time and it is not caused by circumstances, events or general dissatisfaction. Yes, those things can exacerbate it. But no amount of willpower or strength of character alone can overcome depression or anxiety.

Sometimes I am loved up and unstressed, the kids are fine, I've not had any late nights, I've got plenty of enjoyable work, I'm running regularly and eating well and I *still* go under (my term for depression).

The insight I have made into my own psychology through meta-cognition (thinking about my thoughts) and therapy has led to my experiences with depression and anxiety being far less frequent, shorter in duration and diluted in severity.

Would I choose life with depression? Yes. I refer to it as an emotional hard rubbish collection. Every time I come out of depression, I feel my heart is a bit bigger and my understanding of what it is to be human a bit deeper. I feel happiness more keenly and am more grateful. I understand myself and others a little more. It's as if after every bout of depression I get a few more pages of my 'user manual' handed to me.

Anxiety? Would I choose a life without anxiety? Absolutely. Anxiety can fuck right off. It's exhausting and pointless. I haven't suffered much anxiety but it's horrible. It did, in part, lead me to craft, art, creativity, exercise, yoga and music – but so too has depression.

If I had the choice, I would prefer to live with depression than anxiety. I have experienced far more depression than anxiety but the anxiety I have experienced made me feel as if I have less control. It totally overtakes any pleasure or peace. With depression, I can feel peace when I readjust my perspective. It's like a storm I see approaching slowly. I have no idea how long it will descend for or how severe it will be, but I batten down the hatches and bear down. Anxiety is like a motorbike I am strapped to going very fast for a short period until it runs out of petrol.

Give me depression over anxiety any day.

I read this the other day and it really resonated with me:

Depression is not caring about anything,
Anxiety is caring too much about everything.

PART II

THE DISORDERS

6

Depression

Being sad is normal. There are even some benefits to sadness: it helps us recover from life's difficulties. Sadness and pessimism probably have an evolutionary purpose: humanity has been progressed by the cautious, as well as the risk-takers. But at some point sadness can tip over into depression. Depression is essentially sadness that is so persistent and pervasive that it does more harm than good. Some people use the terms 'depression' and 'sadness' interchangeably – but in health care *depression* means a syndrome where sadness has gone too far: it is too severe, is lasting too long and is affecting your ability to function normally.

The potential benefits of sadness

- *Improved memory*. In some ways your brain works better when you are mildly sad.
- *Better judgement*. Judgements we make in social situations are fickle and our interpretations depend on our personal biases. The happier we are, the more these biases influence our judgements.

- *Reduced gullibility.* It's true! Happy people are more gullible. Sad people tend to be more sceptical.
- *Reduced stereotyping.* Sad people are slightly less likely to make judgements about others based on expectations about who they are or what they represent.
- *Better motivation.* Sad people are slightly more likely to persevere at tough tasks. Also, happy people have a tendency to 'self-handicap' by creating artificial excuses as to why they may not succeed, and so give up prematurely.
- *Social benefits.* In some situations sad people perform better. For example, they are more likely to be polite and considerate when making a request, whereas happy people tend to be more assertive in their style.
- *Increased fairness.* In psychological games that test selfishness and fairness, a negative mood results in greater concern for others and an increase in fairness. Happy people tend to be more self-centred.

Determining the cut-off point between sadness and depression is often controversial. Sometimes it's obvious – for example, if someone isn't getting out of bed, is behaving in a much more negative way than their usual state, is worrying constantly and can see no future for themselves, or worse still is suicidal. Sometimes the person diagnoses it themselves – they come to the doctor saying they are not their normal self, they can't enjoy life like they used to, everything feels wrong and they are worrying about things that normally wouldn't cause concern. In these cases, depression is obvious – it's persistent and stopping the person from functioning as they normally would.

More often it's very hard to detect. The depression sneaks up slowly over months or years, and changes in the person's behaviour are so slow and subtle that even their close friends and family don't remember clearly the time when they were not sad, negative and pessimistic. The sufferer explains they are not the type of person who enjoys life: 'It's just my personality, I'm bleak and negative.'

If the person with depression recognises they have a problem, then it's easy for clinicians: we offer help. If, on the other hand, they don't think they have a problem and they are in the consulting room because of the wishes of others, it's much harder – a combination of detective work, listening, clinical judgement and guesswork is required.

Kym

Kym was 21 when she first visited me (Steve) for assessment. She had been a painter since she left school at 17. She wondered whether she was depressed. She said she had never really enjoyed life, even as a little kid. She felt life was a constant struggle – most people annoyed her, she was cynical about almost everything, she wasn't fussed about living and had thought about suicide but never tried it. She had been moderately successful as an artist, but her art was very dark in its themes.

She wore all black. Her mother had taken her to a couple of doctors and even a psychologist, but she'd never engaged. While her mother had suggested this visit, Kym had taken the initiative and booked the appointment. She had started to wonder how much of her dark personality was her true self and how much might be depression.

While Kym did sound depressed, I couldn't in all honesty answer her question. I told Kym a medical interpretation of her circumstances would point to depression, but a more philosophical interpretation might focus on how she was interacting with the world. The choice was hers. I offered her a trial of treatment to see if her mood improved, and gave her the option of therapy or medications. Kym chose medication rather than therapy.

Kym was lucky: the medication did its trick in a relatively short time. Three weeks later Kym returned with a wry smile. She was more animated. She explained that in the last week or so she had started to notice a change. She found more humour in everyday life. She had walked out of her front door a few days ago and noticed how green the trees in her street were – something she said she had never noticed before. She felt positive in small ways. It wasn't a revolution, but she felt different. She was going to buy brighter paints. Her changes grew with subsequent appointments.

Does Kym's result prove she was depressed? If you were a complete believer in the medical model of depression, you'd say it's solid proof. I understand that view but don't entirely agree. To me, her symptoms were vague and she still functioned as an artist. Her outlook was part of her personality. On the other hand, it could have been chronic depression that had hung around so long it seemed like part of her make-up, but was really an abnormal state. Either way, the antidepressants changed her.

Interestingly, Kym came back about a year later because she'd started to wonder whether her new self was her real self. She wanted a trial off the medication to see what happened. She came off slowly, and continued visiting monthly for six months to monitor her mood. She stayed happy. I ran into her about two years later, and she had experienced down times, but not gone back on meds, and the down times had passed. I asked her whether she could answer the question of whether she'd been depressed or whether it was just her personality. She shrugged and said, 'Who knows?' I agree.

Aspects of depression

Depression is common – one in five people suffer from it at some stage in their life. Depression is by far the most common psychiatric disorder that doctors treat. The rule of thumb for diagnosis is five or more symptoms for at least two weeks, with a significant impairment in social or occupational functioning. In reality, most people have had depression for far longer than just two weeks.

The nine key symptoms are:

1. Lowered mood – this means feeling sad. Some people describe crying very easily, others say they feel 'beyond' crying, as if they would cry if they could, but just feel too numb.

2. Lack of enjoyment in usual activities (the medical name for this is 'anhedonia').

3. Change in eating pattern – some people eat more, some less.

4. Change in sleep pattern – most people sleep less, lying awake in bed worrying. Occasionally people with depression sleep more.

5. Fatigue – this is very common in depression, but is also very common in other disorders, and sometimes occurs as a solitary symptom. As a consequence, it's not very useful in discriminating depression from other disorders.

6. Feeling worthless or guilty – depressed people tend to blame themselves for everything that has gone wrong in their lives and those around them, and often feel they are not worthy of help, or are beyond help.

7. Poor concentration – people typically say they can't read a whole page of a book without forgetting what happened at the start, or that they can't watch movies and concentrate to the end.

8. Feeling agitated – this is often described as an inability to relax.

9. Recurrent thoughts of death or suicide.

When doctors examine someone for depression, they look for signs of depression. Often the person's facial expression looks blank (in medical terms, it lacks reactivity), maybe they cry very easily. They tend to pay little attention to personal appearance, or even personal hygiene. Sometimes they are slow in their movements (called 'psychomotor retardation'). Sometimes they are slow in their thinking, with long pauses between sentences. Often they feel hopeless and helpless, meaning they feel there is no hope of improvement and no one can help – these symptoms are particularly destructive, because they stop people seeking help.

Doctors also examine for the medical causes of depression. This is important. While medical causes like low thyroid hormone are uncommon, the list of conditions that may cause depression is long, and if a medical cause is missed it may have serious long-term health consequences. And you may end up embarking on treatments for depression that will never work if the underlying medical problem isn't addressed.

Another area all good clinicians pay enormous attention to is suicide. Suicide is obviously the most feared outcome in psychiatry. While we know that depression is common in those who complete suicide, the precise risk of suicide in a depressed person is difficult to determine. In severe depression the risk is probably around 10 per cent (i.e. very high). So if someone is depressed, a thorough risk assessment is carried out (see Chapter 4).

Types of depression

Depression is divided into various subtypes, and each has a slightly different treatment approach.

Major depressive disorder (MDD)

This is the medical name for what most people think of as depression. It is common: about one in four women and one in six men experience an episode in their lifetime. At least five of the symptoms from the list of nine (above) must be present most of the time for at least two weeks, causing disruption in the way the person functions (usually socially or in their work). Once diagnosed, it is divided into mild, moderate or severe – and this determines the treatment recommended:

- Mild: Usually just five of the symptoms, no suicidal thoughts and only mild impairment in functioning.
- Moderate: More than five symptoms and clear functional impairment, maybe fleeting suicidal thoughts but no suicide plans.
- Severe: Significant suicidal thoughts; and/or almost all symptoms, unable to function normally even for short periods of time.

Dysthymia

This is mild but chronic depression. The person feels depressed but doesn't quite meet all the criteria for diagnosis, so has just two to five of the list of symptoms, but they last at least two years. Dysthymia is less common than major depression, but still fairly common (about 5 per cent of people will experience it in their lifetime).

Bipolar disorder

This is a less common form of depression, occurring in only 1 per cent of the population. It used to be called manic depression.

In bipolar disorder the person has mood swings – they are sometimes depressed and sometimes manic. The swings usually last for weeks or even months, and the person usually returns to normal between episodes. There are 'rapid cycling' varieties where mood can swing within days (or rarely, even hours) but these are less common again.

Whenever a clinician sees a patient with any sort of depression, they will ask questions to explore whether they have ever experienced a manic episode – it's very important, because the presence of mania indicates bipolar disorder and the treatment of bipolar disorder is quite different to straight depression.

A *manic episode* is a period of elevated mood lasting at least a week. An elevated mood is a bit like being super happy. You feel on top of the world and indestructible. Manic people barely sleep, they tend not to eat, they have grandiose plans and ideas, and think they can solve all the problems of the world (alas, usually with plans that are obviously poorly thought out). They are often agitated, talk too much and get easily distracted. Sometimes their mood appears more irritable than elevated, and because their mood is labile (i.e. it fluctuates) mania can occasionally be mistaken for depression. They tend to laugh one minute, cry the next. Mania is dramatic and overwhelming when you first see it – the sufferers are larger than life, taking all sorts of risks and raising all sorts of feelings (from distress to humour) in others. When severe, they can be delusional, sometimes to such a degree that it is hard to distinguish mania from acute schizophrenia. In the days before medications, manic people sometimes died from exhaustion and starvation because they could not settle enough to eat or sleep.

Secondary depression

This is depression that is due to some specific and identifiable cause, usually medication, drugs or a medical illness. It's important to consider, because if there is an underlying cause such as a medical illness, the treatment for depression will fail unless the underlying cause is fixed as well. The most common illnesses that result in secondary depression are hypothyroidism, conditions that cause chronic pain, and conditions that affect the brain, such as Parkinson's disease. The most common drugs that cause it are alcohol and opiates.

Grief

Grief is *not* depression, but it is worth mentioning because grief and depression overlap and can be hard to tell apart. Occasionally grief can lead to depression or trigger a depressive episode.

Grief is the emotional response to the loss of someone or something. The most common cause of grief is the death of a loved one, but grief can also occur after any loss – a failed relationship, the loss of a job, a pet, a possession, or many other losses. It's quite normal for grief to involve a range of symptoms, many of which are typical of depression, such as sadness, crying, loss of concentration and poor sleep. These typically last about six weeks after the loss and then gradually settle down. If they last more than three months, we start to get suspicious that the grief has triggered an episode of depression. In that case we start to consider active treatments, either specific therapy to deal with grief, or simply treatments for depression, such as psychotherapy or medications.

Premenstrual dysphoric disorder (PDD)

Many women report dysphoria in the final week before their period starts. Dysphoria means a profound state of unease or dissatisfaction. It's slightly different to depression. PDD is different for each person, but it usually consists of a mix of mood swings, irritability, anxiety, sadness, poor sleep, poor concentration and tension, which occur for up to a week before the period starts and then disappear soon after.

Postnatal depression (PND)

Depression is common during pregnancy and in the year after childbirth. It often goes unrecognised in the whirlwind of changes that occur after the birth of a child. If untreated, the depression can sometimes worsen and the mother can experience psychotic symptoms such as hallucinations and delusions. This is particularly dangerous and places both the mother and the baby at risk of harm.

Part of the problem in recognising PND is separating clinical depression from the 'baby blues'. The baby blues refers to the tearfulness, anxiety and sadness that is common between the third and tenth days after childbirth (about one in three women experience this). Postnatal depression is when the symptoms are persistent (last longer than two weeks) and interfere with the woman's ability to function. It usually develops sometime between one and twelve months after giving birth. About one in seven women experience PND.

Am I depressed?

Self-diagnosis is hard. Unless you have had previous episodes of depression, you will probably be one of the last people to realise you are depressed. It sneaks up on you. The changes in your mood and behaviour are slow to develop, and you will often think of many possible causes of why you are not your usual self.

The trick to self-diagnosis is to separate causes and symptoms. Don't think about *why* you are feeling sad – just ask yourself: 'Am I sad?' If the answer is yes, then ask: 'For how long have I been sad?' If it is longer than two weeks, run through the list of symptoms above – if you have more than three, if any are particularly severe, or if you feel *at all* suicidal – GO AND SEE YOUR DOCTOR.

There are numerous self-diagnosis tests on the internet. Most only take a few minutes to complete, but take them with a grain of salt: they tend to overdiagnose and misdiagnose. Symptoms of depression overlap with many other problems, especially physical illnesses and anxiety disorders. A better bet is to see a trained clinician, and your GP is the best place to start. The point is to see someone who knows about depression and can take an objective look at you (so not a relative or a friend) and point you in the right direction to get help.

When you see your GP, you must tell them why you have come! Many, many patients beat around the bush, or mention every word *except* depression or don't build up the courage to mention their feelings until the consultation is almost over. Some studies suggest GPs miss the diagnosis of depression about half the time. There are lots of reasons for this – stigma, rushed consultations, patients not recognising their own feelings, and some GPs not being attuned to psychological problems. Sometimes patients are just too embarrassed to mention their feelings, and sometimes they don't want to stress their GP.

If you feel your GP isn't listening, is rushed or hasn't reassured you, try a different GP. It's frustrating that these barriers to getting mental health care exist, and while they are reducing every year, they remain a reality. So don't be put off if your first attempt at raising a response doesn't work – try again.

Also, don't try to work out why you are depressed immediately. The first task is diagnosis, and next comes figuring out the cause. Far too many people get caught up with the *why* before they have figured out the *what*. The best approach is: What is wrong? Am I depressed? What should I do about it? Once this is sorted out, you can start to think about why it happened.

Figuring out the cause of depression is truly tough. It can also be pointless. Blame can distract from dealing with the here and now and getting on with treatment.

Depending on your philosophies and beliefs, you will no doubt have different ideas of what causes depression and how to avoid it. Is it about money? Is it about religion and spirituality? Is it about life's hardships? Is it because of your past? Or your relationships? Are you just in a shitty life situation that will pass?

> *Before you diagnose yourself with depression or low self-esteem, first make sure that you are not, in fact, just surrounding yourself with assholes.*
>
> William Gibson

At the end of the day, depression has many possible causes and figuring out which one is driving your depression is an exercise in educated guesswork. We're not saying that self-reflection isn't important, just that in the early days of depression it's not the main task. It's perhaps best left for once you've recovered and are in a better frame of mind to dispassionately evaluate your life.

Getting help for depression

Getting help for depression can be a real challenge. Depressed people are fatigued, lack motivation, and often feel beyond help and undeserving of care and attention – hardly the formula to get you running off to your local GP. To top it off, they have often burnt a few bridges regarding relationships, so they have fewer people around to help them.

Despite all this, the number of people around the globe seeking help for depression has exploded in recent years. This is due partly to organisations and national programs to reduce stigma and increase awareness, and partly to better funding of mental health professionals and more treatment options.

There are five key steps to consider in treating depression. For mild depression, steps one to three (diagnosis, self-education and psychological first aid) usually suffice. Moderate depression usually requires steps four or five (psychotherapy or medications) as well. And for severe depression, all steps are needed – plus a period in hospital may be needed to address the risk of suicide.

1. Diagnosis

As well as having many different subtypes, depression often overlaps with various other disorders – especially anxiety, drug and alcohol problems, and personality issues. Sometimes there is no simple diagnosis but rather a list of problems, or even multiple disorders. Multiple disorders (called co-morbidity) are actually more common than single disorders. Each problem has a different 'menu' of treatment options. So figuring out the key issues and developing a plan of attack (treatment plan) with different alternatives is essential.

Where you go to achieve this first step is debatable. As for other mental health problems, start with a GP. Other options include your local hospital, a psychiatric nurse, a psychologist or a counsellor. You can't see a psychiatrist unless a GP refers you.

Of course, you may also choose to DIY (do it yourself) – self-diagnose and self-treat. Many would argue this is risky (and it should definitely be avoided if your symptoms are more than mild or if you have *any* suicidal thoughts), but it is not unreasonable as long as you take the issue seriously and set yourself a time limit – if you're not improving in two months, visit a GP.

2. Self-education

Arm yourself with information. Good clinicians will start you on this path on your very first visit. Learn about the treatment options. Read reputable websites. Speak to others who have experienced the same thing.

Part of self-education is learning how to evaluate evidence – this is a skill that will serve you throughout life. Medical science usually divides every treatment into one of five levels of evidence. At the top are treatments that have been studied by different scientists in different countries using the latest scientific techniques – these treatments are the best medical science has to offer at this particular point in time. Of course, not every illness has level 1 treatments available. At the bottom are treatments that lack scientific evidence, or where the results of different studies are conflicting. Look up the treatment you are considering and weigh up the evidence. Professionals are trained to do this, but of course training varies, and some professionals are more prone to personal beliefs and biases than others – so you should always check yourself! Empower yourself with knowledge.

3. Psychological first aid

There are five key planks to good mental health – often called psychological first aid. Everyone should keep these in mind, but if you're depressed, you need to be especially vigilant and work hard to improve them. We go into more detail about these in Chapter 17, but they are:

- good sleep
- healthy nutrition – this includes minimising caffeine, alcohol and drugs
- exercise
- stress management (including problem solving)
- relationships.

4. Psychotherapy

Once you've covered steps one to three, you need to make a

decision about psychotherapy. For depression, the main psychotherapy is cognitive behaviour therapy (CBT). It works in about 70 per cent of depressive episodes, usually takes about one hour per week for three months, and seems to be associated with fewer relapses than medications. Psychotherapy can be carried out by trained clinicians, including psychologists, psychiatrists and some (but not all) counsellors. It takes effort, but is usually well worth it in the long run.

You might also have heard of mindfulness therapy; it's a new take on CBT, with meditation included.

Many people start off by saying they hate the idea of psychotherapy and resist trying it. They've usually got a range of impressions about psychotherapy from movies and TV – these impressions are nearly always wrong! In the long term, most people eventually change their minds, try therapy and in retrospect value the experience. For more details, see Chapter 18.

5. Medications

There are many antidepressant drugs available (see Chapter 19). They are all pretty much equal in terms of effectiveness. They all have side effects. (Every medication ever invented that works has side effects!) They work in about 55 per cent of depressive episodes. If one antidepressant doesn't work after four weeks of being on the right dose and taking it daily, we switch to another antidepressant, usually of a different chemical class. It sometimes takes a number of weeks to figure out the right dose.

Things you need to know if you choose to take an antidepressant

- They take at least two weeks to work, probably more like four weeks. The side effects can start straight away. Don't give up after a week thinking they aren't working – you need to wait longer.
- For benefits to occur, they must be taken consistently every day.
- The clinical course of improvement fluctuates ('three steps forward, one step back'). You need to expect this, so you don't get disheartened and discontinue them when these inevitable setbacks occur.
- Medications need be continued once the symptoms have resolved, usually for about six months if it's your first episode of depression, longer if you've had it before.
- All antidepressants have side effects. Your doctor must discuss them with you. Your pharmacist can discuss them too. You usually get a pamphlet in the packet. Forewarned is forearmed. Most side effects are mild and go away after a week or so. Some require dose adjustment. Some require you to cease the medication. If in doubt, ring your doctor.
- Sexual side effects are particularly common, including reduced libido, decreased arousal, anorgasmia (inability to orgasm) in women and delayed ejaculation in men. The effects are dose-dependent and different

antidepressants have different degrees of them. See
Chapter 19 for more information, and ask your doctor.

- Some antidepressants cause sedation, some cause
  insomnia. Those that cause insomnia are usually taken
  in the morning, and the sedating ones at night. Sedation
  can be helpful if your depression is causing sleeplessness.
- Other less common side effects include weight gain,
  headache and nausea, but the full list is long. The
  upside is that most side effects are short-lived, and
  easy to manage.

Medications or psychotherapy?

This is a common question in moderate depression. In mild
depression you usually don't need either, and in severe depression you need both. In my experience about a quarter of people
come along and say, 'Doc, I'm not interested in all that psycho-
babble-mumbo-jumbo navel-gazing-nonsense. Just give me the
happy pills and I'll be on my way.' About a quarter say, 'Doc, I
know exactly what you shrinks are like, always forcing patients
to take crappy tablets for a quick fix, I want to do this properly, I
want to explore the causes and think it through, I want psychotherapy.' I don't mind which people choose, and so always go
with their choice assuming it is available. In some places it's
very hard to get psychotherapy from trained clinicians simply
because so few clinicians are available. Also, sometimes it's
expensive, so cost needs to be taken into account.

The rest say, 'I don't know, I'll do whatever you recommend.' In this case, if their symptoms are moderate, I recommend starting with psychotherapy – and if that doesn't work, try medications.

Treatment for bipolar disorder

Bipolar disorder is very complex, and I wouldn't recommend trying to treat it without a specialist psychiatrist. Nearly everyone with bipolar disorder requires medications at least some of the time. The medications are complex and some have risky side effects, so careful consideration of the pros and cons is needed. Also, the risk of under-treatment is high. Suicide is common, and there are various other risks, like dangerous behaviours, risky sexual encounters, financial loss from extravagant purchases and so on. Hospital admission is often needed, especially with mania – sometimes against the patient's will (called 'involuntary admission').

When psychiatrists treat bipolar disorder, they work in three key phases:

1. treatment of depressive episodes
2. treatment of manic episodes
3. prevention of further episodes.

Treatment for depressive episodes

This is mostly the same as for depression without bipolar disorder as described above, except that we usually do not prescribe antidepressants alone, as they can trigger manic episodes. So if medications are needed, we start with a mood-stabilising medication, and if that isn't enough, add an antidepressant later.

Treatment for manic episodes

Mania rarely settles without medications, and in fact usually gets worse. There are two classes of medications to consider: anti-psychotics and mood stabilisers. Each has benefits and risks, and sometimes both are needed. Some people also need benzodiazepines (such as diazepam), especially to help with sleep and to settle agitation.

Prevention of further episodes

Mood stabilisers decrease the frequency and severity of further episodes (they rarely stop them all-together). Lithium was the first of these; it is effective but requires close monitoring of blood levels, so is less favoured these days. Anti-epileptic medications are now the most popular, with the common ones being valproate and carbamazepine. Patients other than women of child-bearing age who should not take valproate (NICE guidelines) need to stay on these long-term.

When should you see a specialist psychiatrist or psychologist?

Situations in which referral should be considered include:

- severe symptoms
- high suicide risk
- failure to respond to treatment
- uncertainty about the diagnosis
- possible organic brain disease or dementia
- bipolar disorder
- the need for greater resources (specialist services may include social workers, various peer supports,

and extra funding avenues for more
treatment)
- co-morbidity with drugs or alcohol or
other psych disorders.

What if treatment doesn't work?

This is the most important section of this chapter! Only about
half of the people with mild to moderate depression get better
with their first attempt at treatment. You must have a plan B in
your head. Your clinician must have plans B, C and D in their
head. If you're seeing a specialist, they should have plans B, C,
D, E and F in their head.

When a patient presents with 'treatment-resistant' depression,
these are the questions clinicians explore:
- Is the diagnosis correct? Perhaps the initial diagnosis was
made too hastily; often more inquiry is needed.
- Is there co-morbidity that has been missed? In other
words, is there something else going on that has been
overlooked because of the depression, and it's preventing treatment from working. This is very common –
especially with anxiety disorders and drug and alcohol
problems. Treatments for depression often fail because
the patient is drinking alcohol excessively and hasn't told
their clinician (often because they're embarrassed).
- Is the patient adhering to the treatment? Are they taking
their medications? Are they doing their psychotherapy
homework?

- Is more time needed? Sometimes improvement is slow and we just have to wait longer.

If all of these issues have been addressed, then it's time to consider other options. There are literally dozens of treatments for depression, and each has pros and cons depending on the situation and the unique features of each patient. Some of the things clinicians think about include:

- Is this the right medication? If it hasn't worked after four weeks, change to a different medication or increase the dose. There are a variety of antidepressants to choose from. Different people respond to different medications – there is no 'one size fits all'. Trial and error is the only way to find out.

- Is this the right form of psychotherapy? Just like medications, there are many different types of psychotherapy. Also, sometimes the outcome depends on the relationship between the patient and their psychotherapist (the 'fit'). Sometimes it's worthwhile trying a different therapist.

- Combining treatments. There are medication combinations that are particularly effective in treatment-resistant depression. Medication and therapy can be combined. Different therapies can be combined. Sometimes individual therapy is combined with group therapy. It all depends on the circumstances.

- Second opinion. Sometimes a fresh opinion from a different clinician is what's needed. Each clinician sees the world and their patients slightly differently. A fresh set of eyes is very useful. Note: if your clinician takes offence at you asking for a second opinion, then get a new clinician!

Good clinicians appreciate the extra input and don't get offended.

- Complementary or alternative treatments. The science of psychiatry is in its infancy, so sensible people keep an open mind. If there is an alternative treatment that appeals to a patient, it's often worth exploring. Many so-called complementary treatments, from nutritional approaches to yoga to over-the-counter supplements, are virtually mainstream now. Just be aware that all treatments can interact with each other, so keep all your clinicians informed.

With persistence, nearly everyone gets better. The most common reason people don't get better is that they don't complete their treatments and give up too easily. This is especially common in depression, because one of the key symptoms is hopelessness – the feeling that nothing will help and life is unrelentingly bleak. The very symptoms of depression stop people from persisting with treatment! Lots of support is required. And so is lots of patience – from the patient, the clinician, their family and friends. Don't give up: persistence is the key.

7

Anxiety

Welcome to the anxiety chapter! Dev wants to begin this chapter by defining anxiety, worry and stress. Steve is a little nervous about this, because even after twenty years of practice, he has trouble separating the terms.

The general consensus is that worry is normal and in proportion to a problem, whereas anxiety has a sense of dread attached to it and feels out of control. Worry is specific to an issue; anxiety tends to be more general and about everything. Worry tends to be more realistic and mostly triggers problem solving. Worry tends to be experienced in our head; anxiety is more physical. Worry dissipates when the issue is resolved; anxiety can linger. Worry doesn't damage our functioning, whereas anxiety can.

Stress is a process. Stress occurs when we are under pressure and we think we might fail. It includes some sort of demanding situation and our body's response. The response might include worry, anxiety, depression and a whole bunch of physical responses (our bodies release stress hormones when we're under pressure). Stress can be good or bad – it can trigger solutions, or it can spiral out of control and be destructive. Stress is linked to all sorts of physical illnesses – like cardiovascular disease.

There is a famous law in psychology called the Yerkes-Dodson law. It states that performance increases with physiological or mental arousal, but only up to a point, after which is deteriorates. So as we get aroused, our memory, attention and thinking speed increase. But if it goes too far, we suffer. A little stress is great to get us performing or help us deal with threats, but if we have too much stress we're in trouble.

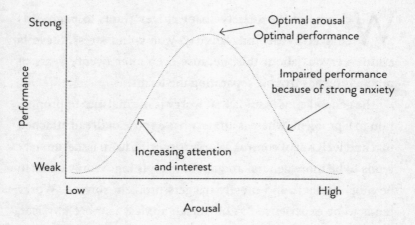

For most clinicians, the distinction between anxiety and worry is a moot point. Most people go to a clinician and say, 'I'm not coping.' The clinician then helps the person figure out whether their symptoms are a normal response to a difficult situation or an abnormal response, in which case we think of it as anxiety.

Aspects of anxiety

Describing anxiety in words is hard – like trying to describe how to ride a bike. Before you read on, close your eyes for a minute, and imagine you are anxious. Try to put into words all of your feelings and symptoms. It might be something like this: *dread, racing mind, uncertain, fearful, nauseous, headachy, preoccupied, dizzy, racing heart, overwhelmed, hyperalert, irritable, snappy, snarky and annoyed.*

Fears and concerns are something that everybody experiences. They're a daily experience for most of us. They're so common we hardly notice the chatter in our heads.

In fact, when people first present to doctors with anxiety, over half begin by describing physical symptoms such as tummy pains, headaches and insomnia, without mentioning they are anxious. Good clinicians are alert to this and ask the right questions to explore the potential diagnosis of anxiety. When we get anxious, we get a mix of thoughts, feelings and physical sensations:

- *thoughts*: a range of fears, especially fear of losing control, going mad, being embarrassed or even dying
- *feelings*: dread, fear, irritability and distractibility
- *physical sensations*: a huge range of symptoms can occur, typically:
  - cardiovascular: palpitations, chest pain, racing heart, flushing
  - respiratory: hyperventilation, shortness of breath
  - neurological: dizziness, headache, vertigo

- gastrointestinal: choking, dry mouth, nausea,
  vomiting, diarrhoea
- musculoskeletal: restlessness, muscle ache and tension

We don't all agree on how the links between thoughts, feelings and physical sensations work. Which comes first, how they interrelate, which drives our response – it's all a little bit of a mystery, despite dozens of theories and decades of speculation. The mind and the body work together. Any change in one, causes a change in the other. The most effective treatments address all three.

Anxiety is a spectrum. Is there a healthy level of anxiety? Most would say healthy anxiety is worry, by definition. Others would say some anxiety is normal and a little is within the realm of healthy. In clinical practice, finding the cut-off point between normal and abnormal anxiety is hard. In essence, we say the anxiety is abnormal if the person subjectively feels it is out of control ('I'm not coping'), and if the anxiety is interfering with their functioning.

Types of anxiety

Anxiety can get out of control for a range of reasons, some known and some unknown. In medicine, we divide the main causes into two categories: primary and secondary.

- Primary anxiety disorders are those where there is no obvious medical cause.
- Secondary anxiety is where the anxiety is due to a clear biological factor. Common causes include physical

disorders (such as hyperthyroidism) or drugs (such as caffeine or amphetamines). When a clinician assesses you for anxiety, they will always ask about other disorders to exclude them. They'll also do a range of blood tests to look for any underlying biological problems.

Primary anxiety disorders are the most common mental health disorders of all, even more common than depression. The typical ones are panic disorder, phobias, obsessive-compulsive disorder, post-traumatic stress disorder and generalised anxiety disorder.

Panic disorder

Panic disorder is a mix of panic attacks and fear of future attacks to a degree the person can't function properly. Panic attacks are sudden episodes of severe anxiety – usually so severe the person thinks they are dying. The first few times they experience a panic attack, people often think they're having a heart attack and rush to hospital by ambulance. They report chest pain, palpitations, a suffocating feeling, dizziness, nausea and more. Attacks can last just a few seconds, but between 10 and 20 minutes is average, and sometimes for up to an hour. After the acute attack settles, people often feel exhausted and apprehensive for hours.

Once a person has had a panic attack, they usually feel fearful of having another for weeks afterwards. Sometimes agoraphobia develops, which is a fear of being in places or situations from which escape may be difficult should a panic attack occur. The most common place people experience agoraphobia is in a supermarket – lights, noise, crowds and the need to pass through checkout to escape. This isn't surprising: if we trace the origins of the word agoraphobia back to the ancient Greek, it means 'fear of the marketplace'!

Once agoraphobia develops, people start to limit their activities. Some stay in their home, with just a few outside places where they feel safe.

Of note, agoraphobia can also occur without panic attacks, but is rare. On occasions people from cities beset by violence (usually cities in the midst of war) can develop agoraphobia, as can people who have other reasons to be fearful when outside the safety of their home.

Phobias

Phobias are fears of specific objects or situations. The fear is persistent, excessive and unreasonable, and results in avoidance of those objects or situations.

A phobia is far more extreme than a simple fear. For example, most people are scared of spiders, and will avoid them and feel fear when they come across a spider. Whereas someone with arachnophobia, a phobia of spiders, will always be on the lookout for a spider – as they enter any new situation, they'll think about the risk of seeing a spider. If they think the risk is high, they'll likely avoid the situation. The mere mention of spiders will cause some anxiety. Reading this paragraph would cause an arachnophobe anxiety.

Social phobia, also known as social anxiety disorder, is the most common phobia. It is the fear of any situation where public scrutiny may be possible, usually with the fear of having a panic attack or behaving in a way that is embarrassing or humiliating.

Social phobia is so common that many people debate whether it is a true disorder or just a part of being human. Not many people can speak publicly without some anxiety – in social phobia, the anxiety is so severe that the person cannot function at an adequate level. This cut-off point will be different for each of us. We all have different levels of acceptance of anxiety and its consequences.

Common phobias

Claustrophobia: Fear of confined spaces
Ophidiophobia: Fear of snakes
Acrophobia: Fear of heights
Cynophobia: Fear of dogs
Astraphobia: Fear of thunder and lightning
Tryanophobia: Fear of injections
Pteromerhanophobia: Fear of flying
Mysophobia: Fear of dirt or germs
Automatonophobia: Fear of anything that represents a sentient being, like masks, puppets, clowns and statues
Phobophobia: Fear of phobias

Obsessive-compulsive disorder (OCD)

As with social phobia, we all have some obsessive anxieties and compulsive behaviours, but in obsessive-compulsive disorder (OCD) they are so overwhelming that everyday life is impaired.

Obsessions are recurrent thoughts, urges or images. For some, it's fear of contamination by germs; for others, it's the fear of being responsible for something terrible happening. Some obsessions are about sexual practices and the person has constant thoughts that they might transgress some sexual boundary. When experiencing obsessions, thoughts go around and around in our heads like a broken record and we become anxious. Compulsions are the actions we perform to reduce the anxiety.

Compulsions are repetitive behaviours or mental acts that the person feels driven to perform. Typical compulsions include washing, checking doors or locks, turning electricity switches on and off, and counting numbers. Some are mental rituals, such as saying something over and over in your head.

OCD is diagnosed when the obsessions and compulsions are particularly time-consuming (usually more than one hour per day) or cause significant distress or impairment in functioning. Approximately 1 per cent of people suffer OCD.

OCD is usually a chronic lifelong problem that waxes and wanes. It typically gets worse at times of stress.

OCD is not well understood. It overlaps with a range of similar disorders – such as body dysmorphic disorder (a preoccupation with an imaginary or slight defect in body appearance), hoarding, hair pulling and skin picking. There is also a link to tic disorders (tics are repetitive, short-lasting movements or sounds), with about 30 per cent of people who have OCD also having experienced a tic disorder at some time in their life.

Post-traumatic stress disorder (PTSD)

Trauma is a common human experience. Traumatic events include witnessing or experiencing wars, physical or sexual assault, terrorism and severe accidents like car crashes.

Nearly everyone experiences traumatic events at some time in their life. How people respond to these events varies for each of us and is partly determined by our past experiences of trauma, our social supports, and the events that follow the trauma.

Emotional reactions at the time of the trauma include fear, helplessness, insecurity and a sense that all order in the world is lost.

After a traumatic event, there are three typical clusters of symptoms that develop to varying degrees. The first cluster revolves around the ways we 're-experience' the trauma. This might be intrusive recollections, nightmares or even flashbacks (brief periods where memories are so vivid it's like the trauma is actually happening again). The second cluster involves all the efforts to avoid reminders of the trauma – things like avoiding talking about it, refusing to watch the news in case similar events are reported, and mental tricks to avoid anything that might trigger memories. The third cluster refers to the changes in thinking and mood that follow a trauma. These include being irritable or angry, feeling on edge and nervous, being 'hypervigilant' for danger in our surroundings, and having poor concentration and disrupted sleep. Depression is also a very common result of trauma.

Post-traumatic stress disorder (PTSD) is diagnosed if the symptoms are severe, last more than a month and disrupt usual functioning. PTSD is common – about 8 per cent of people suffer it at some stage in their life. After experiencing a trauma, the chances of PTSD vary greatly, according to the nature of the trauma and the events around it, but they can be as high as 50 per cent for horrific events such as rape and war.

Generalised anxiety disorder (GAD)

Until relatively recently, generalised anxiety disorder (GAD) had been seen as the diagnosis made if the anxiety failed to fit nicely into any of the other more easily recognisable patterns described above. Recent research suggests that GAD is more common and more disabling than originally thought.

GAD is characterised by excessive, uncontrollable worry about a number of events or activities. The worry is pervasive, difficult to control and out of proportion to the situation. The content of the worries usually involves several life areas, such as concerns for one's family, finances, work and personal health.

Patients with GAD often appear to have a huge bundle of anxiety looking for an outlet. No matter how well things are going, they search for and find things to worry about. When severe, it is very disabling.

How much anxiety is too much?

One afternoon a few years ago, two new patients were booked into my (Steve's) clinic back to back.

The first was Trevor, a 47-year-old male who described over twenty years of anxiety. The anxiety began when he was working as a shop assistant in a large department store. He developed panic attacks on his morning train commute, and after a few months was unable to work. At the time, he saw a psychologist and a psychiatrist. While his symptoms improved a little, he never managed to get back to work. Eventually he received a disability-related pension and settled into a life living at home with his mother and brother. Trevor rarely went out other than to the local convenience store for bread and basic groceries. He'd never had a relationship, had one old school friend he saw most weeks, and his main pastime was watching television with his mother. I diagnosed panic disorder and agoraphobia with severe functional impairment. I recommended medications and cognitive behaviour therapy.

The second patient was Chris, a 31-year-old executive who reported anxiety in social situations, with occasional panic attacks. He'd experienced his symptoms for about twelve months. Chris was the state manager of a transport company. He managed about twenty-five employees and had to travel around the state at least once a week. He found enclosed spaces difficult, never caught lifts, slept poorly the nights before presentations to groups of more than about five people, and avoided plane flights. His panic attacks occurred about once a fortnight, but were brief, and he managed them by finding a quiet place to sit and doing slow breathing techniques. Chris's visit was precipitated by a promotion to national manager. He'd now have to fly interstate at least once a month, and his new office was on the fifteenth floor of his building, so he was going to need to start using lifts. He'd also need to present to bigger groups far more frequently. For Chris, I diagnosed mild social phobia with occasional panic attacks but little or no functional impairment. I thought he'd do fine with CBT alone.

Both patients disagreed with my opinions.

Trevor said he did not need treatment. He was completely happy with his life and anxiety. He enjoyed his time living with his mother, didn't miss work (and thought after twenty years he'd never get another job anyway) and couldn't see the point in changing. He really only came to see me because his mother recommended he look into options. But Trevor said, 'Truth be told, Doc, I think I have a pretty good life. I'm just anxious, but that's just me. I like life as it is.'

Chris also disagreed. While I said his symptoms were mild and psychotherapy alone would be fine, he explained he was ambitious, and any anxiety was too much. He wanted the maximum treatment and as soon as possible. He was excited about his new job and didn't want any anxiety getting in his way. He started medications immediately and booked in for CBT.

Chris had mild anxiety but wanted maximum help; Trevor had severe anxiety but wanted no treatment. Anxiety is a very personal thing. There is no simple formula for when to intervene. Each person makes their own decision.

Anxiety in other disorders

While anxiety often occurs as a standalone issue, it can also occur in conjunction with other disorders. It's often part of another psychiatric disorder or due to the effects of stimulant drugs.

Anxiety with depression is so common that some people argue they are part of the same syndrome. Depressed people are virtually always anxious, but anxious people aren't always depressed. As a consequence, if a person is both depressed and anxious, the clinician will usually not diagnose an anxiety disorder unless it is still present after the depression has gone.

There is also a lot of overlap between the anxiety disorders. Differentiating the syndromes is useful because there are different responses to different drugs, and the psychological treatment options vary.

Anxiety can also result in other problems, most often alcohol abuse. Alcohol is so widely available and such a good elixir for anxiety that most people with an anxiety problem self-medicate with alcohol – and some go on to excessive use.

If you suffer an anxiety disorder, your chances of suffering an alcohol problem increase two- to threefold. The strongest links between anxiety and alcohol abuse are for PTSD, panic and GAD.

Good screening questions to encourage patients to discuss anxiety

- Do you think you might suffer from anxiety? (Always ask the obvious questions first!)
- Do you feel wound up, on edge or nervous?
- Is your anxiety or worry linked with physical symptoms such as a racing heart, shortness of breath and sweating?
- Does your anxiety or worry ever go away?
- How difficult is it to control your worry?

- Is your worry realistic and reasonable, or is it out of control?
- Does your worry help you, or does it interfere and slow you down?
- Is your anxiety or worry predictable?
- Does it only ever happen in certain situations or places? (checking for phobias)
- Do you have anxiety attacks that come from out of nowhere? (checking for panic attacks)
- Do you have any thoughts that come into your head and make you worry? (checking for obsessions)
- Are there rituals or things you have to do to stop feeling worried? (checking for compulsions)
- Have you ever experienced a traumatic event that caused ongoing anxiety? (checking for PTSD)

Getting help for anxiety

Knowing when to get help is not easy for anxiety disorders. We all have different levels of tolerance for concern, worry and fear. Some people with very high tolerance never even consider getting help. They think it is just part of their everyday life experience, or part of their personality. Others have a more philosophical objection to getting help – they see anxiety as normal and attempts to treat it as overmedicalisation of the human experience. They are often especially dismissive of the use of medications for anxiety. They see them as an attempt by 'big pharma' to pathologise normal experiences in the quest for profit.

While we appreciate this view, we tend to favour a more practical approach – if a person has anxiety that is affecting their enjoyment of life or is interfering with their ability to function, then they should at least consider ways to reduce anxiety.

There's a wide range of options when it comes to getting help for anxiety.

First, there is self-help. Anyone can begin by doing some research, including reading self-help books and researching it online. Read widely, think about your anxiety and make your own self-help plan. Consider exercise and relaxation strategies like meditation and yoga. Think about your intake of stimulants, especially caffeine and tobacco, and cut back or quit. Try to figure out what causes you the most stress in your life and make a plan to slowly introduce changes. It sometimes helps to make a list of your problems, then take each one, and write a list of possible solutions. Tackle one solution at a time. Go slow; be patient but persistent. If you're drinking alcohol to help anxiety, cut back, especially because it only lasts for short periods (hours) and often leads to rebound anxiety and tolerance (meaning your body becomes tolerant to alcohol's anxiety-reducing effects, inevitably leading to more drinking).

In terms of seeking assistance, there are many avenues. You can begin by contacting one of the great phone or online services. Lifeline, beyondblue and many other resources online can help you determine where to start in your quest for help.

Alternatively, visit your doctor. Most GPs are very skilled at assessing anxiety, ruling out all the secondary causes (such as physical illnesses) and chatting about local options in your community. Your GP should also know of local psychologists or counselors who work with anxiety. Most are also well informed about alternative approaches to anxiety (see below). Some GPs are a little overzealous with medications. While medications are often required, Steve's own view is that they should be a last resort in anxiety, so if you get pushed down this path as a first line approach, think about seeking another opinion.

Also, don't forget all mental health treatment starts with mental health first aid (see Chapter 17) – this can be addressed alone or with any doctor or counsellor. In particular, minimising caffeine, alcohol and drugs is important for anxiety. Yoga is particularly recommended, and problem-solving can help with stress management.

Psychological approaches

There are a range of psychological approaches to anxiety. The most popular and well researched is cognitive behaviour therapy (CBT). CBT is covered in detail in Chapter 18, but in a nutshell it involves education, relaxation, anxiety monitoring (journaling) and exercises aimed at reducing anxiety. A course of CBT is usually six to twelve sessions of between 30 and 60 minutes duration. Most people begin to see results within about four weeks, and the improvements continue, often long after the therapy ends. The relapse rate with CBT seems to be lower than for medications.

Mindfulness is another popular therapy that has its roots in CBT and Buddhist meditation practices. Mindfulness involves focusing on one's moment-to-moment subjective experiences, learning and practicing meditation and incorporating these into CBT practices. While the research base is not as well developed as for CBT alone, it's gathering momentum but should probably be second choice to CBT until the evidence is better established (of course it may turn out not to be effective – it's too early to tell).

Hypnosis is also popular for anxiety reduction, especially for phobias. Hypnosis is very similar to meditation. Hypnosis requires specialised training, and is usually done by psychologists, some GPs, and some psychiatrists.

Group therapy for anxiety is another useful option. The type of group often depends on the type of anxiety you experience, and it's usually considered as an addition to individual therapy. Again, search the internet or ask your GP or psychologist about local groups.

Eye movement desensitisation and reprocessing (EMDR) is a highly specific psychotherapy developed for treating disturbing memories in PTSD. It involves the therapist gradually desensitising the patient to their disturbing memories using a combination of relaxation and eye movement techniques. While it sounds unusual, the results are very good and it is a well-established therapy for PTSD.

Finally, a range of online anxiety treatments are starting to emerge; some are smartphone apps, such as Headspace (a meditation app), and others combine online learning with online therapy (either via messaging, email or face-to-face video conferencing).

Medication approaches

Medications work very well for anxiety, and there are many to choose from, but in anxiety disorders they should be considered as a last resort, unless symptoms are severe. This is a slightly controversial statement in medical circles. Many clinicians see their good results and the ease of prescribing and use and recommend them as first line. However, as anxiety tends to be fairly chronic, Steve recommends psychological approaches first – as medications have a higher relapse rate once ceased, and carry a risk of addiction (although small if well prescribed and monitored). Also, medications sometimes just provide a partial fix, and they discourage the person from seeking therapy or making the life changes necessary for sustained improvement. This does not mean you should be scared of using medications. If your anxiety is quite severe and impairing your function for day-to-day tasks, then medications can have great results.

There are a number of medications popularly prescribed for anxiety disorders.

- **Antidepressants:** Despite the name, all antidepressants work well for anxiety, and if choosing a medication they are the best option. A good doctor will help you choose which antidepressant is best for you – it depends on the type of anxiety disorder, your specific symptoms (for example, some are better if sleep is a problem) and the side effect profile you are most comfortable with.

  There are a few useful tricks to know when taking antidepressants for anxiety. You often need to start at a low dose and build up slowly (anxiety can sometimes get a little worse when you first start). The final dose often needs to be a little higher than for depression. You need to be prepared to stay on the medication for at least six months from the time your symptoms improve. And beware that *all* antidepressants take at least two weeks to kick in, and sometimes as long as six weeks.

If the first antidepressant you try doesn't work, then you swap to an antidepressant from a different pharmacological family. Overall, each antidepressant has about a 60 per cent chance of working.

Antidepressants are especially good at stopping panic attacks and for obsessive-compulsive disorder. They tend to be less useful in phobias and PTSD.

- **Benzodiazepines:** Benzodiazepines include drugs like diazepam (Valium), alprazolam (Xanax), oxazepam (Serax) and temazepam (Normison, Restoril). For many years they were considered the best medication for anxiety, but their popularity with clinicians has waned, mainly because of the risk of addiction. They work quickly – they are pharmacologically a bit like alcohol (working on similar receptors in the brain). The relaxing effect usually kicks in after 30 to 60 minutes, but once the medication wears off the anxiety returns.

  Tolerance can be a problem, meaning if you take them too frequently the effect diminishes, and you need a higher dose to get the same benefit. As a consequence, if you don't monitor the dose carefully it's easy to become addicted. Addiction is especially common after long-term use. Also, if you have been on benzodiazepines long-term and want to stop, you need to wean off, as withdrawal problems are common – the riskiest being seizures. Cessation after long-term use should be under medical supervision.

For the right patient, with appropriate monitoring, they can be a great circuit breaker to relieve ongoing anxiety. Taken sparingly, they can be really effective. So if your symptoms warrant benzodiazepines, don't be put off by the risks outlined above. Speak to your doctor and use them as prescribed.

- **Buspirone:** Buspirone is occasionally recommended for anxiety. Like antidepressants, buspirone takes a couple of weeks to work. It has very little associated sedation and no withdrawal problems. It's mainly used in generalised anxiety disorder. The main problem is that it needs to be taken three times a day. It tends to be tried when other options haven't worked.

- **Major tranquillisers:** These are a class of drugs mainly used in schizophrenia and bipolar disorder, but they have gained popularity in anxiety. Popular choices include quetiapine (Seroquel) and olanzepine (Zyprexa). They are powerful at reducing anxiety, but have major side effects, including weight gain, slowed movements and many others. They can also increase the chances of developing diabetes.

Combining therapies

Medications and psychotherapy can be used in combination, often with even greater effectiveness than each treatment alone. For example, in panic disorder, the medications are often great at stopping panic attacks, and the CBT is great at reducing the associated agoraphobia and teaching basic life skills to prevent anxiety from reoccurring. Similarly, in PTSD, medications often reduce some of the irritability, nervousness and poor concentration, and psychological techniques such as EMDR reduce intrusive thoughts of the trauma.

Making a plan

As with any mental health problem, you need to have a plan that includes options if your first efforts don't work. Also build in a timeframe – if something isn't starting to work after six weeks, then try the next step.

For anxiety, here is a simple list of things to consider, from easy steps for addressing mild anxiety through to more specialised options:

- self-help and psychological first aid
- yoga or meditation
- seeking an opinion from a professional
- psychotherapy
- medication
- combining therapies
- seeking a second opinion, including from a psychiatrist, if you haven't already done so
- trying different medications or psychotherapies.

*

When it comes to anxiety, it's sometimes easy to accept it as part of life, to become frustrated with treatment and conclude it's just part of who you are. But you don't have to tolerate

anxiety. Treatment works: keep trying until you find the formula that's right for you and your circumstances. Also, even
when treatment works well, anxiety has a habit of sneaking
back at times of personal difficulty or stress – so be prepared.
Keep vigilant for a return of symptoms, and act early. Jump
back into treatment, whether it's self-help, psychological first
aid, medications or therapy. Is there anything you've recently
stopped, that in retrospect was helping keep your anxiety at
bay? No one ever rids themselves entirely of anxiety, but each
time you battle and conquer a period of higher than normal
anxiety you'll get better at it. The battle gets easier each time.

8

Psychosis

Psychosis is the most misunderstood and challenging mental issue. There's a good reason for this – it's very confusing.

Because it's so confusing, the best place to start is by getting your head around the key terms. Trust us – it's worth spending five minutes learning the definitions:

- *Psychosis* means loss of contact with reality. The word comes from ancient Greek via Latin. In Latin, *psyche* means 'mind' and *osis* means 'abnormal condition'. Psychosis is not a disorder – it's a syndrome that's made up of four symptoms: hallucinations, delusions, illogical thinking and odd behaviour. Psychosis always has a cause, and there are many causes, but the most common are schizophrenia and drugs like amphetamines.

- *Schizophrenia* is a psychiatric disorder that causes psychotic symptoms, with an onset in the early twenties. It is mostly long-term and sometimes leads to deterioration in social functioning, personality and relationships. There are lots of subtypes of schizophrenia.

- *Drug-induced psychosis* is psychosis caused by recreational drugs. The most common drugs that induce psychosis are hallucinogens (such as LSD or magic mushrooms), amphetamines of various sorts (including ice – methamphetamine), and stimulants like cocaine. Drug-induced psychosis almost always stops when the drug washes out of the body, unlike schizophrenia.

No one ever forgets the first time they meet someone with psychosis. Interacting with someone who firmly believes crazy things, is agitated and beyond reasoning, feels scary, frustrating and bizarre in equal proportions.

Steve remembers his first time clearly. He was a 25-year-old junior doctor working in a psychiatry ward. His patient was a 19-year-old woman. She had been a highly successful school student whose marks fell away in her final year. She'd gone from being a prefect with straight As to finding study hard and spending hours and hours at home in her room, apparently doing nothing. She barely passed her final year school exams. She was unable to explain what she was thinking about while sitting in her room. Her parents were exasperated. Her younger brother had stopped talking to her. There were vague stories of her behaving oddly (for example, she was staring into mirrors for hours) and asking odd questions – she had at one time repeatedly asked her parents if they had committed crimes in their past and covered them up.

She denied hallucinations and the team could find no evidence of delusions. She seemed illogical in her thinking and lacked her previous drive, but there was little else to suggest mental illness. She denied taking recreational drugs and the family had seen no evidence and drug screens were negative. The head psychiatrist wondered whether she was being abused and was too scared to report it. She denied being depressed, but was she telling the truth?

The team thought she was developing a psychosis, so she was admitted to hospital for observation. After a few days she opened up to a nurse that spies were watching her through the lights in her bedroom at home. She didn't dare speak about it because she thought everything was being bugged. If the spies found out she knew, they would kill her parents and brother. She couldn't explain why. She felt safe in hospital because she believed spies couldn't bug NHS wards. The cause of her psychosis turned out to be schizophrenia.

It was heartbreaking to see this unfold. Schizophrenia is often (but not always) heartbreaking. It usually affects young people; families are often confused and perplexed and the community unsympathetic; there may be difficulty convincing the person to get help; sometimes involuntary treatment is required – it's almost overwhelming.

While this patient was peaceful in demeanour, schizophrenia can present in far more threatening ways. Young, strong men who have paranoid delusions and feel under threat can be frightening. The first time Steve worked in a locked ward (where the sickest, most vulnerable and most risky patients are often treated), he was scared and nervous. He barely left the nurses station for the whole day.

Over time you learn when people are agitated or at risk of committing violence or self-harm and you begin to feel safe. You see people get better – and when they are better, they are different people. A strange-looking dishevelled and delusional man admitted to the ward talking to spirits and responding to imaginary voices will often leave the ward calm, neatly dressed and apologising for his behaviour when he was unwell.

Once the bewilderment of meeting psychotic people wears off, you are left feeling very sad. The consequences can sometimes be devastating – jobs lost, friends lost, families torn apart, criminal charges, and most tragic of all: suicide.

Aspects of psychosis

Psychosis has four main symptoms: hallucinations, delusions, illogical thinking and disorganised behaviour.

Hallucinations are sensations in the absence of a stimuli, meaning people perceive something that is not really there. There are several common types.

- Auditory hallucinations are hearing things that are not real, usually voices, but sometimes music or strange noises.
- Visual hallucinations involve the person sees things like colours or shapes or people or ghosts.
- Somatic (touch) hallucinations can be weird feelings under the skin, such as ants or spiders crawling.
- Olfactory hallucinations are of smells, usually something unpleasant.

Different causes of psychosis tend to result in different types of hallucinations. For example, in schizophrenia auditory hallucinations are the most common, whereas in delirium visual and somatic hallucinations are more common.

Delusions are beliefs or thoughts that are false, fixed or rigid and out of keeping with the person's social, cultural and educational context. It can be very difficult to separate delusions from unusual beliefs. Religious beliefs are a good example. People often present with odd ideas that they claim are part of their religion. Sometimes we need to call in a minister from the relevant religion to talk to the patient. The minister usually sorts it out pretty quickly: 'No, those ideas are odd and none of us believe that' or 'Of course we believe that, we've known it for centuries. God said that.'

Common types of delusion

Erotomanic: The delusional belief that someone is in love with you.
Grandiose: The delusional belief that you have some great, yet undiscovered, talent or insight or idea.
Jealous: The delusional belief that your partner is unfaithful.
Persecutory: The delusional belief that you are being persecuted or conspired against.
Somatic: The delusional belief that you have a physical illness or that your bodily functions have changed.

In psychiatry, illogical thinking is called thought disorder. It can be tricky to distinguish normal illogical thinking (we are all illogical at times), from pathological illogical thinking. Some of the most common types of thought disorder are:

- derailment – the person's train of thought (and therefore speech) moves further and further from the point they are trying to make

- thought blocking – the person's train of thought and speech stop suddenly. When they restart, the topic is often different
- neologism –the person creates new words that have meaning only for them.

Disorganised behaviour includes agitation, silly behaviours, odd movements and postures, or sometimes retardation with little movement at all. Catatonia is a severe version of disorganised behaviour. In catatonia, the person either presents with a loss of spontaneous movement or demonstrates too much movement. In the former, patients can hold a rigid posture for hours, oblivious to external stimulation; in the latter, patients are extremely overactive.

Causes

There are many causes of psychosis.

Organic psychosis

An organic psychosis is caused by brain dysfunction. The most common is delirium. Delirium basically means confusion. It is common in sick people with things like infections, strokes and heart attacks. Walk around a hospital and many patients have some degree of delirium – they are disoriented, have poor short-term memory, their personality changes, and about one third have psychotic symptoms. It's nearly always short-lived (less than a week) and is due to whatever sickness they have disrupting the brain. Fix the brain dysfunction and the psychosis disappears.

Drug-induced psychosis

Psychosis can be caused by recreational drugs. The psychosis caused by these drugs can be indistinguishable from schizophrenia, except that it resolves once the drugs wash out of the person's body (this can take a few hours or days, depending on the drug). There is more on this in Chapter 9. On a Saturday night in the A&E department, nearly all the psychosis will be due to drugs. In a homeless shelter, nearly all the psychosis will be due to schizophrenia. Although sometimes both drugs and schizophrenia are contributing.

Schizophrenia

Schizophrenia usually first emerges in young people. The average age of onset is about 18 to 25 for men, and 25 to 35 for women, but it can develop at any age. About half have slightly odd personalities before the schizophrenia develops.

Once it develops, about a third get better, assuming they adhere to all the treatments, about a third wax and wane, and about a third deteriorate and stay psychotic, often despite treatment.

Schizophrenia affects about 1 per cent of men and women, regardless of cultural and demographic factors such as education or wealth.

The two myths about schizophrenia that most need to be busted are the split personality idea and the link to violence. Schizophrenia has nothing to do with a split personality – it's just movies and novels that propagate this nonsense! And patients with schizophrenia are often also mistakenly viewed as excessively violent – in fact, the risk of violence is only *slightly* higher than the average for the rest of the population. They are far more likely to hurt themselves than others, and far more likely to be the victims of violence than the perpetrators.

While the main symptoms of schizophrenia are those of psychosis (delusions, hallucinations, thought disorder and disorganised behaviour), patients with schizophrenia also have high levels of mood disturbance (sometimes depression, sometimes mania) and also often suffer psycho-social deterioration – meaning over time they seem to change or lose their personality and drift down the social scale – earning less, having trouble with housing, and often unemployed.

For a diagnosis of schizophrenia to be made, the symptoms must be present in some form for at least six months. This is important, as there are many briefer forms of psychosis that do not have the same negative consequences of schizophrenia and have different treatment options.

If the symptoms have been present for less than a month, the term 'brief psychotic disorder' tends to be used. If for more than a month but less than six months, we use the term 'schizophreniform disorder'. This differentiation is useful clinically because it prevents the premature serious diagnosis of schizophrenia before the patient has had a chance to recover. It allows everyone – the patient, family, friends and clinicians, to focus on the immediate goal of regaining sanity before addressing longer-term issues.

Depression and bipolar disorder

When depression or mania becomes severe, it can be accompanied by psychotic symptoms. These can be any mix of delusions, hallucination, thought disorder and behavioural disturbance. Delusions are particularly common.

The delusions usually reflect the person's mood. So, depressed people tend to have distressing delusions, with themes of guilt, failure and worthlessness, and manic people tend to have grandiose delusions of great power or solutions to world problems.

Psychotic symptoms in depression and mania are a clear sign of severity. Most depressed or manic people with psychotic symptoms need urgent hospital admission. They are at risk of all sorts of harm – in depression, the biggest risk is suicide; in mania, the biggest risks are harms resulting from risky behaviours such as financial or sexual misadventures.

Psychotic symptoms make patients unpredictable – so the usual things we do to assess risk, such as ask the patient their intentions and plans, are all unreliable. Psychotic patients can change their minds in the blink of an eye. They can be sitting calmly one minute, and the next have a voice in their head telling them to do something dangerous. Accurate prediction in this situation is impossible. The only predictable thing about psychosis is that it is unpredictable.

Schizoaffective disorder

Schizoaffective disorder refers to a mix of features of both schizophrenia and bipolar disorder. This includes some psychotic symptoms and some mood (either depression or mania) symptoms. If the course of the illness seems to include both for most of the time, then the diagnosis of schizoaffective disorder is made.

Delusional disorder

In delusional disorder the main symptom is the presence of delusions. Other psychotic symptoms can be present, but they tend to be minor in comparison to the delusions. The impact on functioning seems to be much less pronounced than schizophrenia. Also, their behaviour is far less odd or bizarre than in schizophrenia. The delusions must be present for at least a month for the diagnosis to be made.

People with delusional disorder are probably the hardest to engage in treatment. With all the other psychotic disorders, sooner or later people get so impaired in their behaviour or functioning that treatment, sometimes involuntary, becomes inevitable.

In delusional disorder people can continue with their odd beliefs for a long time without ever getting impaired enough to meet the legal criteria for involuntary treatment. This can be tragic for families who see their loved one devoting their life to their delusional beliefs but being told by clinicians they are not impaired enough to trigger involuntary treatment. There is more on this challenge in the section on treatment.

First episode psychosis (FEP)

When a person first develops psychotic symptoms, there are two very important questions that doctors look at:

- What sort of psychosis is it? This determines which treatments to offer and how urgently they are required.
- How can we convince someone who doesn't believe they are unwell to accept treatment?

First episode psychosis (FEP) isn't a diagnosis, but rather a statement of fact that signifies we are in a period of uncertainty. It's a useful term, because it encourages everyone to keep an open mind about diagnosis and avoids the issue of discussing things like schizophrenia (and all the worry that entails) before we know for sure what is causing the psychosis.

In the last decade or so, a group around the world, led by Australian psychiatrist Professor Patrick McGorry, who was Australian of the Year in 2010, has championed this concept and encouraged governments to put resources into responding to FEP, based on the idea that high-quality early treatment reduces the long-term consequences of psychosis.

The message is: the first time someone becomes psychotic is a crucial time to intervene. This episode will set the scene for how they trust and interact with health services. It will set up how they accept and adhere to medications. It will determine how their supports (friends and family) understand and react. Putting in extra effort at this time is expensive, but in the long run it reduces problems and saves money.

Convincing a psychotic person to accept help

In the early stages of psychosis, most people do not accept that they need help. They think the world is the problem, not themselves. As a consequence, getting psychotic people to seek help usually requires the efforts of many – family, friends, health care workers and often police. It often takes days, weeks or even months.

The early efforts to convince someone to see a health care worker often begin with gentle requests, loving explanations and perhaps some pleading, but often end with a degree of coercion, manipulation and trickery.

This sounds harsh, but families and friends are usually desperate – they are watching the person they love deteriorate and put themselves at risk, and they often feel powerless and confused. They are usually desperate to help, but don't know how.

There are whole legal statutes devoted to this problem in most developed countries. They are mostly called Mental Health Acts. Such Acts usually give police the power to take someone to hospital for compulsory assessment if they appear to be psychotic. Once in health care settings, psychotic patients can be held against their will for further assessment. If those assessments suggest the person is indeed mentally ill, at a risk to themselves or others and is refusing treatment, then the Acts also allow for people to be treated against their will. This is called involuntary treatment.

These laws are often controversial. Some people see them as an infringement of individual rights; others see them as too weak and ineffectual. But there are multiple checks and balances in place, such as compulsory second opinions, review boards and tribunals, and lawyers.

We can't cover everything we do to encourage people to get help, or to support families, because every situation is different. But here are some tips if you are dealing with a psychotic person:

- Try not to expend too much energy convincing a psychotic person they are wrong – instead, focus on convincing them they need to speak to a professional. Try something like, 'Everything you've told us is very worrying, you must be under enormous stress, it's no wonder you're upset. Let us help you to organise a doctor to speak to – perhaps they can at least help you with all the stress.'

- Research your local services, and call them to get advice. You can either go online, call one of the many helplines, or visit a GP.

- Find out what crisis services are available. These go by many names – such as CTT or HTT – *Crisis or Home Treatment Teams*. They specialise in seeing people (usually in their home, but also in hospitals) who are at risk of any sort of harm, and assess whether there is a mental health problem.

- When you start trying to enlist help, write a list of all the plans you can think of. Start with the least intrusive options, and work your way forward until you've received help. For example:
  - Plan A: Get the person to their GP.
  - Plan B: Take them to the nearest A&E in a hospital.
  - Plan C: If all else fails, or there is a risk of violence, call the police.

- If there is any hint of suicidality in psychosis, an assessment is essential and urgent. There is no time to take all the gentle approaches – for advice, either visit your GP or ring NHS Direct.

Treatment

To treat psychosis, many tools are used – such as medications, psychological interventions and vocational supports – but how and when they are used depends on the type of psychosis and the phase of the illness.

Medication

Most people with psychosis require medication at some point. A few different types are used:

- **Anti-psychotics** – These are drugs that specifically target the symptoms of the psychosis (hallucinations, delusions, thought disorder and behaviour disturbance). In the old days, they were called major tranquillisers. Common ones are haloperidol, olanzepine, risperidone, quetiapine and clozapine. They come in tablets or injections. You can even get long-acting injections that last anything up to four weeks. In some people they work well, in others they do very little. Luckily, there are many different types of anti-psychotics, so if one drug isn't working we can switch to another drug.

  The big catch with anti-psychotics is that they all have quite concerning side effects. Some can cause movement disorders, some can cause medical problems like diabetes, and nearly all have milder side effects such as sedation or a dry mouth.

  Most people suffering psychosis, especially initially, don't want to take medications. Every time a doctor prescribes an anti-psychotic, they weigh up the risks and benefits. Mostly, the risks of untreated psychosis (further deterioration in symptoms, self-harm, harm to others) far outweighs the risks of the medications – especially with good monitoring.

- **Mood stabilisers** – While these are mainly used in bipolar disorder, they are also often tried in psychoses, especially in addition to anti-psychotics if the anti-psychotics are not working adequately. Common examples are lithium, carbemazepine and valproate. The evidence for their effectiveness is not nearly as good as for the anti-psychotics, so they tend to be saved as a last resort – or if there is suspicion that the psychosis is caused by either bipolar disorder or schizoaffective disorder. They also have a range of side effects, and so require careful monitoring.

- **Benzodiazepines** – These are primarily used to treat anxiety and agitation in a psychosis. Most psychotic people are frightened, can't sleep well, can't sit still or relax, and are very distressed. These medications do *not* relieve the psychotic symptoms, but they help with the anxiety due to being psychotic. They are effective but addictive, so the dose needs to be carefully monitored. Common examples are diazepam (Valium), alprazolam (Xanax), oxazepam (Serax) and temazepam (Normison, Restoril).

Psychological support

Virtually everyone with a psychosis requires both medications and psychological support. Suffering a psychosis is a major trauma in anyone's life. Lots of help is needed to recover. There are various different approaches used depending on the type of psychosis. Here are a few popular examples.

- **Psycho-education** – This is as obvious as it sounds. Arming the patient with information about their problems and the treatment options is vital. Formal psycho-education is more in-depth; you work with a clinician (or sometimes in a small group) to tailor the information to your specific circumstances. Research shows this leads to better adherence to treatment, better outcomes, better management of any future relapse and a greater sense of wellbeing.

- **Family interventions** – Steve once spent a month visiting a large psychiatric ward in a famous Indian hospital. Patients had to have at least one family member staying with them while in hospital. You couldn't be admitted otherwise. The family had to learn about the disorder, the treatments and the services. The Indian doctors knew that without the family being involved in the treatments, problems would develop.

  Until relatively recently in the UK, families didn't get included nearly enough. Now there is solid research to support a range of family interventions, showing they reduce relapse and aid recovery. Most interventions focus on engaging the family in treatment, education, problem solving, reducing distress and creating alliances between families and treatment teams.

- **Cognitive behaviour therapy** – This is described in detail in Chapter 18. In summary, these are therapies that focus on cognitions (thoughts) and behaviours. For psychotic patients, they can include techniques aimed at reducing the distress from hallucinations and delusions, strategies to overcome poor concentration and attention, and strategies to aid decision-making, and much more.

Social support

Social workers and social supports are a key element of treatment for psychoses. As with psychological supports, there are many approaches.

- **Social skills training** – Psychoses usually occur for the first time in young people, so they may miss out on many of the usual experiences to build their social skills. The sorts of skills taught include conversation skills, relationship skills and independent living skills.
- **Vocational rehabilitation** – Employment rates amongst people who have suffered psychoses are low. Vocational rehab aims to address this, either by programs that prepare people for work, or programs that provide support when people first start a job. These are particularly important if the psychosis is due to schizophrenia.
- **Housing support** – People with psychoses have often lost their housing or have trouble securing housing. Homelessness is a common problem in all the psychoses. Housing support includes help applying for housing, help funding housing and help adjusting to independent living.

Care programme approach and case management

A care/case manager oversees all aspects of treatment. They are usually a psychiatric nurse, social worker or psychologist.

The CPA – *Care Programme Approach* – is a system of having a meeting every few months with everyone involved in your care plan. The care/case manager ensures that the patient attends medical appointments, has medication, and gets all the social and psychological interventions. They provide many of the interventions themselves. Care/case managers are highly skilled – both in the clinical support and the practical aspects of helping people with schizophrenia.

Venue of care

Every time a clinician sees someone with a psychotic disorder, they think about the venue of care – should the person be managed outside the hospital in their home, or should they be in a hospital ward?

Some psychoses can be treated in the community, but if there are significant risks – such as self-harm, violence, damage to reputation, vulnerability (sexual or other), absconding or crime – then hospital admission needs to be considered.

Most psychiatric wards look a lot like any hospital ward these days. Thankfully the old days of Victorian-era institutions are over. Steve's career started in buildings that were intimidating and poorly resourced. Everything was of lower quality than general hospitals at the time. The food was cheaper, proper medical equipment was in short supply, overcrowding was common, privacy was rare, and there was never enough staff.

Thankfully the situation has changed. Most governments around the world did two things to improve the situation in the 1980s and '90s – mainstreaming and deinstitutionalisation. Mainstreaming meant the institutions were closed and psychiatric wards were moved to general hospitals. Deinstitutionalisation meant care was moved out of hospitals and into the community. Funding didn't always match ideology, so the process was often less than ideal, but in the long run we ended up with a far better system. The reason this is worth mentioning is that some people don't realise the system has changed and are scared of psychiatric hospitals. But hospital is often the safest and most caring place for a psychotic patient to be treated.

Treating co-morbidity

Co-morbidity simply means multiple conditions. This is common in psychoses. Many people have both a psychotic disorder such as schizophrenia and another problem. The most common co-morbidity is addictions, but we also see depression and many other medical problems.

These disorders often need extra specialists on board. Drug and alcohol problems are so common we have services specifically devoted to people who have both psychoses and drug and alcohol problems – called 'dual diagnosis' services.

Drug and alcohol problems are a challenge alone, but in schizophrenia (and, to a lesser degree, bipolar disorder) they are dynamite. Most people with dual diagnosis require lots of support, help and time.

Is it all doom and gloom?

Absolutely not. Many people have one psychotic episode, get better and it never happens again. Even for those who go on to have schizophrenia, many respond well to treatment and learn to manage their symptoms.

It's a bit like any chronic illness – diabetes, arthritis, asthma – there are challenges along the way, but with a bit of luck and good management, the outcomes with modern treatment practices are way better than most people realise.

Of course, having a disorder where one of the symptoms is that you don't actually believe you are sick is way harder than having a physical problem where simple blood tests can confirm what's going on. But there are many, many more good outcomes with psychotic disorders than bad outcomes. It's not the way people hope their life will go, but it is far from a despairing situation.

9

Addiction

Humans love drugs. We've always used them – sometimes therapeutically, sometimes recreationally. Passions run high when talking about them. The legality and social acceptability of drugs varies widely across cultures. Smoke a joint in Indonesia and you could end up in jail, but in some countries (and some states of the United States) you can buy and smoke it legally.

Drugs are big business. If you include the illegal trade, the legal trade, and throw in the related law and order professions, the drug business must easily be in the top ten industries worldwide.

You will almost certainly know someone who has a problem with addiction. You have a fair chance yourself of suffering an addiction.

The good, the bad and the ugly

Every single drug can have a positive therapeutic or recreational application. Every single drug has the potential to cause devastating health and social consequences.

The positive aspect of alcohol is that it has a range of medicinal uses, from preventing infection to reducing the incidence of some cancers and heart disease. Alcohol is the main drug used to ease social situations, reduce stress and raise spirits. But it is also a leading cause of illness, personal disaster and social disintegration.

Heroin and other opioids relieve suffering and save millions of lives every year in pain-related illnesses and surgical procedures. People get painkillers for everything from headache to arthritis. But heroin and its pharmaceutical siblings also destroy lives, tear families apart and prop up crime-related industries worth billions of dollars throughout the world.

So here's the million dollar question: What determines our perception of good versus bad? In a nutshell, a fickle mix of fashion, culture, religion, politics, the era you live in and your personal pattern of use.

Teasing out the issues is a nightmare skewed by different philosophies and ideologies. Politics, sociology, health care, policing and the law all give different perspectives.

We all want to get to the best possible place with the least amount of damage. Demonising drugs has done more harm than good. The 'just say no' approach closes the door on thinking. Maybe say no, maybe say yes – but whatever you say, base it on knowledge and evidence.

Which drugs are the most dangerous?

It is surprisingly difficult to determine which drugs do the most harm. The laws relating to drugs reflect societal values and politics as much as pharmacology and health risks. Alcohol and tobacco are legal, but they account for about 90 per cent of deaths related to drug use.

A group in the UK recently tried to assess risks based on expert consensus. They convened a group of professionals and scientists from all sorts of fields – addiction medicine, psychiatry, police, pharmacology and forensic science. The experts rated drugs of addiction on three key parameters: physical harm, social harm, and the risk of dependence.

- *Physical harm* assessed three key facets of harm – acute harm including the immediate effects on the heart and lungs and the safety margin of the drugs including the risk of overdose; chronic harm – the health effects of repeated use; and finally the specific harms related to intravenous drug use.
- *Social harm* was measured in three domains. First, the effects of intoxication, such as accidental damage to the user and others. Second, the damage done to families and the social life of the user. Finally, the health-care costs related to the drug.
- The *risk of dependence* was rated according to three related variables: the pleasure the drug caused, the physical dependence and the psychological dependence. Physical dependence looked at the risk of drug tolerance and withdrawal symptoms – both of which suggest the

body has adapted to the drug in a physiological manner that contributes to intense cravings. Psychological dependence was a measure of how difficult it was to stop the drug once the physical factors were removed.

Reaching consensus on the relative scores for each drug wasn't easy. There are no simple measures in any of these fields. Here are some of their key findings – every item was rated on a risk of 1 (low) to 3 (high). These results are the averages for each category (if you're really keen, the original article has lots more data – see References).

Drug	Risk of physical harm	Risk of dependence	Risk of social harm
Heroin	2.8	3.0	2.5
Cocaine	2.3	2.4	2.2
Tobacco	1.2	2.2	1.4
Alcohol	1.4	1.9	2.2
Amphetamine	1.8	1.7	1.5
Cannabis	1.0	1.5	1.5
LSD	1.1	1.2	1.3
Ecstasy	1.1	1.1	1.1

The bottom line is there is currently no purely scientific way to assess the risks of drugs and the damage they might cause. Having said that, based on expert consensus using the current evidence, the riskiest drugs include heroin, cocaine, tobacco and alcohol. It's interesting to note that two of the most dangerous drugs in this study are legal, yet the two lowest-scoring drugs, cannabis and ecstasy, are illegal.

One of the complexities is that different drugs affect different people in different ways. One person might be able to use cocaine in a safe manner with no long-term effects yet get addicted to alcohol and spiral out of control. Some people smoke marijuana and feel relaxed and euphoric; others feel agitated and paranoid.

Alcohol and tobacco carry high health costs, but this reflects the fact that they are legal and use is common. Most people who use alcohol do so in a safe manner. We don't know how many people use heroin in a safe manner, largely because it is illegal and so measuring safe use (that doesn't result in people attending hospital) is almost impossible.

Cannabis is gradually being accepted as much safer than originally thought. Many countries have decriminalised its use; others allow its use for medical purposes and some have gone so far as to legalise and regulate growth and sale. In the United States, currently twenty-three states allow medical use, and four states have legalised recreational use – and the list is growing. Similar movements are occurring in Australia. In the UK, medicinal use of cannabis will be allowed from autumn 2018.

Harm minimisation

You'll hear the term 'harm minimisation' a lot when talking about drugs. Historically, government strategies on drugs have focused on law and order approaches aimed at reducing supply and demand, and health strategies focused on fertilising fear and promoting abstinence. In the UK, from July 2017, a new drugs strategy with a focus on harm minimisation commenced. Harm minimisation (or harm reduction) refers to a range of public policies and cultural attitudes aimed at reducing the potential harms associated with drug use. So, for example, rather than telling teenagers simply to avoid drugs, you might tell them:

> Drugs have risks but nothing is risk-free, and there are very few young people who never try drugs. So if you do try them, remember these simple tips: Don't buy drugs from complete strangers. Start with a low dose, and don't take more until you've given them time to kick in. When you try them, make sure you are in a safe place, and have at least one reliable friend who is sober nearby. If any problems develop, call for help immediately, I promise I wont get mad!

> Other examples of harm minimisation strategies include:
> - good public education
> - advice about safe use
> - needle exchange programs
> - safe injecting sites
> - freely available drug testing kits
> - regulated production and sale of drugs
> - developing a science-based drug policy.

Prevention

What's the best way to prevent drug addiction? No one knows. In Australia about ten times more is spent on policing illicit drugs than on education and health programs to encourage safe use and treat the addicted. Similar ratios exist in other Western countries. Health workers think this is crazy.

While supply is clearly a major driver of addiction, attempts to cut supply (police, lawyers, courts and prisons) are expensive, often fickle (in some parts of the United States you can spend decades in prison for cannabis offences) and rarely successful – drug suppliers always have more resources and tricks than government agencies.

There needs to be a balance. Sensible, cost-effective measures to restrict supply are great, but not measures based on simplistic, attention-grabbing politics. There should be more widespread education about risks, safe use and how to prevent getting into trouble.

And finally, as is obvious to anyone who has ever had even the most minor contact with health services for addictions, we need more resources. People with problems need *fast* access to good quality services. Politics and simplistic, judgemental attitudes get in the way of money reaching these services – yet these services save lives, protect families, prevent violence and crime, and help people in distress.

Treatment

Addiction treatments work. The evidence is clear and unequivocal. Most people who enter treatment either cease drug use or at least significantly reduce their use. Relapse is common, but so is re-entering treatment and further improvement.

There is widespread pessimism about addiction, but it's based on faulty observation and logic. People take great notice of the bad outcomes but they don't see all the good outcomes. Countless people overcome addictions but don't get noticed, or they keep it quiet.

Part of the problem is that there is no 'one size fits all' solution. There are many different treatment philosophies, and many different kinds of practitioners. Some people prefer self-help, others like group help, others go for medical treatment, and others prefer complementary and alternative approaches. Every person's pathway to beating addictions will be different. It depends on personal preferences, the drug (or behaviour), the severity of the addiction, and the social support and services available. Every country, state and region has different services.

The key is information. Information is the best weapon. If you have a problem with addiction, read widely and talk to people who are knowledgeable about it. Keep an open mind. Make a list – not just a Plan A, but a Plan A to Z. Don't give up. List all the treatment approaches that appeal to you, and then put them in order of preference. Start at the top of the list and work your way down.

When to get help

When an addiction starts to affect your health, family, friends, schooling or work, it's time to get help.

Of course, this is a very subjective yardstick. There is no clear line between safe and unsafe use. Plenty of people use drugs in a manner that is no more risky than other lifestyle choices – like your choice of foods, holiday, occupation or even transport! What's riskier – riding a motorbike in busy traffic or smoking an occasional joint? Some people will argue that all drug use is dangerous, but they'll often say so over a beer or a calorie-filled hamburger. We all weigh risks differently.

There are hundreds of quick self-assessment quizzes on the internet to assess whether you have an addiction problem. One of the oldest is the CAGE test. It was originally used for alcohol addiction, but has been adapted to apply to other drugs as well.

Here are the CAGE questions:

- C (Cut down) – Have you ever felt you ought to cut down on your drinking or drug use?
- A (Annoyed) – Have people annoyed you by criticising your drinking or drug use?
- G (Guilt) – Have you felt bad or guilty about your drinking or drug use?
- E (Eye opener) – Have you ever had a drink or used drugs first thing in the morning to steady your nerves or to get rid of a hangover (eye-opener)?

If you answer 'yes' to one of these four questions, you should think about whether you might have a problem; if you answer 'yes' to two or more, it suggests you should seek help.

A model in addiction that is commonly discussed is the transtheoretical model (TTM), popularly called the 'stages of change' model. It describes the stages people go through when contemplating behavioural change. These are:

1. Pre-contemplation – the person is aware their addiction is a problem, but doesn't think they need to stop just yet.
2. Contemplation – the problems are more obvious and the person wants to change but is still ambivalent. They are weighing the pros and cons of getting help.

3. Preparation – here people accept they need to change and are thinking about how best to achieve their goal.
4. Action – the person is actually trying to change or is seeking help.
5. Maintenance – the person has made the change and developed new patterns of behaviour and control.
6. Relapse – this applies to individuals who have achieved maintenance but fall back into a previous stage of use.

The stages are often represented in a circle. But this does not mean relapse is inevitable. A person can stay at any stage indefinitely; hopefully they do so at the maintenance phase.

This model is often discussed by addiction counsellors when assessing a person's readiness to engage in treatment.

The options for treatment of addiction are almost endless. Here are the most popular choices to consider.

Assessment

This is often the first step, although many people skip it by choosing a treatment themselves and jumping right in. Assessment involves seeing a counsellor with addiction experience. This might be a GP, a specific drug and alcohol counsellor or an addiction specialist. Assessment can be done over the phone or in person. Assessment aims to outline the problem and its severity, and then tailor treatment options to the individual. Most services have some sort of assessment process prior to beginning, or they require assessment to be done by some sort of specialist before acceptance into their program.

Counselling

Counselling is very popular and successful. It involves regular sessions with a trained expert who will use some sort of theoretical model to guide an addicted person through the process of recovery. Counselling can be individual or in groups. It can be used while in rehabilitation or while living at home.

Counsellors may have various types of training. They may be a social worker, a psychologist, a doctor or simply a layperson who has done a course (often after recovering from addiction themselves). Some use specific psychological approaches. Two of the more popular approaches are cognitive-behavioural therapy and motivational interviewing. Some also use the twelve-step approach developed by Alcoholics Anonymous (see below).

Rehabilitation

Rehabilitation can take many forms, including home-based or residential (where you live in an institution of some sort while rehabilitation takes place). Residential rehab can be for a few weeks or as long as a year. Some people do rehab near their home, others go away to a place that removes temptation. Rehab in foreign countries is also becoming popular. Countries like Thailand have residential rehab that is a lot cheaper than similar services in countries with more expensive healthcare systems, and often just as good. Rehab aims to explore the reasons for addiction and develop new behaviours and approaches to avoid using drugs.

Withdrawal

Withdrawal (also known as detoxification, or detox) is the process of stopping the drug and getting through the withdrawal syndrome associated with the drug. Some drugs – alcohol, heroin and benzodiazepines – are particularly tough and often require medical support to prevent dangerous complications like seizures. Withdrawal is mostly done in a hospital-like setting, but it can also be done in a structured fashion at home, with clinicians visiting up to twice a day.

Medications

There are dozens of medications used to battle addictions. Some are used to stop cravings, some are used to replace the dangerous drug of addiction with a safer drug (for example, methadone to replace heroin) and some are used to prevent the drug of addiction from working should relapse occur (they block the effect of the addictive drug). There is even a drug used for alcohol addiction that causes nausea and vomiting if the person drinks again (called disulfuram). All of the approved medications have a strong evidence base, but also a range of side effects, so choosing one should involve a risk–benefit analysis with an expert.

Peer support

Alcoholics Anonymous (AA) is the most famous peer support program. These are programs run by people who have had personal experience with addiction. AA was founded in 1935 and has probably been the most successful of all programs. The AA model is used for many other addictions; for example, NA – narcotics anonymous – is for any sort of drug addiction.

Most peer support programs use the twelve-step model developed by AA. These programs are available in most parts of the world, and are essentially free. Most twelve-step programs have a mix of open and closed meetings. Closed meetings are for users only, whereas open meetings allow non-users to attend as observers. If you haven't attended an AA meeting, it is a very worthwhile experience, especially if you want to help someone with an addiction.

There are also peer support programs such as Nar-Anon for friends and family members of addicted people, which provide support and advice regarding how to help someone with an addiction.

Social support

While not specifically aimed at recovering from an addiction, various social supports exist to help people with addiction in various practical ways – including housing support, legal aid and financial support.

Internet and phone services

Many services operate over the phone or internet. A quick internet search will reveal services for drugs, alcohol and gambling. Some are run by government departments, some by non-profit organisations and some by community groups.

What if relapse occurs?

Depending on the treatment program, relapse occurs in 50 to 80 per cent of users after a year. But most who relapse use less drugs than before treatment, so their next attempt at recovery is even more likely to be successful. Also, hopefully they learn from each relapse, making it less likely to occur next time. Multiple attempts at recovery are normal. That's why everyone needs a plan that includes back-ups if things go wrong. On average people attempt to give up about eight times before being successful. This should be an encouraging message: addiction is normal, relapse is normal, recovery is normal. Take heart from the words of Winston Churchill:

If you're going through hell, keep going.

Some of the common reasons for relapse include:
- not sticking to the treatment plan. This is common, especially if the person is still in denial or the pre-contemplation phase. It's also common when there is a lack of support from family or friends.
- inaccessibility of treatment. This is a massive problem. While there are many treatment options, gaining access is not always easy. There are often long waiting lists, but as a general rule, when a person wants to cease drugs it's best to strike while the iron is hot! And there is also the issue of cost. Health insurance doesn't always cover everything that is needed, and many users have no insurance and are financially unable to pay for care.
- psychiatric problems. Some studies suggest as many as 50 per cent of people with an addiction have other psychiatric problems – especially depression or anxiety disorders. Failure to recognise and treat these is a common reason recovery from addiction fails.

- failure to use every treatment option available. Some people require multiple forms of help at once: medications, counselling and peer support. But sometimes rigid philosophies limit care to one type of treatment. Be open-minded and consider all options – 'whatever works' is the best philosophy!

So if relapse does occur, start again. Try the same thing, try something different, or combine treatments – it doesn't matter: just keep trying.

Supporting someone with an addiction

For every person with an addiction, there are typically between one and ten others who are affected by that person's addiction – parents, partners, kids, friends and work colleagues. Most of them have scratched their heads wondering whether they can help, how they can help and should they try to help. Many have actually pulled their hair out.

First, remember that for the most part you cannot force someone to get help. So be wary of trying to force, bribe or coerce them – it usually just results in fights and fractured relationships.

As a support person, your primary role is to be ready to help when the addicted person reaches out. This may take a long time. It doesn't mean you can't try to motivate them, or feed, house and support them in other ways in the meantime – it just means you have to be ready when the critical moment arrives.

To get ready, this is what you need to do:

- Get informed – educate yourself about the drug in question, and the services available in your area to help treat addiction. When the time comes, you will need to help the addicted person navigate the maze.

- Maintain firm boundaries. Boundaries are the imaginary borders between each of us. If you get overinvolved, you will burn out. You can be helpful and still set limits. You could devote your whole life, twenty-four hours a day, to supporting and encouraging an addicted person to enter treatment, and it will probably make only about a 5 per cent difference in the long run. The more likely outcome is that you will get frustrated, burnt out, angry and pessimistic – and then when the critical time does arrive when the person asks for help, you won't be in the right frame of mind to provide it. It's very important to look after yourself.

- When giving help, be consistent, calm and supportive, but beware of doing things that just enable further addiction. For example, bailing someone with a gambling problem or drug addiction out of a financial mess might just lead to further addictive behaviour. This is called 'enabling'.

  Avoiding enabling isn't always easy; sometimes, as a parent or loved one, you feel you have to protect them. There might be court costs or threats from third parties waiting to be paid – but be careful and weigh up your options. Get help and find ways to provide support that doesn't enable further addictive behaviour.

- Try not to respond to crises – respond *between* crises.

The typical time to be asked to help is when there is a crisis like a court case, a legal issue or a personal disaster. Addicted people often feel obliged to make promises about getting help to leverage your support. Once the crisis is over, the motivation can disappear.

Can you force someone to get help?

Forced treatment does work, but it is difficult to force someone to get help.

Treatment mandated by courts has been shown in studies to be successful – it is not quite as successful as voluntary treatment, but it is still successful.

Addictions don't usually fall under mental health acts in most countries. Under a mental health act, if you have depression or psychosis and you are a risk to yourself, you can be forced to get treatment. This isn't the case for addictions alone. If the addicted person *also* has depression or psychosis, then they can be forced to get help, but as soon as the depression or psychosis passes the risk phase, they go back to being voluntary patients – usually well before the addiction is treated.

This often frustrates families – their loved one takes drugs, becomes psychotic, is made an involuntary patient and goes into hospital, but is then discharged once the drug is out of their system and the psychosis resolved. The person then goes back to drug use without getting help for their addiction.

The only effective way to force someone to get help is through a court order of some sort. Many courts will order an addicted person to get help as part of their sentence (or instead of a sentence). There are also programs in prisons.

Of course, mandated care is a last resort; everyone would prefer voluntary treatment, but sometimes it just isn't possible – and any programs that help are worth trying.

*

The rest of this chapter is devoted to definitions and facts about addiction. You may or may not need this information – that's why we have put it at the end of the chapter. Flick through and see which parts are relevant to you, or if you fancy being a true amateur shrink, read the lot!

Key terms and disorders

Different people in the addiction field use different terms. The key terms are listed below. You'll notice some of the terms overlap. It's confusing, but worth knowing because different phases of drug and alcohol problems require different treatments. If you really want to simplify your terminology, the big three terms to remember are intoxication, withdrawal and dependence.

- *Addiction*: Addiction has many meanings. In lay terms, it means a strong and compulsive need to regularly have something, such as a drug, or do something, such as gamble, despite it causing you harm. There is no universally agreed medical definition; in fact, it tends to be a catch-all term covering the whole area of addiction medicine. It's used interchangeably with the term 'dependence'.

- *Intoxication*: Intoxication describes the effects of taking too much of a drug. Each drug has a different intoxication profile. All drugs of addiction cause some sort of intoxication if too much is taken (with the possible exception of tobacco). Intoxication essentially means that significant behavioural or psychological problems have developed from taking too much of the drug – this usually includes things like belligerence, irritability and impaired cognitive function. Alcohol intoxication, for example, has typical signs of slurred speech, poor coordination, unsteady gait, impaired attention and sedation. Chances are you know this feeling! Overdose is where intoxication puts the user's life at risk.

- *Withdrawal*: This is the syndrome that results from stopping a drug after prolonged use. It can even occur after simply reducing the dose. Not all drugs cause a withdrawal syndrome. Like intoxication, the withdrawal syndrome is specific to the drug. For example, alcohol withdrawal comes on after about twelve to forty-eight hours, and causes anxiety, tremor, insomnia, and in severe cases hallucinations and sometimes even seizures.

- *Abuse*: Abuse refers to a risky pattern of drug use without actually being dependant on the drug. For example, the person's functioning might deteriorate as a consequence of the drug use, or they may use it in a hazardous way (for example, while driving). It basically refers to the lifestyle that can go along with drug use.

- *Dependence*: Dependence refers to the severe end of the drug use spectrum. There is a mix of tolerance (needing more drug to get the same effect), withdrawal, using more of the drug than initially intended, persistent and unsuccessful efforts to cut back usage, and persistent use despite knowing it is doing harm.

- *Substance use disorder*: In the DSM-5, the terms abuse and dependence have been dropped as the borderline between them was considered too vague and they often overlapped. Instead, they opted for the umbrella term 'substance use disorders'. This means you are using the substance in a way that is risky and harmful; you have tried to cut back unsuccessfully; you spend large amounts of time either procuring, using or recovering from the substance; it affects many aspects of your life (relationships, work, etc.); and you have strong cravings.

- *Substance induced disorders*: This is also a term from the DSM-5. It refers to all the secondary problems that can result from taking drugs or alcohol, including intoxication and withdrawal, but also all of the psychiatric problems that drugs and alcohol can cause – psychosis, depression, cognitive impairment, anxiety, sexual dysfunction and more. The key principle for these disorders is that they are caused by the drug and go away when the drug is ceased.

Drugs

All the drugs described below have risks. The effects vary from person to person and depend on lots of factors, especially:

- how much you take – and this is often hard to assess because different batches have different strengths
- your weight, size and health
- whether you are used to taking it
- whether the drug is mixed with other drugs.

We've listed the effects as best we can, mainly focussing on the psychological effects. The physical effects are complex and beyond the scope of this book.

Alcohol

Alcohol is by far the biggest drug of addiction in our society, in terms of both individual damage and cost to the community. It contributes to pretty much everything, from a range of diseases to violence and road trauma. It's a mile ahead of tobacco in terms of the damage it does, yet surprisingly it remains relatively untouched by our lawmakers and public health campaigners. This is not to suggest it should be more regulated and maligned; it's just an observation. Alcohol is clearly central to our everyday life.

About 90 per cent of people drink at some stage in their life and about 40 per cent do so on a weekly basis. 20 per cent drink in a way that puts their health at risk. Definitions of what constitutes risky drinking vary, but by and large this means an average of more than two standard drinks a day. In the UK, both men and women are advised to drink no more than fourteen units of alcohol per week, spread over three or four days, with at least two or three alcohol-free days per week. The easiest way to calculate how much you are drinking is to count the units you are consuming. 1 unit is 6g per 10ml of pure alcohol – the amount in one standard 25ml-measure of spirits (40 per cent) or one half-pint of beer (3.6 per cent) or one 100ml-glass of wine. Older people who normally lose muscle and gain fat break down alcohol more slowly are therefore more sensitive to the effects of alcohol. Also, because they naturally react more slowly they can be much more readily affected by the effects of alcohol. About 15 per cent of people get very drunk (more than eleven standard drinks) at least once per year. About 8 per cent drink every day. Problem drinking is twice as common in men than women.

The three really big problems with alcohol are alcohol use disorder (often called alcoholism or alcohol dependence), alcohol intoxication and alcohol withdrawal.

- **Alcohol use disorder (alcoholism):** There is no distinct line in the sand that separates risky drinking from alcoholism. By and large, you fall into the alcoholism category if you are a regular drinker and experience any combination of tolerance, withdrawal and craving. Different people have different patterns of problems – if you're not sure if you are addicted to alcohol, there are hundreds of online self-tests you can try, but the fact you are unsure in itself suggests it's time to seek help.
- **Alcohol intoxication:** This is a mix of slurred speech, incoordination, unsteady gait (walking), impaired attention and sometimes even coma. You can die from

intoxication, but the more common problems are social – trauma and violence.

- **Alcohol withdrawal:** For people dependant on alcohol, withdrawal symptoms usually begin somewhere between twelve and forty-eight hours after their last drink. Symptoms usually include a racing pulse, sweating, tremor, nausea, insomnia and agitation. In severe cases, visual hallucinations and seizures occur. Alcohol withdrawal, if untreated, can be fatal. Permanent neurological damage can also occur. Urgent medical treatment is usually required. The symptoms are relieved with diazepam (or alcohol), which is gradually weaned once the acute risk has passed. The syndrome is usually over within four to seven days.

Alcohol is associated with a wide range of mental disorders, including depression, psychosis, anxiety, insomnia, sexual dysfunction and cognitive impairment. Alcohol can be a direct cause of each of these, although it is often hard to sort out cause and effect. For example, is the person drinking because they are depressed, or are they depressed from the effects of alcohol? Ceasing alcohol is often the only way to find out.

As with so much in addictions (and mental health) no one has really good answers to the problems of alcohol. Attempts at prohibition usually fail and simply create a thriving illegal trade with packed jails and rich criminal bosses.

Various social interventions to encourage responsible drinking, such as laws to limit excessive alcohol purchasing and late-night lock-out laws seem effective, but balancing civil rights against the dangers of alcohol is inevitably controversial.

Alcohol brings in enormous amounts of tax in most Western countries.

Cannabis

In the UK, drug use overall has declined over the past ten years. However, one in three people have taken an illegal substance and 20 per cent continue to take them. Cannabis is the most commonly used illegal drug – about half of 16–19 year olds in the UK have tried it and about 7.2 per cent of all adults report using it at some time in any given year. Debate rages over the dangers of cannabis: many argue it is safer than alcohol and tobacco; others worry it is a 'gateway' drug to more dangerous substances, such as amphetamines. Cannabis does not appear to be very addictive. It doesn't seem to carry the same health effects as tobacco, and nowhere near the violence and trauma of alcohol.

Common names for cannabis include: marijuana, pot, weed, grass, ganja, dope, herb, joint, reefer, mary jane, and bud. It can be smoked (in a joint, pipe or bong), eaten (for example, in cookies, brownies, even ice cream), drunk (for example, as tea) or inhaled (in eCigarette liquid).

Cannabis causes a sense of relaxation and euphoria. Some people report a greater sense of philosophical thinking and introspection. Others experience anxiety and paranoia. Many people have an increase in appetite (often called the 'munchies').

The main problems with cannabis are:

- **Cannabis use disorder (cannabis dependence):** Cannabis is not nearly as addictive as alcohol and other drugs, and full-scale dependence is a little controversial. It is clear that long-term use is associated with declines in social functioning, less education and more mental health problems, especially in younger users (aged fifteen to twenty-five), but tolerance, withdrawal and craving do not seem as prominent as for alcohol dependence.

- **Cannabis intoxication:** Intoxication is characterised by impaired coordination, euphoria, anxiety, a sensation of slowed time, impaired judgement, social withdrawal, increased appetite, dry mouth, racing heart and red eyes.

- **Cannabis withdrawal:** This is a withdrawal syndrome can occur after heavy use, usually with onset within a week. The main symptoms are irritability, anger, aggression, anxiety, sleep disturbance, fatigue, restlessness and depression

- **Various mental disorders:** Cannabis can cause a psychotic episode, ongoing anxiety disorders and sleep disorders. There has been an ongoing debate about the links between cannabis use and schizophrenia. The current belief is that it exacerbates schizophrenia by causing relapses and can precipitate schizophrenia in people who are predisposed, but is probably not a cause in itself.

Cannabis (often called medicinal marijuana) is being studied around the world as a medical treatment for various disorders. Its use is fairly widespread for pain relief, anxiety (especially in terminal illness), muscle spasms, sleep, and for certain relatively rare types of epilepsy. In many countries, medicinal marijuana can be prescribed by doctors.

Stimulants: Amphetamines and methamphetamine

A stimulant is a drug that temporarily improves either physical or mental performance. This might include alertness, wakefulness, endurance, productivity, motivation and cognitive (thinking) function.

There are many stimulants but the most popular examples are amphetamines and methamphetamine (crystal meth). MDMA (ecstasy) and cocaine are also stimulants, but are covered separately below, as they have some significant differences to amphetamines and methamphetamines.

In the UK, home office statistics (2016) note that the use of methampetamines is 0.2 per cent, unlike in the US, Asia and Australia. Stimulants tend to be used as party drugs to stay awake, feel good, dance and socialise. They cause happiness, confidence, increased energy, reduced appetite, and sometimes an increased sex drive.

They can be swallowed, smoked, snorted or injected. Common street names include speed, uppers, whiz, bennies, and dexies. Methamphetamines are also known as ice, meth and crystal meth, among other names.

Amphetamines of various forms have been used for centuries. They remain a key treatment for attention deficit hyperactivity disorder (ADHD) and narcolepsy, and are also used in some diet pills. Amphetamines are the most commonly used drugs in the UK, after cannabis.

Methamphetamines are chemically slightly different. When the body breaks them down, they produce various chemicals, one of which is amphetamine. Methamphetamines tend to be stronger and work more quickly – as a consequence, users are a little more likely to get the dose wrong and take too much, causing various problems related to excessive intoxication. Methamphetamines are rarely used for medical purposes.

Stimulants are popular, with 10 per cent of people having tried one or another in their life, and about 0.6 per cent in the previous year. Of the recent users, it's split about fifty-fifty between those who use methamphetamine and those who use amphetamine.

The main problems seen are:

- **Stimulant use disorder (stimulant dependence):** As in other dependence syndromes, those who are addicted experience various degrees of tolerance, withdrawal and cravings, and so spend large amounts of time seeking the drugs. Estimating the rate of addiction for any drug is difficult because use is illegal, so people rarely admit to their problems. Lots of factors influence the rates, such as availability of the drug, the cost, and access to treatment services. Methamphetamine dependence appears to have been particularly problematic in some countries in the last five years, based on reports in the media, but these reports confuse cases of intoxication with true dependence, and most of the collected data has not yet shown much of an increase.

- **Stimulant intoxication:** Intoxication is a major problem with stimulants, especially methamphetamines. Most of the street drugs sold are produced in 'backyard' labs, so the potency and quality vary enormously. It's very easy to take more than you intended and end up in an

A&E department excessively intoxicated. Typical signs of intoxication include agitation, anger, paranoia and confusion, with physical signs such as racing heart, seizures and blackouts. Intoxication can easily slide into overdose. Death from intoxication does occur, especially if people fail to call for medical help.

- **Stimulant withdrawal:** Withdrawal symptoms will depend on the duration of use. Most people who have used amphetamines for a long time begin developing withdrawal symptoms within about a day, and it takes about a week for the main symptoms to pass, although minor symptoms can last up to a month. Typical withdrawal symptoms include cravings for amphetamines, aches and pains, exhaustion, increased appetite, restlessness, insomnia, anxiety, depression and paranoia.

- **Stimulant psychosis:** Amphetamines are a common cause of psychosis, with any of the typical symptoms: hallucinations, delusions, thought disorder (illogical thinking) and behavioural problems (usually aggression when caused by amphetamines). The symptoms usually disappear after about three days off the drug.

Cocaine

Cocaine is a stimulant that comes from the coca plant. There are three popular forms of the drug. The most common form is a white powder (cocaine hydrochloride) that people mostly snort, but can also mix in drinks, rub into their gums or dissolve in water to inject. Freebase cocaine is a purer form that is usually smoked. Crack cocaine is similar to freebase, but of lower potency, and also usually has impurities. It is also smoked (or more precisely, the vapour is inhaled).

Common names for cocaine include coke, nose candy, toot, blow and charlie. The effects are similar to amphetamines, but it is shorter acting, so the effects wear off quicker. The rates of use in the UK are 2.25% and it is the third most widely used illegal drug. Social classes 1 and 2 make up 40 per cent of users.

The problems with cocaine appear to be fewer than for amphetamines. This may in part be because of its shorter duration of action – meaning people are less likely to take excessive quantities and end up in the A&E department with an overdose. It might also be because of the demographics of the people who use cocaine. Worldwide, cocaine tends to be expensive, and so is used mainly by high-earning people. The pattern of use seems to largely be social users who take it on the weekend and work during the week – this might account for the apparent lower rates of addiction. In countries where it is cheaper, the rates of addiction are higher.

Despite the shorter duration of action, overdose is still possible, especially if the user has a stronger batch than they realise. Cocaine psychosis is also possible, especially with frequent use, but it is less common than for amphetamines.

Ecstasy (MDMA)

Ecstasy is also a stimulant, with the key ingredient being methylenedioxymethamphetamine (MDMA). The catch is that what is actually sold under the name of ecstasy can vary widely. It is often a mix of MDMA and amphetamines, sometimes ketamine and sometimes various other drugs. So describing ecstasy is difficult – it all depends on the specific tablets. 25 per cent of British drug users have used ecstasy and it is the fourth most common drug of abuse in the UK.

This variation in tablet composition makes ecstasy risky – you never know for sure what you are taking. In some countries there are mobile drug-testing labs where the user gets a tiny amount of their drug tested on the spot before they take it.

Ecstasy's psychological effects include feeling happy, energetic and confident. It may reduce inhibitions and increase the desire for sex. Some people also experience hallucinations. It is often used at parties, and is sometimes described as a love drug. It usually comes as a pill, takes about twenty minutes to work and lasts on average about six hours.

Common names include 'E', pills, XTC, pingers, and the love drug.

The main problems with ecstasy are:

- **Ecstasy use disorder (dependence):** It is difficult to estimate the percentage of people who become dependent on ecstasy compared to those who use it in a social manner. There are only a small number of studies attempting to assess this, and they show inconsistent results. Dependence can definitely occur, but how often is unknown. As usual, dependence is associated with tolerance to the drug. People also describe depression, a flu-like illness and anxiety with chronic use.
- **Ecstasy intoxication:** Getting the dose right is hard because the amounts of MDMA in every tablet may vary. Overdose can occur, and usually results in vomiting and

possibly seizures. Deaths from overdose, usually from heart attacks or stroke, are not uncommon. Some people also drink excessive amounts of water on ecstasy, which can also result in death.

- **Ecstasy withdrawal:** While ecstasy can cause a psychological dependence, it is not clear whether it can cause a physical dependence. Withdrawal mainly involves craving the drug, being restless, anxious, irritable and depressed. There is no distinct physical withdrawal syndrome, so medical help to withdraw is usually not required.

Opioids: Heroin

Opioids are a range of drugs that work on specific receptors in the brain (opioid receptors) to produce a broad range of effects – most prominently, pain relief and an intense pleasurable feeling (as well as a long list of physical effects). Most are derived from the opium poppy, but in recent decades a range of synthetic opioids have been manufactured. Broadly speaking, they are classed as central nervous system depressants. They are used extensively in healthcare, mainly for pain relief, but also in the treatment of addictions (methadone is often used to help stop heroin use), and a range of other problems.

Opioids are a major cause of addictions. Heroin is said to be the most addictive drug available, both physically and psychologically. Other opioids are also highly addictive.

Heroin is the major drug of concern for addictions (other than legal drugs such as alcohol and tobacco). In the UK, death rates from most opioids are steady or in decline. However, there are wide regional variations, for example, drug related deaths and addiction are still increasing in Scotland year on year.

It is worth noting that the general decline in heroin use has occurred at the same time that oxycodone, cocodemol and fentanyl use has skyrocketed. These are medically prescribed opioids, mainly used in pain relief. Many people believe oxycodone abuse has replaced heroin, but good data on oxycodone abuse (as distinct from clearly medically indicated use) is hard to obtain.

The most common medical examples of opioids are morphine, pethidine, oxycodone, tramadol, codeine and methadone. All can be abused in addictions, but heroin and probably now oxycodone, are the most infamous.

Common names for heroin include smack, gear, horse, hammer and dope. Heroin can come as a white powder, off-white granules or light brown rock. It is mostly injected, but can also be swallowed, smoked or snorted. The onset of action depends on how you take it, but is usually quick – almost immediate if injected. It usually lasts about three to five hours.

The main problems seen are:

- **Opioid use disorder (dependence):** This is a common problem with opioids. It's very easy to get addicted, with marked tolerance and withdrawal symptoms. Tolerance is such a problem that after a break from heroin, users often misjudge how much they need, take too much and overdose. There are reports of people using heroin socially on and off for many years without any evidence of dependence, but given heroin is illegal, getting data on this is almost impossible.

- **Opioid intoxication:** As with other illicit drugs, it's easy to misjudge the dose and become intoxicated or over-dose. This is exacerbated by heroin dealers often mixing the heroin with variable amounts of other substances depending on supply and profit issues. If there is a high supply, the heroin content increases, and intoxication and overdose are common. Overdose symptoms include sedation, slow breathing, unconsciousness and, if severe, death.

- **Opioid withdrawal:** Withdrawal is a major problem for heroin, especially after long-term use. Withdrawal symptoms include cravings, restlessness, irritability, diarrhoea, cramps, vomiting and depression. Symptoms develop within a day, and are prominent for two or three days, but can last as long as about a week. Medical support is often required. There are medications that can ease the symptoms of withdrawal.

Opioids are also associated with depression and can cause insomnia, sexual disorders and confusion.

Heroin is also notorious for problems related to injection. Injection in recreational settings is often poorly performed, and in the past needle-sharing was common. As a consequence, many infectious diseases were passed from user to user. HIV and hepatitis C were particularly problematic in the 1980s and 1990s. With needle exchange programs and widespread education about injecting techniques, these problems diminished considerably.

Hallucinogens: LSD and magic mushrooms
The term hallucinogen is a little vague. Many drugs can cause hallucinations (for example, amphetamines can result in

psychosis), but in this group of drugs, the experience of hallu-cinations is the primary effect – the reason people take them.

Hallucinogens (also known as psychedelics) cause changes in perception and a person's sense of reality. LSD (lysergic acid diethylamide) is the most common example, but some mush-rooms, known as magic mushrooms, also contain hallucino-gens, called psilocybin and psilocin. Other drugs that are often considered hallucinogens include PCP (phencyclidine or angel dust) and mescaline.

Hallucinogens cause a range of psychological effects, com-monly referred to as a 'trip'. The hallucinations can be in any of the senses – vision, hearing, touch, smell or taste. They also blur senses – for example, the user might feel they can hear colours – and can also distort the sense of time. They cause dissociation, which basically means feeling detached from your body. Most people describe this as a happy and pleasant experience.

The trip usually begins within an hour and lasts about six to twelve hours, but depends on the drug, how it is ingested and then many individual factors, such as size and weight.

Hallucinogens can be taken in various ways:

- LSD is usually swallowed as an LSD-infused piece of paper or a tablet
- magic mushrooms can be eaten raw, boiled or cooked
- PCP can come in tablets or powders, and can be swallowed, injected or snorted.

This is such a broad group of drugs it is difficult to summarise the associated problems. Substance use disorder (dependence) characterised by excessive time spent craving and seeking the drug, with various other features such as tolerance, has been described with hallucinogens, but seems pretty rare, especially with LSD and magic mushrooms. Excessive intoxication is common – it's easy to get the dose wrong and have too much. Sometimes the intoxication, even if not excessive, is deeply unpleasant – often called a bad trip. Some people have suggested this relates to your mood when you take the drug, or the circumstances of where you are when you take it. Another possible problem is 'flashbacks'. These are periods where a person re-experiences parts of the trip long after having taken the drug. They are said to occur after prolonged use of the drugs, but their existence has been questioned, and there is no clear answer as to whether they really occur.

It is also worth noting that in the last decade or two, research into the medical uses of hallucinogens has gained momentum. It looks like hallucinogens might follow the path of marijuana in finding some genuine medical uses. Once the research overcomes the understandable fears relating to the dangers, there are potential benefits for depression, anxiety (especially anxiety related to terminal illnesses) and addictions. There is already a large study from Europe showing benefits in alcohol addiction, and smaller studies in tobacco. The main way hallucinogens seem to be used is by assisting psychotherapy, and promising early neuroscience research is uncovering the various chemical and anatomical mechanisms through which this might work, which in turn may uncover other novel treatment approaches for different mental illnesses. It's exciting, watch this space!

Sedatives, hypnotics and tranquillisers

Many drugs cause sedation, sleep or reduce anxiety as side effects, but this group of drugs has the primary purpose of doing these things. They are used extensively in health care and all have the potential to be abused and can cause addiction. They are legal when prescribed by doctors for health conditions, but are also used recreationally or to 'come down' from various illicit drugs.

The most common group readily available are the benzodiazepines. This includes diazepam (Valium), alprazolam (Xanax), oxazepam (Serax, Murelax), temazepam (Normison, Restoril), nitrazepam (Mogadon) and more. Their street names include benzos, downers, sleepers and various names related to the trade names.

About 5 per cent of Australians admit to using them for non-medical purposes at some point in their life and about 1.5 per cent per year. Some estimates suggest 10 to 20 per cent of Australians regularly take benzodiazepines.

There is no doubt that in the past they have been prescribed too freely, significantly contributing to problems of abuse and dependence. Over the past decade or so, various restrictions on prescribing and education programs have begun to reverse this trend.

These drugs are prescribed for a range of disorders – insomnia, anxiety, epilepsy, muscle spasm and more. There is debate in the medical world about whether benzodiazepines cause addiction when prescribed for clear medical or psychiatric disorders. There is research that suggests when prescribed properly tolerance does not develop. The problem is that they are often prescribed too readily and without adequate warnings about the risk.

The main problems are:

- **Sedative use disorder (dependence):** Long-term use risks dependence, with typical problems of tolerance and withdrawal. Some studies suggest tolerance can develop in as little as a few days, but more typically it's a few weeks. Once the tolerance gets bad enough and people increase their dose, various other problems develop. If too much is taken, cognitive problems that mimic dementia can develop. Steve has seen people diagnosed with dementia, only to fully recover once it was realised they were taking high-dose benzodiazepines and they were gradually weaned off (in fact, this happened to one of Steve's grandfathers!).

- **Sedative intoxication:** Benzodiazepines act a lot like alcohol, so if you take too much you have all the same problems. Longer-acting benzodiazepines (see the table on page 277 in the medication section) are particularly problematic for driving. Overdose is common, but it is usually not by accident – these drugs are commonly used in suicide attempts.

- **Sedative withdrawal:** This is a big problem. Sudden cessation can result in dangerous withdrawal syndromes that can include seizures and brain damage. Other symptoms include anxiety, headaches, insomnia, aching, dizziness, nausea, tremors and paranoia. If a person has been on benzodiazepines for more than about three months, careful weaning is required, often with the help of a doctor.

The rule for thumb for these drugs is to use them for short periods only. If there is some reason you cannot sleep, such as jetlag or a major stress, then a few days of use is fine. If you need them for more than that, have at least one day free for every two days you take them – on the free nights, either expect to sleep poorly or try another sedative such as the various over-the-counter preparations. There is no such thing as a safe medical cure for insomnia!

Other drugs

We have not covered all drugs of addiction here. Others that could be included are tobacco, the various inhalants such as nitrous oxide, alkyl nitrite 'poppers', and other medical drugs that sneak into the recreational and abuse domain, such as ketamine. Refer to the resources section at the back of this book for websites with reliable information about these.

Club drugs

Some club drugs are well known like cocaine, MDMA, GHB, mephedrone, spice and ketamine. However, groups of new club drugs are emerging all of the time. These are known as NPS – *New Psychoactive Substances* – and are made specifically to mimic the effects of already established drugs. In 2015, the UK government introduced the Psychoactive Substances Act, making it illegal to possess psychoactive substances including club drugs (maximum sentence seven years). However, up to 1 million people in the UK are using club drugs and it is increasing. Students, people who identify themselves as 'clubbers' and the LGBTQI community are the most common users. People typically use club drugs for their positive effects including increased energy levels, lifted mood and altered sensations which is why they are popular in social settings but because many of them are relatively new, the harmful effects are still unclear. Toxic reactions, damage to internal organs, overdoses, heart problems, mental health problems, dependence and death have all been seen in club drug users.

Gambling and other behavioural addictions

Traditionally, the term 'addiction' was applied only to chemicals – drugs. In the last couple of decades, the concept of addiction has also been applied to various behavioural problems. Gambling is the most obvious, but others include sex addiction, pornography addiction, shopping addiction and internet gaming addiction. (The World Health Organisation will include this category in ICD–11.) In contrast to addiction to substances where it is possible to conduct other activities simultaneously, behavioural addictions can take up all the physical energy and cognitive space of the sufferer. The belief is that these behaviours activate similar reward systems in the brain, so they share features with drug addiction – things like tolerance (needing to do the behaviour more and more for the same degree of enjoyment), withdrawal (restlessness or irritability when cutting down or stopping) and craving (preoccupation with the need to do the behaviour when not doing it).

In the past, these behaviours were considered more as compulsions or extreme urges. Understanding them as addictions has had all sorts of effects. First and foremost, it brings them into the health domain, which in turn stimulates research and increases efforts at developing treatments. Also, it helps reduce stigma – when seen as simple urges, people tend to apply various judgements to people with excessive self-destructive behaviours – which only serves to alienate the sufferers and minimise their problems.

The DSM-5 only includes gambling as an addiction, as the other behaviours don't have enough evidence yet to support them being called mental disorders.

At the end of the day, it's largely semantics. These are problems that some people suffer, and as a community we should find ways to help. If applying the concept of addictions opens windows to understanding, then it is a useful concept. If it closes down understanding by stopping us from exploring other conceptual models, then it has gone too far.

While many clinicians are yet to be fully convinced behavioural addictions are the same as drug addictions, by applying the concept of addictions to behaviour (especially for gambling) the situation for sufferers and people seeking help has improved dramatically. The jury might still be out, but in the meantime bringing these behaviours into the addiction family has been a huge improvement.

Gambling disorder

To be diagnosed as having a gambling disorder (previously called pathological gambling) the DSM-5 says the person must have four or more of the following symptoms:

- needing to gamble with increasing amounts of money
- restless or irritable when attempting to cut down
- repeated failed efforts to cut back

- often preoccupied with gambling
- often gambles when feeling distressed
- after losing, often returns to chase losses
- lies to conceal the extent of gambling
- has jeopardised or lost significant relationships, jobs or educational opportunities
- relies on others to provide money because of their financial problems.

There are 400,000 problem gamblers in the UK and 6 per cent of the population have used the internet for gambling. Of those who have a problem, poker machines dominate the picture (especially for women). The impacts are dramatic on individuals and families, and overlap with other addictions is common. Only about one in eight people with a gambling addiction seek help to stop.

10

Suicide

Choosing to die by suicide is arguably the biggest decision any human can make. The first question that comes to most people's mind after a suicide is: Why? Why did they do it? Why didn't they seek help? Why didn't anyone stop them?

Suicide is common. The UK suicide rate is approximately 16 deaths per 100,000 for men and 5 per 100,000 for women per year. It's the most common cause of death for both men and women until around the age of forty.

The worldwide figures related to suicide are staggering. The World Health Organization estimates that about 10 per cent of the world's populations seriously consider suicide and about 4 per cent attempt suicide. Somewhere between about 1 and 2 per cent of all deaths are by suicide, and it's the tenth leading cause of death. It's widely accepted that the suicide rate is under-reported, mostly due to the stigma surrounding it.

Men account for about 70 per cent of all suicides, despite women attempting suicide more often. Men tend to use more lethal means (such as hanging). The most common ways people die by suicide are hanging, self-poisoning and firearms. The peak age is mid-forties but no age group from teenagers onwards is spared. Some groups in society are at a particularly high risk; in Australia, for instance, Indigenous and LGBTQI (lesbian, gay, bisexual, transgender, queer and intersex) Australians have higher rates of suicide.

Figuring out why someone has died by suicide is tragically difficult. Those left behind desperately want answers to help with their grieving. Governments and health authorities desperately need answers to minimise those that are preventable. But it's enormously difficult. People have so many secrets, and those secrets die with them. The full truth in any individual case is probably never known.

Researchers who study large numbers of suicide look at both individual and societal factors. The list of individual risk factors is long and ever-growing. It currently includes:

- previous suicide attempt – in the year after a suicide attempt, a person is fifty times more likely to die by suicide than the general population (despite this, the chances are still low; fewer than one in two hundred people die by suicide in the six months following an attempt)
- mental disorders, especially depression and substance abuse
- physical illness: especially if terminal, painful or debilitating
- family history of suicide, substance abuse or other psychiatric disorders
- history of sexual, physical or emotional abuse
- being socially isolated and/or living alone
- bereavement in childhood

- family disturbances
- unemployment, or change in occupational or financial status
- rejection by a significant person: for example, a relationship break-up
- recent discharge from a psychiatric hospital.

The societal factors are even more complex. Social dislocation, poverty, lack of adequate health services, and stigma probably all contribute, but how these interact with personal factors remains a mystery.

Can suicide be prevented?

The simple answer is yes, but it's way more complicated than that. Suicide prevention is the holy grail of psychiatry.

There are essentially three ways societies aim to reduce the suicide rate: universal programs that reach all of society, selective programs aimed at those at high risk, and individual help for those who are considering suicide.

Universal programs
There is no single solution that will prevent suicide. The battle needs to be fought on multiple fronts. Each evidence-based step has a small impact. Here are some of the big-ticket items most governments are slowly working on.

1. *Reducing the means*. Amazingly, in the moments before a suicide, the person is mostly ambivalent. The final moments are often chaotic and skewed by drugs or

alcohol. People are usually distressed, often agitated, not thinking clearly, and right up to the last moment they are weighing the pros and cons. We know this from studies of people who have survived very serious attempts where they would have died if luck had not intervened. Therefore, the more we limit the means of suicide, the more chance there is for the person to change their mind or for someone else to intervene. Putting up barriers on bridges, installing catalytic converters in cars (these reduce the chances of death from carbon monoxide poisoning), limiting access to dangerous drugs, and reducing access to firearms, pesticides, railway lines and dangerous gases all help. It's not inevitable that someone will substitute one method for another if they are thwarted.

2. *Improving access to health care.* Inability to access mental health services is a problem the world over. Financially, mental health services lag way behind physical health services. The easier it is to access mental health care, the more people will seek help and the more we can prevent the consequences of mental illness. The World Health Organization and most governments work hard on this, but public support is minimal – mental illness and suicide remain marginalised problems.

3. *Reducing stigma.* Stigma stops people from accessing help. It also stymies efforts at suicide research and prevention – sadly, it's common for people to feel ashamed when a family member dies by suicide. They hide it, it stays out of the statistics, we can't study it,

politicians don't hear about it – and so little gets done. More on this later.

In the UK, organisations such as the Depression Alliance and The Bipolar Organisation shine light on mental illness but more is needed.

4. *Preventing trauma.* Trauma is probably the most preventable risk factor for mental illness. Trauma is a key cause of nearly everything in mental health – anxiety, depression, eating disorders, and the list grows with every study into trauma. Programs that prevent violence, child abuse and bullying in all its forms are essential. These include better policing, stronger laws and targeted social interventions.

5. *Strengthening communities.* Social isolation occurs everywhere. Anything that can strengthen communities to support the socially isolated helps. Better social services, schools, programs for migrants and the dislocated, relationship supports (such as relationship counselling) and community groups all contribute to lowering the suicide rate.

Selective programs

Selective programs aim to provide support to groups that research tells us are at high risk of suicide. There are thousands of such programs around the world, covering all sorts of vulnerable populations, such as:

- victims of conflict
- war veterans
- victims of disasters

- refugees
- victims of crime
- victims of abuse
- indigenous populations
- prisoners
- LGBTQI people
- the bereaved.

In order for these programs to work, the various gatekeepers need training. Gatekeepers are people who are in a position to recognise that someone from a vulnerable group might be suffering. This includes primary health-care providers, teachers, community leaders, police officers, social welfare workers, prison staff and many others. Gatekeeper training aims to improve knowledge, attitudes and skills, as well as equip the gatekeepers with the required links to enlist professional support when needed – especially crisis support services.

Crisis support services are resources people can turn to when they are concerned about suicide. Sometimes they are helplines: The Samaritans is the most well known in the UK, but there are many. Sometimes they are clinical services that people can access over the phone and clinicians can be sent out to help where needed. And some police forces now include trained clinicians to attend call-outs with police where mental health problems are likely.

Individual supports

The final part of the jigsaw is high-quality interventions for those who have become suicidal. Interventions begin with skilled assessments and extend to reliable community follow-up programs. In between, evidence-based, effective treatment programs must be available. Mental health treatments do work and they reduce the risk of suicide – but they have a fair way to go. We need more effective treatments with less side effects. And they need to be more affordable and accessible.

Why the secrecy around suicide?

Every family has a right to privacy. And losing a loved one to suicide is a tragedy almost beyond comprehension. Family and friends often feel like they have failed. Why didn't they recognise the problem? Why didn't they do more to prevent it? Blame is often thrown around freely. Guilt and grief are powerful, sometimes overwhelming emotions.

Some religious practices encourage secrecy. Suicide is a sin in some religions, forbidden in others, and often the funeral and burial practices are different if death was by suicide.

There are also legal implications. In some countries suicide remains a criminal act, and in some circumstances families can be penalised. There may also be implications for insurance and other legal matters. In the UK, suicide and attempting suicide are no longer crimes, although assisting or encouraging suicide are.

Another contributory factor is fear in the media around discussing suicide because of the risk of copycat suicides. There is some evidence to support this view. But media reporting guidelines have softened in the past two decades, from a point where suicide was barely mentioned to the current state, where it is reported, but sensationalism is minimised and contact details for support services are provided.

Some of the key principles of current media reporting guidelines are:

- Avoid terms that sensationalise suicide, such as 'suicide epidemic'.
- Don't be explicit about the method.
- Beware of glamorising suicide – especially with celebrity suicide.
- Beware of interviewing the bereaved – they are at risk themselves.
- Include information and contact details for helplines such as the Samaritans and other support services.

Finally, there is the language around suicide – it evokes images of crime and guilt. The word 'commit' – she *committed* suicide – has negative connotations, implying a crime. We commit murder, we commit rape – we don't commit marriage, nor childbirth. Suicide should not be included in acts we *commit*.

Stopping the secrecy

Let's be clear – the reasons for the secrecy are entrenched and complex. No one wants to criticise families for making up stories – how could we, when they're in the midst of such grief and sorrow? The decision to disclose must remain theirs and theirs alone.

But ignorance will never shift the elephant in the room. We need to be aware that every time we hide suicide, we contribute to the secrecy, the stigma and the knowledge gap around suicide. If we as individuals and a community talk freely, without prejudice or sensationalism, then we will slowly lift the veil. We might finally make some progress and – like the toll from road accidents – the rates might finally fall.

How is suicide risk assessed?

Assessing suicidal patients is relatively straightforward; clinicians essentially do a standard psychiatric assessment, as outlined in Chapter 4. We pay particular attention to what's known as the suicide (or self-harm) risk assessment – although nearly all good-quality studies tell us this doesn't actually predict who will go on to die by suicide, and in reality this needs to be done for every patient, regardless of whether they have stated a wish to die. Put simply, there is no way to predict the future – the best we can do is look for problems that we can fix and take measures to make sure people are getting the help they need.

These are the sorts of questions we ask people who have attempted suicide:

- What did you do?
- How serious was the attempt?
- Did you plan it for long?
- Did you think you'd die?
- Did you take measures to avoid being stopped?
- Have you been depressed lately?
- What other problems are going on?
- What supports do you have?
- Do you plan to try again?

- Will you accept help?

We look at the risk factors – age, sex, support, drugs, alcohol, past attempts and various other things. We weigh up the risk of another attempt to help decide the next step. But, there is no simple combination of factors to predict the future. The Nobel Prize-winning physicist Neils Bohr said, 'Prediction is very difficult, especially about the future.' He was right.

We try to engage the patient and family (if appropriate) in a treatment plan.

We balance our legal and medical responsibilities.

A typical risk assessment divides people into low, medium or high risk of further attempts in the short term, but at best this is educated guesswork.

- Low risk – low lethality attempt (such as taking relatively harmless medications or not taking enough to do serious damage), no efforts to avoid intervention, minimal prior planning or a spontaneous decision, denies ongoing suicidal ideas, accepts treatment.
- Medium risk – somewhere in between the two extremes
- High risk – high lethality attempt (for example using a firearm or attempted hanging) with efforts to avoid detection, prior planning, preparations for death (such as a suicide note, will or funeral instructions), ongoing plans to try again, severe mental illness and refusing treatment.

High-risk patients are usually admitted to hospital for further assessment and treatment. Low-risk patients are managed according to their personal preferences (usually in the community, but not always: some choose hospital).

The most important thing at the time of assessment is to try to establish rapport with the patient – build trust and communication. We need the patient to engage in treatment. If we admit them involuntarily, using a Mental Health Act, this can damage rapport – so it's a high-wire balancing act.

Decisions about how to treat a suicidal person are some of the most complex decisions in psychiatry, and most services require senior staff to review or sign off on the plan.

Suicide attempts

Mostly the stories about suicide we hear are incredibly sad – life can go wrong so easily. It's hard being human. Sometimes the stories are maddening – people doing stupid things for stupid reasons and hurting themselves and others in the process.

The stories of survival can be amazing – huge jumps off bridges; branches of trees breaking to thwart a hanging; chance interventions by strangers.

Thankfully, many people who have made very serious attempts immediately regret it and the event is a watershed moment – a turning point. On the other hand, sometimes the attempts are half-hearted, but the person unknowingly chooses a dangerous means and the consequences are far worse than they intended.

Some suicide attempts get labelled as a 'cry for help' or 'attention seeking'. Sometimes people diminish these attempts, as if they somehow deserve less attention. But there is no such thing as a suicide attempt that doesn't deserve attention. People fear that by providing attention they will encourage more attempts, but this risk is small, and far outweighed by the risks of missing an opportunity to assess and intervene appropriately. Every suicide attempt needs a response – assessment, support and intervention by a professional.

When you ask people with no mental health problems whether they have ever considered suicide or thought about what circumstances would lead them to suicide, most say 'yes'. It seems we all think about it at some point. "What if I became paraplegic? What if my child died? What if I had terminal cancer? Or dementia?" Most of us run through these scenarios at some point.

There are also people who say they would like to die but something stops them from considering suicide. Occasionally it's religion. Often it is a responsibility: 'My life is horrible and I'd like to die, but I couldn't do it to my family – they'd be devastated.' Sometimes it's fear.

For doctors, the task is to determine if the person has a mental illness. By far the majority of people who try to kill themselves do have a mental illness – usually depression, sometimes schizophrenia, anorexia or severe anxiety. There is often an associated drug or alcohol problem. Sometimes there are huge personal issues at play, such as gambling, relationship problems or financial ruin.

Occasionally the problems are easy to treat; sometimes they are very difficult.

If the person has a mental illness with ongoing suicidal ideas and refuses treatment, the laws of our country say we must treat them against their will – involuntary treatment. Mostly this works well, but not always.

Sometimes the person has no mental illness. They have just decided that they want to die. They are not depressed, they understand the issues, and they believe it is their right to die. It might be related to a terminal illness (euthanasia) and on rare occasions a political act, or simply just a balanced decision about the pleasure they are getting from life. As difficult as it is to digest, sometimes we need to honour and respect an individual's personal agency and their wishes.

The aftermath

The hardest part of dealing with suicide is supporting family members. It is tragic seeing them try to make sense of it all. Complex issues, confusion, feeling like a failure, being scared, not knowing what to say – in the midst of dealing with doctors and nurses. They are confused, they are grieving, and they know this tragedy will stay with them. The lucky ones get support from each other, but not everyone is so lucky.

Good clinical services aim to provide support to those left behind – but it is often difficult. Sometimes the families and others blame the service for not preventing the suicide. Sometimes it's true – there have been clinical failings – and sometimes there are various consequences for the service – lawsuits, investigations and changes to practice.

It's a confusing, anxious and sad time. Families grieving, clinicians feeling guilty, administrators reviewing processes, investigative bodies wanting reports – and everyone (friends, families, clinicians) asking: 'What more could I have done?'

What should you do if you think someone is suicidal?

This is a common problem. We are often faced with a friend or family member who has said or done something to indicate that they might be suicidal but are not getting the help they need.

Every situation is different, but here are a few tips:

- Tell them you are worried, and ask them directly whether they are suicidal. In the old days, people thought asking might make matters worse by giving the suicidal person the idea to do it. No one believes that now.
- Tell them they need to get help. Tell them they at least need to talk to someone. Offer to arrange it or offer to go with them if you feel comfortable doing so.
- Get them to ring a crisis service – either the Samaritans or their local hospital.
- Arm yourself with information. Ring a crisis service yourself, explain the situation and ask for suggestions. You can do it anonymously if you feel nervous about breaking confidences.
- If all else fails, think about referring them yourself without their knowledge (most crisis services are used to this request). Your loved one may be angry at you, but it's better than losing them.
- If you think they are right at the point of ending their life, just call the police.

It doesn't always turn out well, but more people regret the things they didn't do than regret the times they tried to help.

In Australia, a Sydney man called Don Richie was known as the Angel of the Gap. He lived 50 metres away from a famous suicide location – the Gap – a cliff where many people jumped to end their lives. Over the years he was estimated to have saved over 200 people. He simply approached people with a smile and asked, 'Is there something I can do to help you?' He often took them to his home and offered a cup of tea or a beer. He suggested they seek help. Don said: 'A conversation can save a life.' This is a small illustration of how acts of kindness and care can make big difference. Of course, acts like this are not going to prevent everyone from ending their lives, but it's a reminder that sometimes action, no matter how simple, can prevent suicide.

11

Eating Disorders

Eating is threaded through all aspects of our daily life – our social interactions, our celebrations, our culture, our identities and our emotions. It's so ubiquitous that we rarely consider its complexity. At its simplest, we need to eat in order to live, but there is much more to eating than nutrition. We begin life being fed, then we learn to eat independently, and once we're older we learn to feed others. Nearly every relationship involves eating. Food is a pillar of every economy. Every culture has rituals and practices related to eating. Every emotion has an impact on eating. Our eating practices and our weight are key aspects of how we define and view ourselves and others. Furthermore, like it or not, they impact on how others view us and relate to us.

Feeding and eating behaviours can be used as a communication. They can express positive attitudes like nurturing, love and belonging. They can also express anger and punishment – feeding prisoners gruel; no dessert for misbehaving teenagers. We can eat to relieve uncomfortable emotions, and we can eat to reward ourselves. Nearly every medical and psychiatric disorder has some impact on eating and weight – and vice versa.

With food meeting so many complex needs, it's no wonder

eating disorders are some of the most mysterious of all mental health problems.

The key eating disorders are anorexia nervosa, binge-eating disorder and bulimia nervosa. Obesity, while described as a major community health problem, is not considered to be a mental disorder.

Assessment

It's rare to find a person who at some stage hasn't stressed about their eating or weight. Unfortunately, most of the stress has nothing to do with health – it's usually about looks and acceptance. And most of the obsession with weight is built around an illusion that we'll be happier at a different weight.

Weight ranges recommended by health bodies are only guides. What is a healthy weight for you depends on your body type, your genetics and various other factors. Also, weight is just one of the many risk factors that affect your health – things like smoking, sedentary lifestyles, exercise levels, drinking, pollution, risk of road trauma and travel habits. There is a growing belief that worrying about weight does more harm than good. The medical evidence around weight, especially obesity, is not iron-clad.

In clinical practice, when assessing eating disorders the key things investigated are eating patterns, weight and body image. These form the crux of the three eating disorders.

Assessing eating patterns is pretty straightforward. We ask about the types of food, eating behaviours, feelings while eating, calorie counting, and any purging behaviours such as vomiting or laxative abuse. Past diets are important, as is information about weight concerns and efforts to lose weight.

Assessing weight is largely based on measurements such as the Body Mass Index (BMI), fat measurements and waist circumference. None of these are ideal, but they are the best we've got.

BMI is by far the most common measure. The formula is:

$$BMI = kg/m^2$$

where kg is a person's weight in kilograms and m^2 is their height in metres squared.

Here is the standard way BMI is assessed in adults:

- below 18.5 – underweight
- 18.5 to 24.9 – normal
- 25 to 29.9 – overweight
- over 30 – obese

Assessing body image is much harder. Essentially, we ask how you feel about your weight and size. Do you think you look thin? Are you worried about how you look? People with anorexia nervosa believe they look fatter than they are. However, many are used to the questions and, especially at first, say they look thin, before they develop trust in the person asking.

Specific screening questionnaires have been developed for eating disorders. A popular one is SCOFF, which has five simple questions:

- Do you make yourself Sick because you feel uncomfortably full?

- Do you worry you have lost Control over how much you eat?
- Have you recently lost more than One stone (14 pounds or 6.35 kg) in a three-month period?
- Do you believe yourself to be Fat when others say you are too thin?
- Would you say that Food dominates your life?

Two or more answers of yes is suggestive of an eating disorder.

Anorexia nervosa (AN)

The first time you meet someone with anorexia nervosa you're hit with a cascade of mixed feelings. Typically, you're confronted with a perplexed but somewhat determined and reluctant young woman. She is thin and sick-looking. She emphatically denies the extent of her problems. There is nearly always a parent there too – scared and frustrated. The exasperated parent has, by some means or other, organised and insisted on the assessment. The problem has usually been going for at least a year. Initially, everyone thought it was just normal dieting but at some point worry kicked in. The patient is now engulfed in a complex system of people and opinions, many contradictory. You can't help thinking, 'If only she'd just eat. This would all go away. Life could return to normal.' But anorexia nervosa is nearly always far more complicated than that.

Anorexia nervosa affects 1 per cent of the population. At least 90 per cent of sufferers are women, with an average age of onset of eighteen. The name anorexia is a misnomer – anorexia means loss of appetite, and this usually doesn't occur in anorexia nervosa.

There are three key clinical features of AN:

1. restriction in food intake leading to an abnormally low body weight
2. an intense fear of gaining weight or becoming fat, usually with persistent behaviours that prevent weight gain
3. a disturbed body image, such that the person underestimates how thin they are.

All three criteria must be met for the diagnosis. Being thin alone does not mean anorexia nervosa. There are many causes of being excessively thin, the most common in the world being a lack of food. Anorexia is the combination of being thin, fear of weight gain, and a distorted body image.

Once anorexia nervosa is diagnosed, the severity can be graded according to weight:

- mild: BMI over 17
- moderate: BMI under 17
- severe: BMI under 16
- extreme: BMI under 15.

For the average British woman, with a height of about 162 cm, this approximately means moderate is under 44.5 kg, severe under 42 kg, and extreme under 39 kg. In clinical practice, we see people with weights as low as 30 kg.

No one really understands the causes of anorexia nervosa, but we have some ideas. Some of the ideas studied include:

- genetics – it runs in families (even when family eating customs are taken into account, there is evidence of a genetic factor as well)

- hormonal changes
- negative body image
- low self-esteem
- personality traits of perfectionism
- childhood abuse
- culture, and society's emphasis on weight and body image – anorexia is more common in Western cultures
- media and digital manipulations of female body images
- dysfunctional family relationships
- athletic-oriented sports
- behavioural addiction, such as gambling or internet addiction, but the addiction is dieting
- sexist societal attitudes that a woman's value is linked to her weight
- body dysmorphia – the person is preoccupied with an imaginary deficit in appearance (being overweight).

The list of associated symptoms is endless: preoccupation with food and cooking, fear of certain foods, complicated rituals around eating, purging behaviours such as vomiting after meals or laxative abuse, social withdrawal, anxiety, depression, restlessness, excessive exercise, poor sleep, absent sex drive, inflexible thinking and more.

One of the most exhausting and heartbreaking things about AN is the fractured relationships from deceit and lying. Patients are usually battling against treatment – the patient wants to stay thin; the family and clinicians are aiming for weight gain. Deceit and lying are a protective response that prevents the patient, practitioners and loved ones from overcoming this devastating syndrome.

The medical complications are also many and varied. Heart problems, reproductive abnormalities, hormonal problems and gastric problems are the most common.

The mortality rate in AN is estimated to be between four and fourteen times higher than expected. The lower the weight, the higher the risk of death. Half the mortality is from medical complications and half from suicide.

Anorexia nervosa, once established and diagnosed, is often chronic. About a third of sufferers get better, a third fluctuate in and out of anorexia, and a third don't really ever recover. There are also many people with mild anorexia who never get to the point of diagnosis and treatment, and they probably do better, but they don't make it into the statistics.

Anorexia presents many challenges to the patient, the family and to treatment services. The patient usually just wants to be left alone – for them, the big challenge is control over their health and treatment. The family is usually racked with questions: How did this happen? Did we contribute? What can we do?

Treatment

Treatment for anorexia nervosa is multifaceted and inter-disciplinary. It usually requires at least a nutritionist, a mental health clinician and a general doctor, working in partnership. Different facets include individual psychiatric support, family support, medical support and nutritional support. Most patients with AN are treated by services specialising in anorexia nervosa.

The options chosen depend very much on the severity of the disorder.

Nutritional support, sometimes called nutritional rehabilitation, includes education about healthy eating and dieting, re-feeding strategies, attention to the medical complications of low weight, and behavioural strategies to gain weight. To begin, an assessment is carried out and goals are set. Depending on the patient's weight and the duration of the illness, the goal is usually around 0.5 to 1.0 kg weight gain per week. A nutritionist will begin by helping develop an eating plan with enough calories to meet the goal and providing the necessary supplements to avoid medical complications. If re-feeding is too rapid or unbalanced, there are further medical risks, so attention to detail is important.

Re-feeding can be done as an outpatient or inpatient. Inpatient care is chosen if the risks are high – usually meaning if the patient's weight is very low or there are already medical complications or high psychiatric risks such as self-harm or suicide.

Behavioural strategies to support this phase include setting rewards for successful weight gain. There are many approaches to this, but most include various incentives attached to gaining and maintaining weight.

While everyone agrees psychotherapy is an essential part of the management of AN, no one form of therapy has been shown to be the most effective. So the choice of psychotherapy is based on availability, age, patient preference and cost. The options are:

- *Cognitive behaviour therapy (CBT)* – addresses the thinking, feelings and behaviours around eating and helps develop goals and strategies to eat in a healthy manner. It is time-limited, practical and engages the patient in homework and exercises to reach their goals.

It is especially popular for younger patients, and can be delivered by a range of clinicians, although psychologists are often the clinicians of choice. It is suitable for inpatient or outpatient settings, and can include group therapy.

- *Psychodynamic psychotherapy* – addresses conscious and unconscious thoughts and feelings. While traditionally psychodynamic psychotherapy is long-term, more focused forms have been developed for eating disorders, and like CBT may include group or individual approaches.
- *Supportive psychotherapy* – using various techniques borrowed from other therapies and taking a more general approach to helping the patient address their problems and goals, supportive psychotherapy is often very useful especially in the early phases of treatment.
- *Family therapy* – aims to address the problem from a 'systems' perspective. This means the patient and their problem is seen as part of a system (the family) and understanding and addressing the way the family functions is the goal of treatment. Family therapy is also useful to help support family members, who can feel isolated and left out when all the efforts are aimed at the patient alone. Understandably, it is especially useful for adolescent patients or patients still living in the family home.

There are no specific medications to treat AN, but medications are often used to help with various associated problems, such as depression, anxiety around eating and dangerous behaviours such as self-harm. Some clinicians also use small doses of anti-psychotic medications, which help with dysfunctional thinking and also have the side effect of weight gain. However, the evidence base for their use is minimal, so they are usually reserved as a last resort.

Very low weight is life-threatening, so physicians experienced in nutrition and weight problems are an essential part of treatment. Their role is to monitor the medical complications of anorexia and re-feeding. Medical doctors also play a vital role in keeping the treatment coordinated and ongoing. Since patients with AN are often reluctant to accept mental health care, the primary physician is often the only clinician who can stay engaged over a long term, and call in the necessary support when needed.

Bulimia nervosa (BN)

Bingeing on food is fairly normal; most people do it from time to time. Bulimia nervosa is when the bingeing is excessive and associated with various behaviours to compensate for the binge-ing, and a self-evaluation that is excessively influenced by body shape and weight.

Distinguishing normal bingeing from BN is challenging. Criteria have been set to help clinicians with the diagnosis. First up, a binge is defined as eating an excessive amount in a discrete period of time – usually about two hours. Excessive means more than normal for the circumstances – so a Christmas lunch wouldn't count, but eating a big meal at 11 pm with dessert and then more food to follow would. A binge also feels out of control, as if you just cannot stop.

The most risky compensatory behaviours are self-induced vomiting and taking medications such as laxatives or diuretics to reduce weight. Other behaviours include fasting and excessive exercise.

A typical pattern develops: diet, then binge, then vomit. Some people get so practised that they can vomit on demand. They will describe being constantly worried about their shape and weight; they will diet all day, then go out with friends, eat a meal, pop into the toilet afterwards and induce a vomit, and then re-join their friends, who are totally oblivious to the behaviour. Later that night they might feel ashamed and binge and purge again.

Bulimia nervosa is diagnosed when bingeing and any of the compensatory behaviours occur on average about once a week for three months. Both males and females suffer BN, but it is three times more common in females. Rates are probably underestimated because many people keep it secret, but estimates suggest about 1.5 per cent of women and 0.5 per cent of men suffer BN at some time in their life, usually while young (the average age is eighteen).

Medical complications are common, especially from vomiting and medication abuse. Vomiting can lead to dehydration, tooth decay and stomach problems. Laxatives and diuretics can cause various biochemical abnormalities that can alter heart function. Chronic laxative abuse can also cause problems with bowel and stomach emptying, leading to chronic constipation. The risk of diabetes is also doubled in bulimia nervosa.

Most people with BN have a roughly normal weight, or are

mildly overweight. If their weight is low, in the anorexia range, then a diagnosis of anorexia nervosa is made instead of bulimia nervosa.

People with BN are intensely ashamed of their behaviour and commonly keep it secret for years. Since their weight is normal, friends and family usually don't have a clue. The problem usually starts as a teenager, and typically in association with dieting. The binges are especially common in times of stress.

It seems that only a small minority of people with BN (probably around 15 per cent) develop anorexia nervosa. Bulimia, like anorexia, tends to be chronic, with up to a third of patients still having symptoms after ten years. As with anorexia, the risk of dying is increased, both from medical complications and from an increased risk of suicide.

Bulimia is also often associated with other problems, the most common being depression, substance abuse and anxiety disorders.

Treatment

The treatment of bulimia nervosa is similar to anorexia nervosa, although inpatient care is rarely needed unless there are significant medical problems. The key elements are:

- thorough medical assessment for medical complications
- nutritional support – as with anorexia, this includes education, meal planning and strategies to overcome the compensatory behaviours.
- psychotherapy – cognitive behaviour therapy is the most well-established therapy for bulimia, and is usually the first choice.

- medications – these have quite a prominent role in bulimia, and can even be used in the absence of psychotherapy if psychotherapy and nutritional support are not available. The main medications are the antidepressants which have been well researched. The most popular choices are fluoxetine (Prozac) and the other selective serotonin reuptake inhibitors (SSRIs).

Binge eating disorder

Binge eating disorder is essentially bingeing without the compensatory weight-loss behaviours of bulimia nervosa. For the diagnosis as defined in the DSM-5, the person needs to binge on average at least once per week for three months.

Binge eating disorder is estimated to occur in about 2 per cent of people during their lifetime, and is twice as common in females as in males, with an average age of onset of twenty-three. On average 50 per cent of patients with binge eating disorder are overweight, which is a similar rate to the general population. It's commonly associated with anxiety disorders, depression or addictions. There are many medical complications, often related to being overweight.

It is difficult to diagnose binge eating disorder because most sufferers binge in secrecy. The diagnosis should be considered when patients have a pattern of large weight fluctuations and evidence of depression. Sensitive and skilled questioning is usually required to help patients feel comfortable enough to reveal their symptoms.

Treatment

Treatment follows the same line as for bulimia nervosa described above, but the role of medications is less prominent (psychotherapy is better studied and superior in binge eating disorder). The first line is cognitive behaviour therapy, although forms of interpersonal therapy and dialectical behaviour therapy have been developed for binge eating. These are often combined with family therapy, self-help, and of course solid nutritional support, including healthy weight-loss behaviours if obesity is a problem.

*

Weight, health and body image continue to be worldwide obsessions. Anorexia nervosa, bulimia nervosa and binge eating disorder are the current identifiable manifestations of the interplay between our psychology, culture, media and food. Culture, media and food are changing rapidly – it will be interesting to see how these disorders change with time and whether new disorders emerge.

Personality Disorders

Personality refers to the combinations of characteristics that describe a person – their ways of thinking, motivations, emotional range and behaviours. A human is made up of a body, an intelligence and a personality. Personality may sound simple, but it's the most complex part of mental health. Understand personality and you understand people.

Scientists, philosophers and people in pubs have for centuries tried to explain what makes people tick. We all analyse other people's personalities, but we can only ever do it from the standpoint of an outsider – we don't know what's going on their heads.

On the other hand, if we ask someone to describe their own personality, we know it will be coloured by their own biases – understanding oneself doesn't seem to be much easier than understanding others.

Personality is important to shrinks because many people present with problems that seem to be due to their personality. Sometimes they are said to have a personality disorder.

Personality disorders are some of the most criticised diagnoses in psychiatry. They are seen as unreliable. Ask five shrinks to assess a person with a personality disorder and you'll get five different descriptions of their personality. It's almost as if shrinks are just like normal people – they each draw different conclusions depending on their own beliefs, experiences and personality.

Personality disorders are used in a stigmatising, often unhelpful, way. It is common for people to attempt to undermine a person through descriptions of their personality: 'He's a narcissist', 'She's a hysteric.' Clinicians are not immune to this trap – if a clinician dislikes a patient, they're more likely to diagnose them with a personality disorder.

Despite these obvious shortcomings, they are common diagnoses – 6 per cent of the population are said to have a personality disorder.

My (Steve's) own view, which is not a majority view among my fellow psychiatrists, is that they are a fairly useless group of diagnoses. I agree that certain personality types run into problems because of their personality, and I agree that *sometimes* a shrink can help, but to say a patient is disordered in their personality strikes me as unhelpful. I think this is one area where diagnosis is likely to do more harm than good. The diagnosis can get in the way of a person receiving help, especially in mild to moderate cases.

On the other hand, for some people, gaining insight to their own personality can provide enormous understanding – 'Now I understand why I have caused so much drama.' Even more significantly, a personality disorder diagnosis can be an epiphany for those around the individual with the personality disorder. It can be like a light has been turned on in a room – finally some sense can be made of the way a loved one or friend behaves.

Understanding personality

Personality is inherently tough to describe and understand. And like anything in psychiatry (in fact, all science), the less we understand something, the more competing theories there are to attempt to explain it.

Our best current models of personality describe it as a series of traits. A trait is a characteristic. Each trait develops throughout childhood and should be (more or less) enduring once we enter adulthood.

Each of us has a different amount of each trait; that is, each trait has a spectrum. You could think of them as primary colours (blue, red and yellow), which together can make up millions of other colours, depending on how they are mixed. Everybody is composed of a mix of traits, each to a greater or lesser extent, that when combined create our personality.

Hans Eysenck was one of the first prominent psychologists to try to nail down the number of key traits that create a person. He initially proposed two key traits, but later added a third:

- Extraversion – this is all about obtaining gratification from things that are 'outside the self'. The other end of this spectrum is introversion. Extraverts are enthusiastic, talkative, assertive and gregarious. Introverts, on the other hand, are more reserved and reflective.

To oversimplify, extraverts like parties, introverts like reading.

- Neuroticism – this describes how emotionally unstable and responsive to stress each of us is. A highly neurotic person would tend to be reactive, anxious and easily angered. A person low on this spectrum would be even-tempered and calm.

- Psychoticism – this describes the degree to which we are aggressive and interpersonally hostile. High psychoticism includes being reckless, cold, creative and impulsive. Someone at the opposite end of the spectrum would be warm, submissive, rule-oriented and sympathetic.

It can be deflating to think that just three basic characteristics make up every personality in the world – and yet each of us is supposedly unique! But remember how many colours you can make from just three primary colours. Other personality theories tend to stretch the number of traits – some with as many as 4000!

The most prominent current theory is the five factor model, which uses the acronym OCEAN:

- Openness – this is about imagination and insight. It includes being adventurous, curious, artistic and open to unusual ideas. The opposite is being consistent, cautious and pragmatic.

- Conscientiousness – conscientious people are dependable and organised, appreciate self-discipline, are goal-directed and have good impulse control. The other end of the spectrum includes being flexible, spontaneous and free-spirited.

- Extroversion – this is similar to Eysenck's concept above.
- Agreeableness – this is the degree to which a person is compassionate, cooperative, trusting and altruistic. The other end of the spectrum includes suspiciousness and antagonism.
- Neuroticism – this is also similar to Eysenck's concept above.

No matter which model you subscribe to, the key thing to remember is that for each trait, we all each sit somewhere on a spectrum from a little to a lot.

We also have our intelligence (which has many dimensions) and our body (size, shape, colour, looks, hair, etc.), which all combine to make us who we are and influence how we interact with other people, our environment and our cultures. Sex and gender provide yet another component to consider. There are so many different permutations and combinations that it is no surprise that with only 7 billion of us, no two of us are the same.

Human = body + intelligence + personality

Disorders

A personality disorder is defined in the DSM-5 as an enduring pattern of inner experience and behaviour that deviates markedly from the expectations of the individual's culture, is pervasive and inflexible, and leads to distress or impairment.

Classification systems, like the DSM, have struggled to create a system that is easy to use clinically, but also reliable – meaning different clinicians can make a diagnosis about someone separately and come to the same conclusion. Given we all have various degrees of each trait, this is hard. It's fair to say that the current system is a work in progress (that's a polite way of saying it is poor).

Rather than focusing entirely on traits, the DSM-5 defines ten disorders, and divides them into three groups, or clusters – often jokingly called the mad, the bad and the sad.

Cluster A: The odd or eccentric group

- Paranoid personality disorder – a pattern of distrust and suspiciousness such that other people are interpreted as malevolent. People with paranoid personality disorder tend not to confide in others due to mistrust, and are often suspicious or jealous in relationships.
- Schizoid personality disorder – a pattern of detachment from social relationships, with a restricted range of emotional expression. People with schizoid personality disorder are often described as loners and lacking close friends.
- Schizotypal personality disorder – a pattern of acute discomfort in close relationships, with odd or eccentric behaviours. Paranoia is common and close relationships are usually only with relatives.

Cluster B: The dramatic, emotional and erratic group

- Anti-social personality disorder – a pattern of disregard for and violation of the rights of others. This is sometimes called psychopathic personality disorder. As you might expect, this is the most common personality disorder diagnosed in gaols.

- Borderline personality disorder – a pattern of instability of relationships, poor and unstable self-image, impulsivity and highly fluctuating moods. Self-harm and suicidal threats are common.

- Histrionic personality disorder – a pattern of excessive emotionality and attention-seeking behaviour. People with histrionic personality disorder are often dramatic and theatrical and tend to consider relationships to be more intimate than they actually are.

- Narcissistic personality disorder – a pattern of grandiosity, need for admiration, lack of empathy for others, and self-entitlement. Sufferers often exploit others.

Cluster C: The anxious and fearful group

- Avoidant personality disorder – a pattern of social inhibition, feelings of inadequacy and excessive sensitivity to negative evaluation. As a consequence, people with avoidant personality disorder tend to avoid others and be very restrained in relationships.

- Dependent personality disorder – a pattern of clinging behaviour and fear of separation in relationships, with an excessive need to be taken care of by others. People with dependent personality disorder prefer others to make decisions, and often seek nurturance from others.

- Obsessive-compulsive personality disorder – a pattern of preoccupation with orderliness, perfectionism and interpersonal control. People with obsessive-compulsive personality disorder are often preoccupied with details, rules and lists and excessively devoted to work.

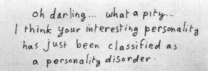

As you may have noticed, many of the disorders overlap with each other, and with other psychiatric disorders. For example, the cluster B disorders often go together – people who are anti-social are often narcissistic. The cluster A disorders are often closely related to possible diagnoses of schizophrenia and related disorders. And cluster C overlaps heavily with anxiety and mood disorders.

There is also undeniable gender bias at work in personality diagnoses. Men rarely get diagnosed as histrionic or borderline, and women rarely attract diagnoses of narcissistic or antisocial.

It's worth remembering that the whole point of making a diagnosis is to aid understanding and offer help. If a personality disorder diagnosis is being used to account for annoying beha-viour with no offer of help, then seriously question the person making the diagnosis. By and large, all personality disorder diagnoses should be taken with a grain of salt.

Assessing personality

Personality is tricky to assess well. It's often done over a number of sessions and then ideas are further refined as the clinician gets to know the patient better. If necessary, personality tests can also be carried out.

Before going any further, try to describe your own personality. Write down as many words as you can think of. Write how you think others would describe you. Then take each of the words and give yourself a score from one to ten. Don't focus on how you want to be, focus on how you really are – no one other than yourself will see the list! Be honest.

One of the curious things about self-assessment of personality is that it is often the opposite to self-assessment of physical characteristics. When we look in the mirror, we tend to exaggerate even the most minor imperfections. We look fat, our skin is marked, our hair is not quite right. But when we self-assess personality, we usually minimise every imperfection. We justify our behaviour, and claim good intentions and motivations even for our biggest sins. We turn a blind eye to our weaknesses and follies. In short, we are poor at self-judgement. We often say we are our own harshest critics, but it's rarely true.

The main clues to an individual's personality come from questions about their life so far: their childhood, friends, responses to things such as schooling and significant events, their relationships, their work history and the way their family functions. Any history of drugs, crime and self-harm is also relevant. Of course, we also ask people to describe themselves, and sometimes to say how others describe them. We look for recurring patterns of behaviour and emotional responses.

Personality tests can sometimes be helpful. There are many to choose from, including hundreds of online tests. The quality varies enormously. Most of the free online tests are not much more than light entertainment. In clinical practice, the most popular is the Minnesota Multiphasic Personality Inventory (MMPI).

The MMPI was first developed in 1939 and it has had various improvements since then. It consists of over five hundred questions that can be done on computer or with pen and paper. It takes an hour or two. The responses are interpreted by trained psychologists, who compare the person to standardised results from thousands of others who have previously completed the test. The results are presented as positions on various scales that represent different personality traits – the MMPI has ten standard traits, reflecting (to various degrees) the big five traits (OCEAN) discussed above.

However, understanding someone's personality is only part of the challenge. A clinician must also decide if personality is the cause of the person's problems.

Regardless of assessments of the *type* of personality a person has, there must first be evidence that the patient's personality is causing problems. The DSM-5 sets some criteria to help make this decision:

- The patient must show evidence of enduring patterns

of experience and behaviour that deviate from the expectations of their culture, such as ways of perceiving and relating to others, emotional responses, interpersonal functioning and impulse control.

- The pattern must be inflexible and pervasive across various situations, and date back to at least early adulthood.
- The pattern must result in distress or impairment in functioning.
- The pattern must not be the result of another mental health problem (such as depression, schizophrenia, head injuries or addictions).

Treatment

For decades, treatment of personality disorders was considered difficult, and mostly futile. Part of the problem was that only people with very severe personality disorders ever came for treatment, and usually because they were having their arms twisted in some way, such as by law courts or frustrated loved ones.

The main intervention in the 1970s and '80s was considered to be long-term insight-oriented psychotherapy. This consisted of one to five sessions per week, on the couch, with a highly trained psychodynamic therapist. This took a minimum of two years, usually more like five years. Each session cost between £40 and £200 depending on insurance. Needless to say, the patient had to be highly motivated and rich. Not many people with personality disorders were highly motivated and rich. Fortunately, the situation has changed.

These days there is a range of interventions used to treat personality disorders. The type of intervention used depends on the personality disorder and the most problematic issues, for example self-harm, relationship problems or work difficulties.

Borderline personality disorder is the most common personality disorder that clinicians treat. People with antisocial or narcissistic personality disorder are often reluctant to see mental health clinicians. They don't trust doctors, they usually don't believe they need help, and they usually believe therapy is futile anyway.

Cluster A people (the odd and eccentric) rarely request treatment, and if they do, the interventions are usually a combination of supportive psychotherapy, occupational therapy to engage them in work and social activities, and perhaps a trial of medications, usually anti-psychotics in case there is some underlying psychotic disorder, such as schizophrenia.

Cluster C people (the anxious and sad) are more likely to seek help, and treatment is usually psychotherapy, with an emphasis on behavioural approaches to overcome problems socialising. Clinicians also look carefully to make sure there is no underlying depression or anxiety that might be contributing to the avoidant behaviours.

Medication

Sometimes medications can seem to change personality because they alter our emotions or dilute our emotional responses, but there is no medication that changes a person's personality per se.

There are no medications to specifically treat personality disorders, but some medications assist in relieving associated problems – especially depression, mood swings, impulsive behaviours, addictions and psychotic symptoms.

Almost always, prescribing medications is a case of trial and error. There are studies of medications used in patients with personality disorders but, to be quite frank, they are inadequate. It's a profoundly difficult area to research. A lack of successful studies doesn't mean medications don't work (absence of evidence isn't evidence of absence), it just means there is no science to guide us.

As a general rule, the balance of evidence right now would suggest psychotherapy is the best option for all personality disorders, and medications should be used sparingly, for specific indications (such as depression), with lots of discussions about the pros and cons, and careful attention to the risks of over-prescribing, such as addiction and overdose.

Psychotherapeutic treatment for borderline personality disorder

It's worth taking a closer look at the therapy for borderline personality disorder, as there have been some significant advances in recent times. The therapies are problem-focused. Typical problems that patients present with include:

- recurrent self-harm
- dysfunctional behaviour – relationship breakdowns, housing crises, work problems
- health engagement problems – meaning the patient wants help and is seeking assistance from clinicians, but is running into problems such as arguing with doctors, having trouble accepting the rules of hospitals and clinics,

or chopping and changing clinicians impulsively without giving them a decent trial

- legal problems – such as needing support defending charges in court.

Management begins with a thorough treatment plan that the patient helps develop and modify to suit their specific needs, goals and level of engagement. This must include an honest and open discussion of the diagnosis and the associated challenges – especially the stigma the diagnosis attracts.

There are many possible elements to treatment, including self-education, individual or group therapy, and attention to co-morbidities such as addictions or depression.

The current range of therapies have been specially designed for borderline personality disorder, or adapted from other approaches. They share common features, although each has a slightly different focus. Most include elements of psychoeducation, social skills training, training to help regulate emotional instability, help with addressing impulsivity, and relationship counselling.

Some examples are:

- dialectical behaviour therapy (DBT) – this is a variation of cognitive behaviour therapy designed for BPD. It usually includes individual sessions and group sessions. There is a strong focus on addressing suicidal ideas. It has been well studied and is probably the most effective and popular therapy.
- mentalisation-based therapy – this is a combination of psychodynamic principles, cognitive-behavioural techniques, and mindfulness.

- cognitive-behaviour therapy (CBT) – this uses a combination of behavioural techniques and cognitive exercises aimed at addressing the dysfunctional thoughts and behaviours associated with borderline personality disorder.

*

As we said at the start of the chapter, personality is complex. Understanding personality is a work in progress. There are some significant research developments that show enormous promise – in particular genetics and epigenetics (epigenetics describes how our own personal experiences alter how our genes are expressed), and also work examining the impact of traumatic experiences on the development of personality. However, these advances are still a good way off changing the actual experience of treatment for people with personality disorders. Despite this, there have been some impressive advances, especially in borderline personality disorder, the treatment of which has totally changed in a single generation. As difficult as treating personality disorder is, we've come a long way in a short time, and the future looks very promising.

Psychosomatic Disorders

Psychosomatic medicine is endlessly fascinating. The relationship between the mind and the body is one of the great mysteries of human understanding. Everyone from philosophers to scientists has had a go at uncovering it but, alas, the puzzle remains unsolved.

In its broadest definition, psychosomatic medicine refers to the relationship between psychological symptoms and physical symptoms. In medical circles, the term is used slightly differently – psychosomatic medicine usually refers to illnesses with a clear physical cause, but where psychological factors are believed to play a part.

Disorders where the presence of a clear physical cause is thought unlikely are called somatic symptoms disorders, or somatoform disorders. In somatoform disorders, the patient has physical symptoms (called somatic symptoms), but the cause is thought to be either purely psychological or at least mainly psychological. Confusing, eh?

Psychosomatic illnesses

Heart disease is a classic example of a psychosomatic disorder. Among the risk factors like smoking, obesity and high blood pressure, stress is also believed to play a role. Social isolation, a lack of support and depression are each believed to increase the risk of some heart problems threefold. But just how much are these the cause of heart disease, and how much are they the effect? Perhaps high blood pressure, smoking and obesity cause stress, or perhaps some other unknown factors – maybe personality, or some particular genetic make-up – cause you to feel stressed, so you smoke and eat excessively and therefore have high blood pressure?

To add to the confusion, most physical illnesses get worse when people are suffering mental illnesses. But again, cause and effect are hard to determine. We know when people have mental illness they also don't manage their physical illnesses well – they are more likely to delay seeking help, less likely to take medications as prescribed, and less likely to carry out rehabilitation programs.

Some illnesses that were thought to be strongly psychosomatic have turned out to have biological causes that were simply undiscovered. Stomach ulcers are a great example. Prior to the 1990s, ulcers were thought to be due to stress, spicy food and excessive stomach acid. They were chronic and hard to treat. Many ulcer patients saw shrinks to reduce stress. Then a couple of Australians in Perth, Barry Marshall and Robin Warren, discovered that a common gut bacteria, Helicobacter pylori, was the major driver of ulcers. They won a Nobel Prize, and ulcer patients stopped being referred to shrinks to reduce stress (now they are ulcer-free, but still stressed!).

These days, doctors are less inclined to debate whether stress or psychological problems are causing an illness, and instead just go ahead and treat both the illness and the stress. Regardless of whether mental illness is adding to the physical illness, treating the psychological component will help the patient feel better, manage their treatment better and have greater quality of life.

Somatoform disorders

This group of disorders is characterised by prominent somatic (physical) symptoms that cause significant distress or impairment, where psychological factors are believed to be the main cause of the symptoms. In DSM-5 they've been renamed somatic symptom and related disorders, which is too much of a mouthful, so we've stuck with the old term.

These disorders are challenging for everyone! Imagine this scenario: A patient visits their doctor complaining of abdominal pains. They report that the pains have been present for about a month. They come and go. Sometimes the patient has diarrhoea, sometimes nausea. They report that this happened once before, when they were going through a divorce. At the time, the doctor did a series of tests but no cause was found and the symptoms settled with time and eating less meat.

The doctor does an examination but finds no abnormalities. They order a series of tests – blood tests, an abdominal X-ray and an abdominal ultrasound. All are normal. They next order a gastroscopy (a camera on a tube fed into the stomach). The results of this are also normal, except for some mild inflammation in the lining of the stomach, which is reported as within normal limits and not likely to be the cause of the symptoms.

The doctor asks about stress, and the patient reports there have been some problems with bullying at work and they do feel stressed but think it is under control and not the cause of the symptoms. They ask to have more tests.

The doctor suspects the stress is significant, and probably the cause, but refers the patient to a specialist to be certain. The specialist (a gastroenterologist) reviews the patient and the tests, and also thinks the stress is significant. They recommend seeing a psychologist, but just to cover all bases, they also recommend a trial of medication to reduce the stomach inflammation, but this doesn't seem to help.

Where does this leave the patient? They've been through about four weeks of tests and doctor's visits. They are being told the abdominal symptoms are stress-related – a somatoform disorder. But naturally they will have doubts. They have probably been stressed many times in their life, and this is only the second time these symptoms have appeared. They are probably doubtful and would rather have more tests before seeing a psychologist.

As for the doctors, it is likely they think the patient is more stressed than they are acknowledging or realising. They are likely a bit perplexed. Either way, they will probably look into more tests, but also ask the patient to see a psychologist to address the stress issue.

Here is the problem – getting to the bottom of symptoms is

hard. Studies suggest up to a third of symptoms remain unexplained despite good-quality medical examinations and tests (perhaps even more, if you consider medical consultations are often done in a hurry and tests are often rationed due to the high costs). Also, stress and psychological problems are very common – about 20 per cent of people in any given year have a significant problem. So there is bound to be a large overlap between unexplained somatic symptoms and stress – even if the stress isn't causing the symptoms.

The result? Diagnosing somatoform disorders is hard. Knowing whether the psychological stress is definitely the cause of the somatic symptoms is impossible. It might just be a coincidence.

Doctors get frustrated. Patients often feel they are being dismissed as crazy and their somatic symptoms are being ignored. Doctors are sometimes reluctant to tell patients that they think stress is the cause – they fear the patient will just change doctors. All in all, the diagnosis and management of somatoform disorders is tough!

The above example, or variations of it, occurs daily in thousands of medical consultations throughout the country. But sometimes the problems become more chronic, and then there are a few particular somatic symptoms disorders that might be diagnosed if the pattern of symptoms fits neatly into one of these categories.

Somatic symptom disorder (SSD)

Somatic symptom disorder is a relatively new disorder, having been added to the DSM in the most recent (fifth) edition. SSD is the presence of one or more somatic symptoms that are distressing or significantly disrupt daily life for at least six months. The symptom is associated with excessive thoughts, feelings or behaviours, such as a disproportionate belief relating to the seriousness of the symptom, high anxiety levels or excessive time and energy devoted to the symptoms.

There are usually many symptoms, and often the problems have been going on for years. The symptoms often change and sometimes are mixed with coexisting medical illnesses. The symptoms often become the main focus of the person's life – including efforts to find medical causes, various attempts at different treatments, and long periods of frustration trying to find doctors who understand and can help.

While SSD is new, it replaced another disorder, called somatisation disorder. Somatisation disorder included long lists of symptoms that needed to be met for the diagnosis, so was quite rare, at about 0.5 per cent of the population. Given SSD has 'loosened' the criteria, it will likely be a more common diagnosis.

One of the reasons somatisation disorder was replaced was confusion around the term 'somatisation'. Somatisation was most commonly used to describe the psychological process of expressing distress in somatic ways. So, for example, if you were stressed before an exam and felt dizzy and nauseous, this was called somatising. If you did it for months on end, and had symptoms in various systems (gut, neurological, sexual, various pains, etc.) it was called somatisation disorder.

Illness anxiety disorder (IAD)

Originally the term for people preoccupied with fears of illness was 'hypochondriac'. But the term hypochondriasis has now been removed from the DSM. Hypochondriasis was described as a preoccupation with fears of having a serious disease based on the misinterpretation of bodily symptoms. It was a confusing term, often misinterpreted by doctors and invariably greeted with frustration by patients. Research suggested most people with hypochondriasis fitted better in the diagnosis of SSD, but that there was also a subgroup who had little in the way of actual somatic symptoms but were very anxious about having or acquiring a serious illness – this subgroup has been given the name illness anxiety disorder (IAD).

In IAD the actual somatic symptoms are minimal – but the fear is prominent. The person performs excessive health related behaviours, like repeatedly checking themselves for disease, or being phobic about health issues. It must be present for six months to be diagnosed, and significantly interfere with the person's functioning.

Conversion disorder

Conversion disorder is the most mysterious of all psychiatric disorders. It is the presence of a neurological abnormality (either a motor or sensory problem) without any evidence of an underlying neurological disorder. The examination and investigations of neurological function do not match the symptoms. It's sometimes called functional neurological symptom disorder, or psychogenic disease. Prior to Freud, it was known as hysteria. Freud coined the term conversion, meaning anxiety was 'converted' to a physical symptom. In reality, we don't know the cause; however, it is assumed to be psychological.

Typical motor symptoms include weakness, paralysis, abnormal movements and unusual walking. Typical sensory symptoms include altered sensation, vision, or hearing. Sometimes people have episodes almost indistinguishable from seizures – called pseudoseizures. Speech problems are also common.

The onset is usually sudden and can be quite dramatic. A famous sign that is sometimes present is called *la belle indifférence*, from the French meaning beautiful indifference – this refers to the patient often being relatively unconcerned by the seriousness of their symptoms.

When a person presents with neurological symptoms that don't add up (on examination and tests), the psych team is brought in to look for evidence of conversion. They look for evidence of psychological problems. Past abuse is a very strong clue, as is any other form of trauma. Evidence of depression or a very stressful recent experience also suggests the diagnosis. But the reality is that we often do not know.

In this case, we provide psychological support (usually concurrent with physiotherapy) and wait and see if it helps. Sometimes hypnosis is used, and the symptoms usually improve under hypnosis.

Body dysmorphic disorder (BDD)

BDD describes a preoccupation with one or more bodily features that are either not present or only slight. The preoccupation leads to repetitive behaviours such as checking in the mirror, skin picking, excessive grooming and seeking reassurance. People with BDD often make repeated visits to doctors and sometimes have ill-advised plastic surgery.

The particular bodily feature can be anything, but the most common sources of preoccupation are the nose, abdominal fat, thighs, skin and hair. Sometimes the preoccupation becomes so severe it becomes delusional – meaning the person is convinced, beyond any doubt, and won't even tolerate any attempts at reasoning (when this occurs is it called a somatic delusion).

In the DSM-5, BDD was removed from the section on somatic symptoms and added to the chapter on obsessive-compulsive disorders, as this was felt to be a better fit. Time will tell if it this works better for patients and clinicians. The move also sits better with treatment approaches, which tend to favour cognitive behaviour therapy and medications commonly used to treat anxiety or depression.

Factitious disorder (Munchausen syndrome)

In factitious disorder the patient feigns (fakes) a disorder. The disorder may be a physical illness or a psychological syndrome. They purposely pretend to have an illness and often do things to support it – such as put blood in their urine, take drugs to induce illness, or purposely infect wounds. The deceptive behaviour is done *without* any obvious external rewards such as money or to escape some consequence like jail. When there is an obvious 'secondary' gain, it is called malingering. Malingering is simply faking illness for some personal gain – the most common example being faking an illness to get sick leave from work. Malingering is not considered to be a psychiatric disorder, but rather a form of fraud.

The assumed goal of factitious disorder is to get the benefits of being sick, such as attention, sympathy and care. Differentiating between factitious disorder and malingering is sometimes impossible. Knowing the patient's motivation is not possible unless they declare it in some way. In factitious disorder, we usually assume the motivation is unconscious – whereas in malingering there is a clear, conscious goal, but it is often not until later that a goal becomes apparent, such as a claim for compensation.

A diagnosis of factitious disorder or malingering is always very challenging because clinicians are not lie detectors; they often don't know when a patient is faking. The suspicion that faking is occurring usually comes from either clinical staff noticing suspicious behaviour, failure to get better with treatment, or test results that don't make clinical sense. Sometimes patients fake medical records to support their claims.

Factitious disorder by proxy occurs when a person presents someone under their care as sick (usually their child). This is particularly dangerous, and is a form of child abuse.

Treatment

Unravelling the causes of somatic symptoms in a medical world where uncertainty is the norm is obviously a challenge. Medically unexplained symptoms are common. Many illnesses with a clear underlying biological (or pathological) cause take time to declare themselves. Sometimes years pass before the biology becomes evident. Trying to determine if a symptom is due to psychological factors or is being feigned is a clinical skill that can elude anyone.

As a consequence, much care and sensitivity is required when psychosomatic problems are suspected. The usual plan follows some careful principles:

- *Involving the relevant experts.* Usually this requires a multidisciplinary team. Clinicians who understand the primary symptoms (such as specialists in the relevant system – neurologists or gastroenterologists, for example), plus psychiatrists or psychologists with expertise in psychosomatic illnesses, and allied health staff who can help manage symptoms with uncertain origins.

- *Clear explanation.* The patient needs to understand that multiple possible causes for their symptoms are being considered and addressed. This requires high levels of sensitivity. Explaining that you are worried there might be a psychological cause can raise anger and frustration in patients who are not 'psychologically minded'. But phrasing this explanation in a way that conveys the clinician is simply keeping an open mind and trying to help is possible with good communication skills.

- *Treating any mental health problems.* Whether they are contributing to the somatic symptoms or not, problems such as depression and anxiety need to be treated.

- *Maintaining consistency of clinical staff.* If patients go from doctor to doctor looking for explanations, the same tests and procedures (which are often unnecessary and carry risks of complications) get repeated over and over. A consistent clinical team who get to know the patient and develop a strong sense of when to intervene is necessary.

- *Being aware of the possibility of new symptoms representing new pathology*. Even if patients have a long history of symptoms that turn out to be due to psychological causes or feigning, they can develop new illnesses. Falling into the 'boy who cried wolf' trap is a real risk. New symptoms must be taken seriously.

- *Providing active treatment*. Even somatic symptoms with psychological causes will respond to physical therapies such as physiotherapy. Usually a rehabilitation approach is taken, where the patient receives a mix of psychological and physical therapy.

- *Providing psychotherapy where possible*. Psychotherapies of various types have been used successfully to help patients appreciate the links between their minds and bodies.

While we began this chapter saying psychosomatic medicine is endlessly fascinating, by now it's probably obvious it's endlessly confusing as well. Separating which somatic symptoms are due to an organic cause (physical pathology), from those that are thought to be psychological (in the *mind*) is often educated guesswork. Especially when there are sometimes elements of both in the mix.

Efforts to make this distinction sometimes seem futile – why not just offer a mix of psychological and physical treatments? For the clinician, patients who are resolutely fixed in their belief that their symptoms are purely physical and refuse psychological interventions can seem frustrating. It is equally frustrating for patients who feel the clinician is in some way diminishing their experience by insisting psychological factors are causing their symptoms.

The best approach is for everyone to keep an open mind, and explore all the treatment options until symptoms improve – but sometimes this is easier said than done. All of us (humans) can be stubborn, we don't easily change our belief systems!

Child and Adolescent
Mental Health

The field of child and adolescent mental health has grown faster than any other area of psychiatry in the last couple of decades. This is partly because the rates of various disorders have increased (more due to better recognition than any true increase) and partly because there has been growing awareness of the importance of recognising problems early and treating them before they have too significant an impact on the child's development.

This growth has brought with it an ever-expanding list of challenges. To put it plainly, child and adolescent mental health is hard! Diagnosis is harder, because young people don't communicate verbally as well as adults, so it requires more interpretation of behaviour and other symptoms – all of which can be misleading. Furthermore, all the disorders must be viewed through the prism of the child's developmental stage – the way a child with depression presents at age five is very different to how a fifteen-year-old with depression presents. Separating normal behaviour (such as teenage angst) from abnormal problems (such as depression) is sometimes impossible. Uncovering hidden problems, such as child abuse and bullying, is fraught with difficulties and these issues often remain a secret far longer than they should. Finally, treating children and adolescents often carries greater risks than treating adults – especially with medication, as side effects on the developing brain are less understood. With all these challenges come strongly held, often contradictory, views, and passions in the field run high.

This complexity has led to subspecialisation within the child and adolescent field. There are even some clinicians who specialise in problems of the foetus. Infant psychiatry, child psychiatry and adolescent psychiatry are often practised by separate groups of clinicians. But there can be overlap: for instance, adolescent psychiatry can extend into early adulthood. It can all seem mind-boggling.

Assessment

Assessment of children and adolescents requires more effort than for fully functioning adults. More sources of information are required – family, teachers, carers and others. Screening tools are used more often: questionnaires are given to significant people in the child's life to gauge opinions and rate the severity of symptoms.

It takes longer to complete an assessment for a child– usually about four sessions: the child is first seen with their family, then alone, then the parents or significant carers are seen without the child, then the whole family again to wrap up and plan treatment. For adolescents who are independent (emotionally or financially) the assessment is more likely to follow the adult model.

Assessments for children and adolescents are usually carried out by a multidisciplinary team, including doctors, psychologists, social workers and allied health professionals. Paediatricians also play a key role, especially if there are any physical problems to be explored. Some paediatricians specialise in behavioural and emotional problems in kids, and they are often the primary clinician.

The wide range of options and approaches to treatment can make the field confusing for families. Beware of any clinician that offers a quick fix or skips the thorough approach – children and adolescents are too complex for a quick one-off session and treatment plan. Also, medications should not be prescribed at the first appointment except in extreme emergencies. Unfortunately, this happens far too often, usually with poor outcomes and unnecessary distress.

Disorders

Nearly all the disorders discussed in this book can present in young people. In this chapter, we look first at disorders that typically present in young people that haven't been covered in the other chapters. All of these disorders can extend into adulthood and require ongoing care and treatment. We then consider the specific issues surrounding anxiety and depression in children.

Autism and Asperger's syndrome

Autism and Asperger's syndrome were barely heard of a generation ago. Their growth has been fuelled by extensive medical research and cultural curiosity. Dozens of movies and popular books have featured characters who have various degrees of behaviours that are characteristic of the disorders. The popular depiction of these disorders has resulted in greater recognition and treatment, but also a significant amount of misinformation. It's now popular to hear people described as 'a bit aspy' or as 'on the spectrum'. This is unfortunate, as it misrepresents the seriousness of these disorders and adds to the confusion around diagnosis.

To add to the confusion, the medical terminology has changed since these conditions were first identified in the mid-twentieth century. Initially, Asperger's was described as a milder form of autism. Then, from about the 1980s onwards, it was thought to be related to autism, but different. The wheel has now turned full circle and Asperger's is again considered a mild form of autism. In the DSM-5, Asperger's has been removed and is subsumed under the combined term autism spectrum disorder (ASD).

ASD is described as a neurodevelopmental disorder (meaning its cause is rooted in abnormal brain development), characterised by problems in two key domains:

1. social communication and interaction
2. behaviour, where children have restricted and repetitive interests and activities.

ASD affects around 1 to 2 per cent of children and is possibly four times more common in boys, but the numbers of girls with

ASD is increasing following the recognition that their presentation may be different from boys. About half of the children with ASD have some degree of intellectual disability, about a quarter have seizures, and about a tenth have a related genetic disorder.

The cause isn't well understood, but there are strong genetic links, convincing evidence of neurological abnormalities and small links to problems during pregnancy and birth (especially infections and exposure to various toxins). Links are often drawn between ASD and immunisation, but no scientific evidence for this has been found.

The range of symptoms is huge, as every child with ASD expresses their problems slightly differently and at different ages.

The social problems can manifest in various ways:

- delays in language development
- lack of desire to communicate
- lack of social reciprocity – meaning they don't respond to the communication of others
- lack of empathy for the emotions of others – meaning they don't recognise and respond to the emotions of others
- impaired ability to use and recognise non-verbal communication such as eye contact and facial expressions
- failure to develop relationships with similar-aged children.

The behavioural problems include:

- repetitive movements, such as hand flapping, twisting, rocking, head rolling or unusual walking
- insistence on sameness, with an intense dislike of change.

Routines become rigid and inflexible. It may mean particular things need to be done in the same order, such as always eating, dressing or travelling the same way.

- restricted and repetitive interests, such as a love of certain topics (often nature or science-based), such as the weather, dinosaurs, cars or trains. There is often difficulty shifting attention to other things, called cognitive rigidity.

- the ability to process sensations is usually impaired, and children are often sensitive to particular noises, smells, textures and tastes.

The age of diagnosis depends on the severity of symptoms (the spectrum is large) and the social demands on the child. Once the child reaches school and needs to socialise far more, the symptoms often become more obvious. Kids on the milder end of the spectrum might not be recognised until the early teenage years.

The severity of ASD ranges widely. At the mild end, children have a few symptoms in each major domain (communication and behaviour) requiring some support but largely capable of independent living, and progress in school with a small amount of extra support. At the severe end, children require substantial support, including specialised housing and education.

The diagnosis of ASD requires specialised services – it's not a disorder that can be assessed and managed optimally by a single clinician. A range of assessments (cognitive, educational and behavioural) are needed to uncover the range of symptoms, many of which can remain hidden until the demands of life overcome the child. The earlier they are recognised, the earlier treatments that limit the impact can begin. Also, screening for related disorders such as depression, intellectual disability and seizures is required.

The management of ASD is also complex and is usually coordinated by a primary clinician who brings in the full range of services offered by specialised teams. Given the range of severity, management needs to be carefully tailored to the individual child's needs.

The earlier intervention can begin, the fewer long-term consequences. Various treatment modalities are often employed. Educational support is vital to maximise learning. Behavioural interventions help with repetitive behaviours at home and school. Parental support and training assist the parents to cope and to guide and teach the child. On top of these basics, there are programs and approaches to help with various specific symptoms. The type of program also depends on the age of the child. The range of strategies is endless.

The outcome for ASD depends on the severity and the amount of help available. About a quarter of cases have a good outcome, meaning the child goes on to live independently and gain employment. About a quarter require long-term support and don't work or live independently. The rest lie somewhere in between, requiring long-term help in at least some domains, but being independent in others.

Attention deficit hyperactivity disorder (ADHD)

ADHD is one of the more controversial child mental health problems. The rates of diagnosis have increased dramatically in the last two decades, especially in developed countries. It's not clear whether this is due to better recognition, a true increase in the prevalence of the disorder, or simply loosening of the diagnostic criteria so that previously subclinical cases now get diagnosed.

Either way, it is common. Roughly 8 per cent of school-aged kids have ADHD. It is four times more common in boys. It is usually diagnosed in children between the ages of six and twelve, but can also be picked up in preschoolers or in older children. It is often associated with other psychological problems, especially conduct disorder, depression, anxiety and learning problems.

The key symptoms are:

- hyperactivity – this can take many forms; the most common are fidgeting, talking too much, difficulty remaining seated, noisy playing and restlessness.
- inattention – such as difficulty waiting turns, disruptive behaviour, and intruding on others
- impulsivity – this is not always present, but when it is, it includes being easily distracted and forgetful.

Under the DSM-5, for a diagnosis of ADHD to be made there must be significant evidence of symptoms for at least six months, beginning before the age of twelve. The symptoms must be present in more than one setting (for example, school and home) and interfere with functioning, such as school performance, social interactions or development.

Treatment for ADHD is the most controversial aspect of the disorder. Some people believe medications are prescribed far too readily for the condition – and it is true that in some places the rates of medication use appear very high. Others report amazing results with medications and argue they should be prescribed more.

Treatment begins with careful monitoring of the symptoms in different settings. The family and teachers should document the problem behaviours and their frequency – this is essential to monitor progress and assess whether treatment is working. Careful consideration should be given to whether other problems (depression, learning difficulties and so on) are present, as they are easily missed.

In younger children (especially preschoolers), behavioural approaches are tried first. These include the use of schedules; setting small, reachable goals; rewarding positive behaviour; developing charts and checklists – and, finally, calm and clear discipline. Parents often enrol in parenting classes. This does not mean they have poor parenting skills, it simply reflects the reality that parenting ADHD kids is tough and lots of parenting skills are required.

In school-aged kids, medications are often preferred. The drugs used are stimulants, which sounds odd given the aim is to reduce stimulation, but these drugs actually help in ADHD. It's a paradox! There are many versions, the most common being amphetamines and methylphenidate. They work in about 80 per cent of kids with ADHD.

There are many other approaches as well, including complementary treatments such as massage.

Whatever approach is adopted, consideration should be given to engaging teachers and extra help at school. It is also essential to monitor progress with regular questionnaires to see if the treatments are helping. There is no point continuing medications, or any other treatment, unless there is clear evidence of improvement.

Conduct disorder and impulsive, disruptive behaviours

These are a group of disorders where the primary feature is bad behaviour that violates the rights of others or brings the child into conflict with the expectations of their community. Of course, a certain amount of bad behaviour is completely normal, especially if the child has other problems, such as ADHD or depression. But in these disorders the behaviour is the primary problem and is not the result of difficult circumstances or other psychological problems.

These disorders are poorly understood and the names have changed and the criteria have been refined over the last decade. Families and clinicians worry that these disorders are precursors to antisocial personality disorder in adults, but how strong this link is remains unclear.

Conduct disorder refers to kids with repetitive behaviours that violate others and break rules. Examples of such behaviour include bullying, starting fights, being cruel to animals, using weapons, destroying property, theft, and ignoring rules. To be diagnosed, the pattern needs to be repetitive and continue for at least twelve months, and lead to significant disruption in the child's social or academic functioning.

Oppositional defiant disorder is a pattern of angry and irritable moods with defiant behaviours, such as tantrums, or being easily annoyed, resentful, vindictive and argumentative.

Intermittent explosive disorder is recurrent aggressive behavioural outbursts or tantrums. There is usually a mix of verbal and aggressive outbursts, and they are not premeditated or planned to achieve anything.

Kleptomania refers to recurrent stealing, with a sense of pleasure from the act.

Pyromania is fire setting, with tension and arousal before the act and pleasure afterwards. It is usually associated with an intense curiosity and fascination with fire.

All of these disorders can overlap with each other (and other psychological disorders). Sometimes they are so extreme that the diagnosis becomes obvious pretty quickly, but mostly it is hard to separate normal amounts of bad behaviour from disorders. It's also hard to figure out whether there is some other factor, such as depression or abuse, behind all the behaviour.

Treatment for these disorders is usually a mix of behaviour therapy, parental skills training to help manage the behaviours, and efforts to better integrate the child into their family and school. Individual counselling or therapy for the child is also very helpful.

Intellectual disability (ID)

Intellectual disability is a complex problem requiring extensive specialist support and evaluation. ID affects approximately 1 per cent of children. It is usually diagnosed young, although if mild may not present for years, and even go unnoticed into adulthood. The typical presenting problems are language delays, immature behaviour, or difficulty learning. Sometimes ID is picked up on routine child screening of developmental progress at health centres, or increasingly through genetic testing.

ID is defined in the DSM-5 as limitations in:

- intellectual functioning – such as reasoning, problem

solving, planning, judgement, abstract thinking and
learning from experience

- adaptive behaviour – meaning a failure to meet
developmental independence and sociocultural
standards for personal independence and social
responsibility.

Onset must be in the developmental period of childhood and
adolescence.

Various tests are done to explore causes (which are not always
found) and to look for associated problems. The associated problems may be medical, such as seizures or sensory problems in
vision and hearing, or the full range of mental health problems,
especially autism, depression, ADHD and behaviour problems.

Clinical assessment obviously needs to be thorough and cover
a range of domains. Multiple clinicians are usually involved
– including specialist paediatricians, occupational therapists,
educational experts, family support workers and psychiatric
clinicians.

Treatment planning is similarly extensive, and specialist services are highly recommended. The outcomes depend on the
severity and the availability and affordability of supports but,
much to the surprise of people outside the field, are often very
good. In mild ID, as many as two thirds end up working, having
a home and forming long-term relationships.

School refusal

This is not a diagnosis, but rather a description of a fairly common behaviour where kids simply refuse to attend school, or
experience severe emotional distress attending school. There are

multiple possible causes and it can occur at any age – although it's most common in primary school. It's particularly common after major changes at home or school, after holidays, after illnesses or at times of high stress.

Typical behaviours include frequently claiming vague physical illnesses on school days, tantrums and refusing to attend school, anxiety, and calls to be bought home from school.

It is important to address the problem promptly. The longer it persists, the harder it is to get the child back to school. Help usually begins with a visit to the GP to rule out any underlying physical problems, then an assessment to explore causes such as anxiety, depression or bullying at school.

Anxiety in children

Anxiety is a normal part of growing up. Fears and worries are universal, and part of normal human development is learning to tolerate anxiety and develop coping strategies. But sometimes the anxiety is persistent, excessively distressing and leads to problems, most commonly educational delays. The borderline between normal anxiety and clinical anxiety can be tough to determine, but it is important because failure to recognise clinical anxiety in kids can lead to the problem becoming chronic, affecting learning and spilling into adulthood.

Anxiety disorders are the most common mental health problems in children. A little over one quarter of kids develop a disorder, usually social anxiety (about 10 per cent of all children) and phobias (also about 10 per cent). When present, these conditions are often associated with other problems, especially ADHD, depression, conduct problems, and school refusal. They don't always present in the ways typically seen in adults, as kids cannot express their emotions as clearly. Anxiety disorders in children often include physical symptoms (such as tummy pains), sleep problems, avoidance of various situations (especially school), eating problems and poor school performance.

The good news is that kids respond well to treatment. The first task of treatment is a thorough assessment to look for causes and other problems. Once the anxiety is understood, treatment is usually psychotherapy-based. Specific kinds of cognitive behaviour therapy (CBT) have been developed and researched for all childhood anxiety disorders. CBT in kids includes education, reassurance, relaxation and sleep training, exposure techniques and more.

Medications are also used, but the research base is less well developed and they tend to be reserved for kids with more severe disorders.

Parental support and education about anxiety is also essential. And sometimes extra support at school is needed.

Depression in children

Depression in children often goes undiagnosed and untreated. This is probably due to the challenge of separating depression from normal sadness and to widespread beliefs that it's normal for kids to get down and depressed. But it's worth remembering that from the age of fifteen onwards (until about forty), suicide is the most common cause of death.

Depression in kids can be typical 'unipolar' depression, or the rarer 'bipolar' depression that includes episodes of mania.

Studies suggest that about 2 per cent of kids under ten suffer unipolar depression, with the rate rising to about 8 per cent by the age of seventeen. As with adults, unipolar depression is twice as common in females than males. The rates of bipolar depression are harder to determine. The lifetime rate is 1 per cent, with an average age of onset of eighteen, so children sometimes get diagnosed in their adolescent years.

Kids who have depression have the same symptoms as depressed adults, but they may manifest differently depending on the child's age. Irritability, somatic (physical) symptoms and behavioural problems are particularly prominent.

Recognised risk factors for depression in children include a family history of depression, low birth weight, family problems, abuse, stressors, and concerns about sexuality (in particular gender identity and homosexuality).

Depression can affect many aspects of development, with school performance and relationships with parents and peers being the usual casualties.

Overlap with other disorders is also common, especially drug and alcohol problems, anxiety, conduct disorders, and ADHD.

There are many well-developed treatment options for kids with depression. As usual, treatment begins with a thorough assessment of causes and exploration of other problems. Careful exploration of suicidal ideas is essential. If the risk appears high, hospital admission must be considered. Education for both the patient and their family and carers is also particularly important. Depression in kids is frightening to all involved, so the more time spent educating and supporting the patient and family in the initial phases, the better.

It is also useful to consider specialist referral early in the course of treatment. Kids are complex, and considerable expertise is required. Specialist services often have a range of staff too – including doctors, specialist child psychiatrists, psychologists, social workers, educational specialists and occupational therapists – and they all need to work together.

Psychotherapy is usually the first option for treatment. All types have been used successfully in kids, and are widely available. These include cognitive behaviour therapy (CBT), interpersonal therapy (IPT), psychodynamic psychotherapy, family therapy, dialectical behaviour therapy and supportive therapy. Only CBT and IPT have a strong evidence base in kids, so these tend to be favoured as first approaches.

Medications are also often employed, especially in moderate or severe depression. There are extra risks in kids, in particular an increased risk of worsening suicidal ideas, so referral to a specialist is wise if medications are considered necessary. When used, they are mostly combined with psychotherapy.

The management of bipolar disorder in kids is complex and always requires specialist input.

The outcome for the treatment of depression in kids is good; the vast majority improve. But ongoing monitoring is important because relapse is not uncommon.

Brain Disorders

*The human brain starts working the moment you are born
and never stops until you stand up to speak in public.*

George Jessel

Who doesn't love the brain? Of all our organs (and depending how you count them, we have seventy-eight), the brain is probably the most mysterious. It's almost impossible to believe a lump of meat can do so much.

We know a lot about the brain, but not enough. We know it plays a central role in processing information, perception, muscle control, arousal, motivation, learning, memory, emotions, and general control of the body – but understanding of exactly how it does these things is only just emerging in the last few decades.

With so many functions, when something goes wrong with the brain, there are many possible symptoms.

Given the multiple roles of the brain, it is not surprising that lots of different clinicians focus on the neurological disorders:

- neurologists: doctors who specialise in neurological (brain) disorders

- geriatricians: doctors who manage people over the age of sixty-five, which is when many brain disorders first emerge
- psychiatrists: doctors who manage the psychological 'brain problems' (especially schizophrenia, and all the emotional disorders)
- neuropsychiatrists: psychiatrists who subspecialise in brain problems
- psychogeriatricians: psychiatrists who specialise in people over the age of sixty-five
- psychologists: like psychiatrists, they treat all the psychological aspects of brain problems
- neuropsychologists: psychologists who subspecialise in the brain and its functions.

Many other clinicians – including GPs, social workers, occupational therapists, physiotherapists and more – manage people with brain problems, and some do extra training to subspecialise. Which clinician you see depends on the underlying disorder and what symptoms are most prominent and problematic.

From a mental health perspective, the primary brain disorders mental health clinicians manage are dementia, delirium and other neurological disorders with prominent psychological symptoms. Clinicians often work as part of a team – with a physician managing the primary problem, say dementia, while the psychiatrist focuses on the mental health side. A handful of clinicians are trained across disciplines to manage all aspects of brain disorders.

Dementia

Dementia basically means your ability to think and remember is no longer adequate to function in your various roles. Most people's thinking and memory deteriorate a little as they get older, but the changes are mild, and they usually find ways to compensate. That's normal. Not all cognitive impairment is dementia. Dementia is when it's so bad simple things become a problem – like remembering stuff that would normally be routine, getting lost when you go out, leaving on the stove and risking burning down the house, and losing language abilities. Distinguishing between normal decline and dementia is important.

Dementia is defined formally in the DSM-5 as evidence of significant cognitive impairment in at least one of these domains:

- learning and memory
- language
- executive function – higher brain functions, such as problem solving and planning
- complex attention – the ability to focus attention
- perceptual-motor function – the ability to perceive and interact with the environment
- social cognition – the ability to interact socially.

The impairments must be a decline from previous levels of functioning (as distinct from being born with an intellectual disability); they must interfere with independence in everyday activities; and they must not be due to other problems such as delirium or depression.

The risk of dementia increases exponentially as we age. About

1 to 5 per cent of people will have it at sixty-five and about 25 to 40 per cent at eighty-five.

Causes

There are multiple possible causes of dementia. The main ones are:

- Alzheimer's disease (AD) – the most common cause, responsible for more than 60 per cent of all dementias. The pathology is pretty well understood (the brain becomes clogged up with 'plaques' and 'tangles'). There is a rare hereditary form of AD as well. The onset of AD is slow and insidious.
- Vascular dementia – between 15 and 20 per cent. This is basically due to multiple small 'strokes' – vascular events in the brain. The onset can be sudden or gradual.
- Lewy Body Dementia (LBD) – about 10 per cent. Lewy bodies are microscopic spots in neurones that damage their function. LBD has a gradual onset, but is often characterised by the addition of hallucinations, clinical fluctuations and features of Parkinson's disease.
- frontotemporal dementia (FTD) – about 5 per cent. This is dementia that starts in the frontal and temporal lobes of the brain. Prominent early features include changes in personality and social behaviour (including disinhibition, loss of empathy and compulsive behaviours). It's also sometimes called Pick's disease, or just frontal dementia.

There are lots of other illnesses that can cause dementia, including HIV, Parkinson's disease, traumatic brain injury and Huntington's disease.

Features

Most dementia starts gradually. The early signs are subtle, and relatives and friends spend a lot of time wondering, before time passes and in retrospect it is obvious. Detection is especially difficult because mild cognitive deterioration that doesn't progress or interfere significantly with functioning is common in the elderly. Only about half of the patients with mild cognitive deterioration progress to dementia.

When it does progress, typical early symptoms include:

- forgetfulness – mainly forgetting new things, such as trouble remembering events or forgetting where they've put things. A poor memory in general and forgetting names are not typical signals of dementia: in fact, they're a normal part of life for many people, even young people.
- trouble handling complex tasks such as the household budget
- difficulty with thinking and reasoning
- language problems – especially trouble finding the right word for something
- changes in behaviour – sleeping different hours, eating differently and more
- getting lost, especially in new environments.

The different forms of dementia have distinctive presenting features – but as the dementia progresses, they all merge into a tragic final phase – global brain failure.

Many dementia sufferers develop various behaviour disorders along the way. These are usually a mix of:

- wandering
- resistive behaviour

- verbal and physical abusiveness
- calling out and shouting
- sleep disturbance
- psychosis – a third of people with dementia have either hallucinations or delusions.

Dementia slowly progresses to the stage where the patient is bedbound and eventually dies. The rate of progression varies enormously – some die quickly, in about three years from the time of diagnosis; for others, it takes up to twenty years. Ten years is about average.

It's also worthwhile noting at this point that, despite how awful dementia sounds, many people with dementia are happy and continue to lead lives they enjoy. Depending on their stage, relationships can still be fulfilling, and people with dementia often find new forms of enjoyment. It's also often a time for families to come together, especially in the early stages.

Assessment

Getting a good-quality assessment is essential. It is often carried out by a multidisciplinary team – doctors, social workers, neuro-psychologists, occupational therapists and more.

The first step is a clinical assessment looking for reversible causes of cognitive decline that might mimic dementia. This includes a thorough physical examination and tests to determine the type of dementia and to look for other causes of cognitive decline. Common problems that may be mistaken for dementia include delirium, depression and the adverse effects of being on too many medications. It's obviously essential to find the reversible causes, as they can be treated and reversed.

Next, cognitive function is usually formally measured with neuropsychological testing. There are a range of quick bedside tests of cognitive function, but detailed formal testing is better. It does a few things: establishes a baseline to track further deterioration; helps with diagnosis; helps determine the type of dementia; and can establish strengths and weaknesses around which occupational therapy programs can be tailored.

Formal assessment of functional ability by an occupational therapist is also very useful. This explores how the person is functioning in their own environment – can they catch public transport, cook meals, manage money and so on? This determines how much help is needed and whether the person can live independently.

Next, a range of tests – including neuroimaging (either structural, such as MRI – *Magnetic Resonance Imaging*, or functional, such as PET – *Positron Emission Tomography*) – help confirm the diagnosis and look for any other brain disorders that might be present and treatable.

In the elderly, it is also important to consider certain age-related issues that usually need careful attention, in particular social isolation and functioning; and legal issues – especially consent and advanced care planning before the patient has lost the ability to express their preferred plans for treatment and end-of-life care. It is important to optimise physical health and for clinicians to work closely with family or carers. Those treating the patient must be careful with medications – every extra medication increases the chances of drug interactions and unexpected side effects.

Treatment

While dementia carries a poor prognosis, there are many treatments along the way that can slow its progression or at least minimise the functional effects.

Medications can help slow the course of dementia. They don't work in all types of dementia, so aren't always used. There are also medications to treat various symptoms (for example, antipsychotic medications help with delusions and hallucinations) and sometimes to relieve the behavioural symptoms. All have risks, of course, so both the doctor and patient must carefully consider the pros and cons.

Attention to nutrition is essential. Many patients with dementia lose the ability to plan and prepare well-balanced meals. Poor nutrition can hasten the course of illness, so careful consideration and assessment of eating patterns and weight, often with the help of a dietician, is important.

Rehabilitation is the mainstay of treatment. Cognitive rehab in the early phases of dementia aims to maintain as much function as possible and to find ways to compensate for lost abilities. Exercise-related rehab aims to improve physical functioning and slow decline. Occupational therapy aims to improve functioning in activities of daily living, especially in the home, to maintain independence for as long as possible.

A diagnosis of dementia can seem hopeless, but this is far from the truth. With careful, well-planned treatment from a range of professionals, daily functioning can be maintained and life can be extended for many years.

Delirium

You're more likely to read about delirium in medical or neurological textbooks than psychology books. It's usually managed in hospitals by specialists. Delirium is basically when the brain is so disrupted it's failing to function at even a basic level – the person is confused, doesn't know the time or where they are, and often has hallucinations or delusions.

The reason it's important to know about delirium is that it is easily missed when mild and easily mistaken for other things (especially dementia, depression and psychosis). This is dangerous – not only because delirium can be life-threatening and urgent treatment is needed, but because doctors, family members and carers can make the wrong decisions about the patient's future. They might plan dementia care, or fail to recognise the risks to the patient posed by their delirium, or admit them to the psych ward instead of the medical ward, or discharge them when they cannot cope at home.

Delirium is common, especially in the elderly when they are sick in any way. About a third get delirious at some point. When it happens, about half don't get recognised! Yes, you read that right – about half (and up to 70 per cent in some studies) of delirium cases don't get recognised at all. It's one of the most dangerous missed diagnoses in hospitals.

Recognising delirium

The key feature of delirium that separates it from the other brain disorders is that it is an *acute, confusional state* with *altered consciousness*. This means it comes on reasonably quickly – acutely

– within hours or days (rather than weeks or months, as in dementia, depression and psychosis). The patient is *confused*, meaning they mistake where they are, who they are and the time. Finally, they are *not fully conscious* and their consciousness fluctuates; they are alert one hour, sleepy and hard to rouse the next. Delirium is always worse at night.

Depressed and psychotic patients are not confused. Dementia patients don't have an altered consciousness (unless it's very advanced).

About a third of delirious patients have psychotic symptoms – either hallucinations or delusions. Most of these patients are scared stiff – it's often described afterwards as like being in a nightmare. They often think the nursing staff or family are attacking them in some way. This is quite dangerous, as they can assault staff or run away. They also do dangerous things like try to jump out of windows or harm themselves to escape their imagined attackers.

Causes

The list of things that cause delirium is as long as your arm. Anything that makes you sick can make you delirious. A simple mnemonic to remember the possible causes is:

- D – drugs, especially ones that affect the brain
- E – endocrine causes such as hypothyroidism
- L – lung causes, especially anything that makes you lack oxygen
- I – infection: virtually all of them if they become systemic (get into your blood)
- R – renal: lots of kidney abnormalities cause delirium

- I – ischaemia, meaning tissue damage from oxygen depletion, such as in heart attacks
- U – unknown: this is the most common cause! In about 30 per cent of cases, no specific cause is identified.
- M – metabolic, meaning anything that disturbs metabolism.

It's a shame the word delirium doesn't include an 'N', because there are many neurological causes of delirium as well.

The take-home message is that the cause isn't always found. You'll often hear doctors say, 'We've done the tests and no cause came up, so we don't think this is delirium.' If they say that, get a second opinion! They do not understand delirium (and this is sadly common). An absence of cause does *not* exclude delirium. Delirium is a clinical diagnosis, not one made by tests – acute onset plus confusion plus changes in conscious state is nearly always delirium, regardless of what shows up in tests.

What to do

Delirium nearly always gets better once the underlying illness improves. Mostly this is pretty quick – a few days or a week. Sometimes it drags on for more than a week – and sometimes the full recovery of cognitive function takes up to a month or more.

In the meantime, clinicians sit tight, look after the patients (usually in hospital to keep them safe), provide support for nutrition and hydration, and keep looking for reversible causes (using blood tests, brain imaging or tests for hidden infections).

There are also a range of behavioural measures that help calm the patient – a quiet room, pictures of family on the wall to foster familiarity, a notice with the date and place to help for the brief periods the patient is alert, assistance with mobility (falls are common in delirious patients) and efforts to avoid overstimulation.

Knowing about delirium is useful. In elderly patients who become delirious, the family often thinks their loved one has become demented or psychotic. They are worried stiff and start to rearrange their lives to provide support. But they don't need to! Delirium should get better. The patient should be able to go home to their previous life. So don't make any changes – sit tight and wait to see the outcome before making major decisions.

Other brain problems

The list of brain problems that can cause psychological symptoms is obviously long, but there are a few that deserve special mention because they are relatively common and illustrate the complex interplay between brain disease and mental health: HIV, Parkinson's disease and Huntington's disease.

Human immunodeficiency virus (HIV)

HIV is primarily an immune disorder; however, the brain is one of the main organs affected. The ramifications of big events usually take decades to become evident. AIDS was first recognised in 1981, when a case report of five young gay men with a rare form of pneumonia was published. The term AIDS (acquired immune deficiency syndrome) was coined the next year. Those Australians who remember the 1980s will recall the 'Grim Reaper' commercials, which were first aired 1987, designed to raise public awareness about the disease. The first really effective treatments for AIDS began in 1996.

When HIV first emerged, all the attention focused on lung diseases and certain cancers. Within a decade it became apparent that a range of neurological problems were also common, especially once HIV infection progressed to AIDS.

The most prominent manifestations of HIV that involve mental health clinicians are cognitive decline, depression and mania. The cognitive decline associated with HIV mirrors that of age-related cognitive decline. There can be mild cognitive changes that do not affect the person's ability to function – or HIV dementia, with all the features of dementia described above.

Since the introduction of effective treatments for HIV, the incidence of HIV dementia has dropped dramatically and it mostly only occurs in people with advanced disease who are not on treatment. In contrast, the milder cognitive decline is still common, affecting about a third of HIV-infected individuals at some point in the course of their illness.

The main differences between HIV dementia and other dementias are that HIV dementia is often slower in its onset, it fluctuates a lot, and it is associated with prominent mood symptoms – either depression or mania. The first clue to diagnosis can be recurrent depression or mania in a person who previously didn't suffer mood problems. The cognitive symptoms are also slightly different. They tend to follow what's known as a subcortical pattern – memory deficits, poor concentration, apathy and mental slowing. Treatment with anti-HIV drugs often reverses the problems.

Depression is also particularly common in HIV. This is probably due to a mix of factors – HIV's effect on the brain, the psychological stress of having HIV, and treatments that can have this side effect. Luckily, depression in HIV responds to treatment as well as depression without HIV.

Mania is also more common in HIV than we would expect based on normal rates in any population. Early research showed that this was because of the subtle effects of HIV on the brain. It usually occurs late in infection, and is associated with HIV dementia. Treatment with HIV drugs reduces the risk. If it does occur, as well as standard mania treatment, HIV drugs are reviewed to ensure those that get into the brain are included.

Parkinson's disease (PD)

Parkinson's disease is a degenerative neurological disorder that becomes more common with age. It begins to emerge in forty-year-olds, but is most commonly diagnosed in people in their seventies. The key symptoms are tremor, slowness of movement (bradykinesia) and rigidity (an increased resistance to passive movement).

There are many other manifestations and lots involve mental health.

Dementia is common, occurring in up to 70 per cent of sufferers, especially late in the illness and when elderly. There is also a milder syndrome of cognitive impairment without significant functional decline.

Depression is the most common psychiatric disturbance seen in PD. About half of PD sufferers become depressed at some point. It's important to recognise depression, because it exaggerates the functional impairments associated with the muscle problems. Anxiety disorders are also common. Psychotic syndromes, especially with hallucinations, are frequent, occurring in around a third of patients.

All of these syndromes improve with standard psychiatric treatments, but it is very important to include the neurologist in care as many of the Parkinson's treatments can also affect mental health – both in a positive and negative way.

Huntington's disease

Huntington's disease is a relatively rare genetic disorder that causes abnormal movements, dementia and psychiatric problems. It is an autosomal-dominant inherited disease, which means if one parent has it, all offspring have a 50 per cent chance of also having the disorder. Genetic testing can reveal whether offspring have the abnormal gene, but the age of onset can be difficult to predict (although the more of the abnormal gene you have, the earlier you are likely to get the disorder).

Symptoms develop slowly. The movement disorder is complex; it is mostly characterised by rapid, involuntary movements involving the face, trunk and limbs. These movements progress as the disease develops.

The dementia is progressive and inevitable. It initially presents in the typical frontal pattern, with problems related to planning and making decisions, but eventually affects all cognitive domains. Patients end up bedbound, and die from complications of immobility, usually between ten and thirty years after the onset.

The psychiatric symptoms are diverse. Depression is common, as are a range of problems related to socialising, probably in part due to the dementia. Apathy and anxiety are often reported. Some people develop obsessive-compulsive disorder, and a small number (about 10 per cent) develop psychotic symptoms, especially hallucinations and delusions. Suicide is a significant risk.

One of the worst features of this tragic illness is the waiting. Some people find out well before the onset that they have the gene, so they are left wondering when it will affect them. Naturally this is enormously stressful and can lead to all sorts of mental health problems. It also raises the issue of gene testing for relatives – each individual must decide whether they want to know and therefore whether to undergo the gene testing.

There is no definitive treatment to reverse or prevent Huntington's disease at this point in time, although with recent genetic advances hopes are high for a range of possible treatments. Despite this, there are many treatments that help relieve the symptoms of the various problems that develop. Some medicines help with the movement disorders. Psychiatric medications are moderately successful in relieving depression and psychotic symptoms. Many other medications are being trialled.

A major focus of treatment is supportive therapy – meaning helping the person deal with the effects of the disease. Counselling, physiotherapy, rehabilitation, occupational therapy, nutrition and speech therapy all play key roles. In-home care and, later, nursing home care is usually required.

*

Brain diseases are often considered some of the most frightening of all health problems. This stems from the fact that the brain is arguably our most complex and poorly understood organ, and dysfunction strikes at the very core or our identities – our personality and our memories. Despite this, recent advances in understanding the anatomy and biology of the brain through incredible progress in brain research (especially brain imaging and genetics) are offering exciting and promising solutions, more so than in any other time in our history.

Not so long ago, most brain disorders were thought of as virtually untreatable. Now this is false – many are reversible, and many can be slowed or improved. This highlights the importance of early diagnosis and accessing the various specialists who manage brain problems. We began this chapter by stating the brain was the most mysterious of all our seventy-eight organs, we can now add that advances in brain research are finally unravelling the mysteries and offering some of the greatest advances in all of health care.

PART III

THE TREATMENTS

Psychiatry: Where We Are Now!

Religions die when they are proved to be true. Science is the record of dead religions.

Oscar Wilde

Every generation basks in the glory of knowing that they are at the cutting edge of medical science. They are living longer than ever before. They have the best treatments to fight the ravages of disease. They are smug in the belief that medical understanding is at its greatest point in history and they are part of it. Those poor bastards in the past!

But then something predictable yet horrible happens – the next generation comes along. Half the stuff the previous generation believed turns out to be not quite true. They look back on the old medical truths with a mixture of conceited amusement and disgust. They laugh at the simplistic explanations, condescendingly smile at the treatments that were thought to be revolutionary, and are outraged by discovering that some treatments did more harm than good.

The generation after them do the same. And on and on it goes.

Medical knowledge mimics life – it grows. It starts off imma-ture, has an adventurous adolescence that involves nail-biting experimentation, then reaches adulthood, gets older and wiser, and eventually retires and dies to be replaced by different knowledge. In typical narcissistic human fashion, we always think we are in the peak time, the salad days, the golden age of humanity. But in reality each medical specialty is at a different stage of life. It's hard to estimate exactly where each is at right now, but here's a guess. Feel free to disagree:

- Infectious diseases: rough age – 40. Great advances have been made with the discovery of various types of bugs. Antibiotics for bacteria are wonderful, but resistance is emerging. Antivirals for viruses are just beginning. Vaccination covers many but not all infections. Major pandemics are still a high risk.

- Cardiology: rough age – 35. The heart is a relatively simple muscle and we understand its physiology pretty well. We know the risk factors for most cardiovascular diseases but are struggling to control them as a community. Still a leading cause of death.

- Gastroenterology: rough age – 30. We know a little about the physiology, but only recently discovered the role of the microbiome (the 100 trillion or so microbial cells in your gut). We are just beginning to learn the role of the gut and biome in health – especially immunity.

- Neurology: rough age – 25. The brain is still a bit of a mystery, despite the advances of imaging, especially MRI and PET scanning, which have uncovered lots of hidden secrets. Many treatments have emerged for brain disorders such as Parkinson's and epilepsy, but we still can't prevent much except strokes (and even then it's mainly via cardiovascular improvements). We only recently learnt that neurones might be able to regenerate, but we don't know how. We are still figuring out the roles of the various other types of cells in the brain. How the damn organ delivers consciousness is anyone's guess!

- Surgery: rough age – 18. Surgical technique is always improving, and anaesthetic improvements have been amazing. Safety is also pretty good, especially infection control. But our studies of the benefits of surgery are limited by short-term trials with inadequate control treatments against which to measure them. We are still trying to figure out what surgery to do and when. Not nearly enough money is invested in surgical research (hint, hint government funders!)

- Psychiatry: rough age – 10. (Please, friends and colleagues, don't shoot the messenger.) We have reasonable treatments, but they don't work nearly well enough and many of the side effects limit their use. Psychiatric services lag way behind general medical services in terms of both funding and research. We don't really understand emotions and behaviour – they are just so frustratingly hard to study. The Heisenberg uncertainty principle states that the mere act of measurement changes that which is measured – this is just as true in human behaviour as it is in quantum mechanics, and this stuffs up nearly every psychiatric study!

Very few doctors have an interest in pointing out the limitations of science and health care. Why would they? It would only make everyone anxious and suspicious. But knowing a little about the limitations helps you understand why choosing a treatment isn't as simple as 'doctor knows best'.

So the challenge is to be alert but not alarmed. Don't throw the baby out with the bathwater.

A brief history of psychiatry

Here's the briefest potted history of psychiatry ever.

Treatments for mental illnesses date back to a few centuries BC. Early ideas mostly blamed supernatural powers or some sort of moral weakness on the part of the individual. Despite this, there were various attempts to understand psychosis as an illness at different times in various cultures. There are reports of psychiatric hospitals in India as far back as the third century BC.

Hippocrates revolutionised medicine around the third century BC. He thought illnesses were naturally caused, rather than the work of gods. He separated medicine from religion. He contributed to the theory of 'humors' (four distinct bodily fluids thought to cause most illness), which turned out to be wrong, but he was on the right track. He also introduced professionalism in medicine – many still take his oath today!

Now, we have to jump forward 1600 years to find any significant further innovation.

Bethlem Royal Hospital in London opened in the thirteenth century and is often cited as the first of the modern 'lunatic asylums'. Bethlem was an early attempt to separate the mentally ill from criminals and provide treatment (although this struggle still continues today). While the intentions were probably good, many of the treatments were still more custodial, rather than therapeutic. The 'lock them up and throw away the key' approach dominated.

In the seventeenth century a range of private asylums opened up. The public were slowly recognising the extent of mental illness in the community and trying to sort out solutions.

The UK's *Lunacy Act 1845* explicitly established that mentally ill people should be treated as patients as opposed to undesirables, outcasts and criminals. The United States followed suit and the first big hospital for the mentally ill opened in New York in 1843 – the Utica Psychiatric Center. The director established the first psychiatric medical journal, *The American Journal of Insanity*. These were the early underpinnings of a true medical approach to mental illness.

The Europeans started to write about classification and describe mental illnesses in more detail. In the early twentieth century, German psychiatrist Emil Kraeplelin turbo-charged the process and wrote about 'nerves' while promoting the idea that there were different types of mental illness and they had biological causes. In 1908 the term 'schizophrenia' (meaning a split in the mind) was coined.

Freud was also hard at work in the early twentieth century. He developed psychoanalysis to treat psychopathology. With the exception of hypnosis (which had limited applications) this was the first real talking therapy (psychotherapy) and it led to an explosion in attempts to help people through talking. While the popularity and use of psychoanalysis dropped off after the 1970s, psychotherapy remains useful to this day.

The first successful biological therapy was psychosurgery. After some early attempts in the nineteenth century, the leucotomy, a surgical procedure where the connections to and from the prefrontal cortex are cut or scraped away, was developed in the 1930s by Portuguese neurologist Egas Moniz. He won a Nobel Prize for his work. The practice was embraced in the US and overused to the point of abuse, which led to a serious and deserved backlash. While it is still used today, it's restricted to very severe illnesses and is closely regulated.

Next, in the 1940s, came electroconvulsive therapy (first known as electroshock treatment). ECT was based on the observations that people with mental illnesses seemed to improve after a seizure. Electricity proved to be the safest way to induce a seizure. At the time this was a revolution. It was the first truly successful physical therapy. For the first time ever, thousands of patients in hospitals all over the world emerged from their chronic mental illnesses. Many patients living in institutions could be discharged.

But there were also problems with ECT. The technique took decades to be refined. Early attempts used too much electricity, leading to significant memory problems. And it was done without anaesthetic – leading to complications from the seizure, like bone and teeth fractures. Modern ECT is always done with an anaesthetic. As ECT was the only viable treatment available at the time, it was overused. There weren't clear ideas about which illnesses responded and which didn't – everyone got a try. At some institutions it was routinely given to all patients. There were claims that at times ECT was more a punishment than a therapy; its reputation nosedived.

Apart from psychosurgery, ECT carries more stigma than virtually any medical treatment. Patients who have ECT are often reluctant to ever admit it to anyone. In one famous case, a 1972 US vice-presidential nominee, Thomas Eagleton, apparently withdrew from the election race after the press reported he had received ECT in the past (although, just like everything in the history of ECT, there are various conflicting accounts of why he quit). ECT almost certainly does not deserve the stigma it carries, but it is persistent. Stigma is the main reason the use of ECT is limited today.

It's worth noting at this point that the life cycle of all medical treatments typically goes something like this:

New treatment gets developed
↓
Extreme excitement and publicity
↓
It gets tried in a range of circumstances/illnesses
↓
Overuse
↓
Complications and side effects get noticed
↓
Backlash & negative publicity
↓
Underuse
↓

Further research & clearer ideas about uses and indications

↓

Repeat cycle at least once or twice

↓

Final indications for use and its place in medical
treatment is established.

It's a bit like a pendulum slowly finding its equilibrium point.
It happens for everything from antibiotics to surgery to psychotherapy. Sometimes the pendulum swings wildly – ECT and
psychosurgery were two such cases.

The 1950s saw the next big advance – the beginnings of phar-
macotherapy (medications). At this point in history, ECT was
the main treatment for psychoses and severe depression, but it
had reached the point where there was a backlash and problems
were emerging. Many patients in the large institutions were still
very unwell. Even if they responded to ECT, they often relapsed.
Something better was needed. A couple of surgeons and chem-
ists in France were searching for better anaesthetic drugs. One
that they developed and trialled was chlorpromazine. They
found it had a distinct calming effect. They gave it the trade
name Largactil – from the French for 'large activity'. They suggested to psychiatric colleagues to give it a try in psychosis. The
rest is history!

Psychotic patients began regaining their sanity. The death
rates from serious disorders in major institutions worldwide
plummeted. Chlorpromazine largely replaced ECT, psychosurgery and other experimental treatments of the day. Haloperidol,
a related compound, followed about five years later.

Of course the life cycle of both these new treatments went through a few rounds. Side effects and efficacy problems emerged, but over the next half century came improvements. It became evident which illnesses responded to them. The dose ranges were refined. New and safer versions of the drugs were developed. We now have over twenty to choose from. There are still problems, but these drugs have saved millions of lives and, perhaps just as importantly, have made millions of lives more tolerable.

Around the same time, an Australian psychiatrist, John Cade, experimented with lithium in rats and noted its calming effect. He tried it in patients with mania. The results were dramatic. Because it was toxic in high doses, the rest of the world was slow to catch on, but research in Europe and the United States helped refine its use. It took about twenty years for its full benefits to become apparent. This lead to the class of drugs known as mood stabilisers, which are essential in the modern management of bipolar disorder. Lithium and its related compounds have saved lives and restored sanity to millions of people with bipolar disorder. The article Cade wrote in the *Medical Journal of Australia* is the journal's most cited article. Cade received one of Australia's highest honours – an Order of Australia. He probably should have received a Nobel Prize too. But we might be biased!

Slightly later in the 1950s came the first antidepressants. Prior to the 1950s doctors had tried opioids and amphetamines for depression, but their addictive properties limited their use. In 1952 some doctors trialling new drugs for tuberculosis found some patients had an improvement in mood (as well as in their tuberculosis). Vigorous research followed and in 1957 the class of drugs known as tricyclics emerged – the first medication for depression.

Tricyclics became hugely popular, but had a significant flaw – if taken in overdose, they were lethal. This limited their use, as doctors were reluctant to give depressed and potentially suicidal patients a weapon to end their life. Also, they were tricky to prescribe – you had to start with a low dose and build up slowly. Doctors (and patients) hate tricky treatments.

In the late 1980s this problem was overcome with the introduction of fluoxetine (Prozac). This medication had the same antidepressant effects, yet was relatively safe in overdose and easy to prescribe. In 1992 Prozac made the cover of *Time* magazine.

While all this pharmacology was exploding, other changes were afoot. The big hospitals were raising concerns. The concept of 'institutionalisation' emerged. This was the recognition that if a person spent too much time in a hospital (institutional) setting, they lost the ability to function in the community. The Italians led the way with this idea. Governments the world over jumped on board and the big psychiatric hospitals began being replaced by smaller wards in general hospitals and intensive community care.

This period also saw huge improvements in psychotherapy. First up came the behaviour therapies in the 1950s, which then morphed into cognitive behaviour therapy, interpersonal therapy and the even newer mindfulness-based therapies. Psychoanalysis morphed into psychodynamic therapy, and this gave birth to treatments such as dialectic behaviour therapy. Research techniques improved and the indications and limitations of each therapy emerged. Psychotherapy is now favoured over pharma-cotherapy for many disorders.

All in all, the future is beginning (ever so slowly) to look bright. Research is ever-expanding, and new treatments, such as magnetic therapies, are emerging each year. Stigma is melting. Services are improving. Governments are getting on board. But there is a long way to go.

Some bits we didn't tell you

Okay, we left out huge hunks of the history of psychiatry. But, remember, this book is the start of a conversation – not the end. Jump on the internet if you want to know more.

The only things we feel a little guilty about leaving out are the abuses. Psychiatry has been used for some dreadful purposes – for political purposes, for profit, for primitive and unethical research purposes, and more. There have been failed trials of treatment that, quite frankly, are distressing to read about. The main reason we left this out is because it's just too hard to document and understand without some serious scholarly activity. Also, this book is about telling you where we are right now. There are plenty of others who will gladly tell you the problems.

Our own view is that psychiatry and psychology and all the other health sciences are trying to do their best with limited resources in a field that is in its infancy. Nearly everyone is well intentioned; at least, that's our experience. We are all trying to get to the best possible place with the least amount of damage. So let's focus on that.

Getting Started

There's no real street directory for treatment, which is a shame. It would be great if you could simply plug in your condition and have a computer spit out a set of instructions, but it's never that easy. Treatment needs to take into account the disorders (it's usually more than one), the person and their beliefs, their life and its complexities, their family and friends, and their culture. Also, the range of services available varies – between countries, between cities, even between suburbs. The pathways are endless.

It can feel overwhelming at the start. So, take a deep breath, step back and break it down.

The first thing to remember is there is no right or wrong answer. You weigh up as much information as you feel ready to handle, find a clinician you think you can trust, and get started somewhere. Anywhere. Trial and error mixed with per-severance is the key.

The good news is that making the decision to start treatment is the start of things turning around. The moment you start, you will see attitudes around you change. People who have been worried about you, frustrated with you or oblivious to your problems will immediately re-evaluate their attitudes. Once they know you are getting help they will start to understand your problems in health terms, rather than possibly judging you.

Chances are you will feel a great sense of relief – perhaps for the first time you will meet people who understand what you are going through and can offer help. Hopefully you will see that your problems have answers and solutions. Feelings of hopelessness will diminish and light will appear at the end of the tunnel.

First steps

Pretty much every mental health clinician begins with the same steps – they develop a treatment plan, provide information and address psychological first aid.

Treatment plan

A treatment plan is exactly what it sounds like – a list of things to do and options to consider. It usually begins with tests and investigations that they think might be necessary to find the cause of your problems – things like blood tests, scans or psychological tests. These are not always necessary, and sometimes the GP has already done them. Next they gather more information, sometimes through more time talking to you, sometimes by speaking to your relatives and partners, friends or other important people in your life – such as teachers if you are still studying. But rest assured, they never do so without your permission (legally they must get your permission first).

They will also address any specific problems that need urgent attention, like providing a medical certificate for time off work or finding safe housing.

Generally a plan will include steps to address any risks (like self-harm) and then possible treatment approaches like psychotherapy or medications.

The plan is written down, but is not exhaustive; everyone recognises more problems and options will emerge as treatment progresses – the treatment plan is just a guide to get started. Some doctors give these plans to the patient; others prefer not to because they can seem overwhelming early on.

Psychoeducation

Psychoeducation is all about explaining the ins and outs of the disorder you have and the treatment options. It usually takes a session or two, as there is a lot to absorb when you first see a shrink. Your clinician will probably also direct you to reliable websites – those run by governments (because they are all carefully reviewed by experts) or the big philanthropic organisations.

At the end of this process, you should have a basic overview of your situation and answers to some key questions:

- What is your main problem?
- Do you prefer medications or psychotherapies, a mix of the two, or something else, such as alternative therapies?
- What services exist in your area?
- What can you afford?
- How urgent is the problem?

Psychological first aid

Psychological first aid goes by various names, but it essentially means addressing the five pillars of good mental health: all psych treatment should begin here.

- **Sleep.** Your clinician should give you advice about the basics of getting a good night's sleep – often called sleep hygiene. Things like minimising caffeine before bed; having a routine for sleep; making your bedroom suitable (quiet, stable temperature, etc.); using your bedroom just for sleep (not watching television, for instance; sex is obviously an exception); and relaxation techniques.

- **Exercise.** Physical activity is surprisingly good for mental health. More and more studies support this obvious advice. Begin with a simple routine like walking, then build it up – gym, running, swimming, cycling – choose whichever you prefer but get started. This has flow-on effects for nutrition, weight, sleep and relaxation. Some conditions get better with exercise alone!

- **Nutrition.** It's hard to overstate the importance of nutrition: it is essential. This begins with basic advice about eating a healthy diet – and this advice is simple and you probably already know it. Stuff like eating fruit and vegetables, eating in moderation, making sure you're getting the right nutrients and so on. Equally important is cutting back on the bad stuff – caffeine and alcohol are the biggest problems. The simple step of reducing caffeine can fix some anxiety problems. And alcohol is even more obvious – you can't fix depression if you're drinking yourself to sleep every night.

- **Stress.** Stress and the problems driving it should be a key focus of any early treatment. Your clinician should give you advice about problem-solving and relaxation. This often includes specific training in how to relax – from meditation to suggesting other useful approaches such as yoga.
- **Relationships.** Humans are social animals! You cannot treat any mental health problem without paying attention to relationships. A good clinician helps you think constructively about which relationships are working, which are worth fixing, how to do it, and when to quit toxic relationships.

While this all sounds simple enough, it's usually enough work for the first few weeks of treatment. Often other approaches are begun simultaneously. For example, you might start medications while you are discussing psychological first aid in the first few sessions with your clinician. Psychotherapy usually takes a little longer to get organised, as a suitable therapist needs to be found (unless the primary clinician provides it) and booked, and there are usually waiting lists.

Second opinions

Second opinions are very helpful. The field of mental health is full of differing views and clinicians have various levels of expertise – so seeking other opinions can be very useful. Most clinicians love second opinions and will help organise them. They recognise the benefits of using other experts and getting a broad range of ideas and options. It's also true that some clinicians dislike second opinions – either because they see them as the patient searching for answers they want to hear rather than the truth, or because they dislike having their own opinion questioned. If this is the case, remember you are in charge! You can explain that it is important to you and request for it to be organised. Of course, you can also do it yourself (on the quiet without telling the first specialist) and simply ask a GP to refer you to another specialist. This is okay, but not quite as good because sometimes the best results come from the two specialists discussing their respective opinions with you, so you might want them to be aware of each other and consider each other's opinions.

Second opinions are especially useful when:

- Your disorder is particularly severe. You can seek the opinion of someone who 'sub-specialises' in your disorder. Mild problems can be treated by most clinicians, but severe problems often require someone who sub-specialises in that field.
- Your disorder is rare. Some problems are simply too unusual for the average clinician to ever see enough cases to maintain their skills. It is usually possible to find someone who is an expert, but you may need to travel to get the second opinion, especially if you live in a rural or remote area.
- Your disorder isn't getting better. There are many reasons problems don't improve, but one reason to consider is that something has been missed. A second set of skilled clinical eyes can often see something that was initially overlooked.

Inpatient versus outpatient care

The vast majority of mental health problems are treated in the community, but sometimes treatment in hospitals is required.

There are pros and cons to hospital admission. The pros are:

- Most problems can be assessed and helped quicker in a hospital.
- Risks can be minimised but not removed. Risks include self-harm, suicide, damage to reputation and the risk of harming others. Inpatient settings can drastically reduce these risks through closer observation.
- Medications can be adjusted quicker because clinicians are on hand to monitor and treat side effects.
- Several different clinicians can get involved quickly without the need for booking and travelling to appointments.
- Test and investigations can be completed more quickly.

The cons are:

- It's expensive in private, and in NHS beds are always in short supply.
- It takes you out of your usual environment, which can be overwhelming and remove you from your usual support systems. Also, it can remove you from the very problems you need to address – a double-edged sword.
- It can become too 'comfortable', making it hard to readjust to the community when the time for discharge arrives. It's easy to become dependent on hospital care.

If you have access to private hospitals (usually through health insurance), then there are more options. If not, the NHS system comes down to risks – admission is reserved for patients at high risk, where usually the Mental Health Act kicks in.

Finding extra services

While we covered choosing a clinician in the early chapters, there are also some tricks to finding extra help when you first start treatment. For any given problem, you can access help from a range of people:

- a general clinician – a psychiatrist, psychologist, counsellor, GP, or community mental health team member.
- a clinician who sub-specialises in a particular disorder – many clinicians have areas of special interest, often with extra training and degrees.
- NHS trusts have a mental health department that treats everything (within the limitation of budgets and waiting lists). Staff will include the full range of professions – psychiatrists, psychologists, nurses, social workers, occupational therapists, etc. If they cannot help, they will give suggestions of other options, or refer you back to your GP.
- specialised NHS services – big cities usually have a series of specialist services for particular disorders that, when severe, are outside the scope of the general services. They are classified as 'tertiary care' and are called 'centres of expertise' and they provide second opinions, advice and sometimes ongoing care. Specialist services usually exist for complex neuropsychiatric disorders, eating disorders,

depression, anxiety, intellectual disability, dual diagnosis (this refers to combined mental health and drug and alcohol problems) and forensics problems (medicine and the law). To find out about these, either ask your GP, your local hospital or search the internet.

- crisis services – many community mental health teams include a crisis/home treatment team. These are teams of clinicians that respond to crises, mostly suicidal behaviour. They assess people rapidly, usually in their homes, provide expert risk assessment and often manage people at high risk without admission to hospital. The GP will ring on your behalf.

- A&E (Accident & Emergency) services – these are linked to a general hospital, and are emergency services that do an assessment and help explore the range of treatment options.

The take-home message here is that there is a comprehensive NHS service, as well as many private options out there. Exploration is hard if you are unwell. If the idea of this seems overwhelming, consider getting someone close to you to do the legwork for you. Ask them to make the calls or search the internet to draw up lists of options. Perhaps get them to visit a GP with you – they'll probably feel more confident asking questions on your behalf. And remember that all the helplines, especially the big ones like the Samaritans, have trained counsellors sitting on the line with massive lists of services and options in front of them (Steve knows; he did this for a couple of years while at uni).

Mental Health Acts and involuntary treatment

Pretty much every developed country has a Mental Health Act and they usually say roughly the same thing:

You will be treated involuntarily (meaning against your will) if:

- You have a serious mental illness.
- You are at risk to yourself or others.
- You are refusing treatment.

The UK Mental Health Act

The Mental Health Act says when you can be taken to hospital, kept there, and treated against your wishes. This can only happen if you have a mental disorder that puts you, or others, at risk.

You should only be detained under the Mental Health Act if there are no other ways to keep you, or others, safe.

Being detained under the Mental Health Act is sometimes called being 'sectioned', because the law has different sections.

Your rights under the Mental Health Act depend on which section you are detained under. You can only be detained if you have a 'mental disorder'. The Mental Health Act does not say exactly what can be classed as a 'mental disorder'. So, when they're using the Mental Health Act, health professionals will decide if someone's mental health meets this definition.

You cannot be detained for drug or alcohol addiction. But you can be detained if alcohol or drugs cause mental health problems. For example, if you have delusions because of using cannabis. Usually, three people have to agree that you need to be detained. But this may not be the case if the situation is urgent.

The three people are normally an AMHP – *an Approved Mental Health Professional*; a doctor who has special training in mental disorders called a Section 12 Approved Doctor and another doctor. If all three people agree that you need to be detained, the AMHP will apply to a local hospital for a bed.

Your nearest relative can also apply for you to be detained, but this is rare. AMHPs are mental health professionals who carry out certain duties under the Mental Health Act. They are given specialist training to do this.

An AMHP might be a social worker, nurse, occupational therapist or psychologist. A doctor cannot be an AMHP. The assessment might take place at your home, in a public place, or in hospital.

The AMHP can apply to court for a warrant if you refuse to let them in, or if they think it's necessary for another reason. A warrant lets the police enter your home to take you somewhere safe. This is called a Section 135. If your home can be made a safe place, you may be kept there while an assessment is arranged.

If you are away from home in a public place, the police can take you to a safe place under Section 136. A safe place might be your own home, a hospital or police station. When you are safe, the professionals will decide if you need to be detained. They will ask you questions, and think about all your circumstances. If you are detained and not already in hospital, the AMHP will arrange for you to go there as soon as possible. Sometimes the police will go with you.

Staff should tell you which section you are detained under,

and what your rights are. They should also give you a Patient Information Leaflet about your rights. It is likely that you will be taken to a specialist ward for people with mental health problems. They may call this an 'acute ward' or a 'psychiatric ward'. In most hospitals, the door to the ward will be locked.

Sometimes the hospital might be a long way from home, but guidance says that the AMHP should try to find you a hospital bed as close as is 'reasonably possible' to where you would like to be.

In hospital, you will be introduced to your 'responsible clinician'. This is the person who is in charge of your care and treatment. They are usually a psychiatrist, but they can be other health professionals too.

Your doctors should start planning your discharge as soon as possible, and you should be involved.

Aftercare

When you leave hospital, health professionals should plan your care including where you will live, what medication will help you, what social support you will have and which mental health services can help under the CPA – *Care Programme Approach*, if there's a high risk that your mental health will get worse without ongoing care.

If you have been in hospital under section 3, you are entitled to free aftercare under section 117.

CTO – *Community Treatment Order*: A CTO means that you can leave hospital, but you stay under the Mental Health Act. You have to meet conditions to stay in the community. You may be taken back to hospital if you don't meet the conditions in the CTO, or you become unwell. This is sometimes called 'supervised community treatment'.

You may go on a CTO if you are discharged from Section 3. You can't go on a CTO if you are under Section 2, or if you are not detained.

Section 2 – Assessment

Under Section 2, you can be kept in hospital for up to twenty-eight days. An approved mental health professional (AMHP) is more likely to use Section 2 than Section 3 if you have never been assessed in hospital before, or you have not been assessed for a long time.

Section 3 – Treatment

Under Section 3, you can be detained in hospital for treatment for up to six months. But it can be extended for longer. An approved mental health professional (AMHP) needs to apply to hospital. Your nearest relative can also do this, but this is rare.

Section 4 – Emergencies

Section 4 is used in emergencies, where only 1 doctor is available at short notice. Unlike a Section 2 or 3, you can be detained with a recommendation from only one doctor. You can be kept for up to seventy-two hours. This gives the hospital time to arrange a full assessment.

Section 5 – Holding powers

Section 5 allows a doctor or nurse to stop you from leaving hospital. They may do this if you are in hospital voluntarily, and you want to leave but they think you are too unwell to leave.

Doctor's holding power – section 5(2)
A doctor can hold you in hospital for up to seventy-two hours, if they write a report explaining why you need to be detained, and send this to the hospital managers. A doctor can do this in any hospital.

Nurse's holding power – section 5(4)
A mental health or learning disability nurse can keep you in hospital for up to six hours if they need to immediately stop you leaving hospital, for your own health or safety, or for the protection of others, and it is not possible to find doctor who can section you under Section 5(2).

Independent Mental Health Advocate (IMHA)
You can get help from an IMHA if you are under Sections 2 or 3 of the Mental Health Act.

*

It's fair to say that Mental Health Acts attract controversy. In decades past (and still in some countries) they have been overly restrictive with inadequate checks and balances. There have been examples where they have resulted in abuses of human rights. In extreme cases in some countries they have been used systematically to abuse rights, sometimes for political purposes, and sometimes simply as an excuse to remove mentally ill people from the community. Thankfully, this is mostly in the past, but we all must remain vigilant. Lawyers are needed to help ensure services are following the Acts correctly. Also, governments and politicians need to be pressured to ensure adequate funding – when funds are tight, patient rights are often the first casualties.

Furthermore, to balance the comments about the abuses of patient's rights, it's also worth remembering the many millions of lives that have been saved because of Mental Health Acts. Mental Health Acts allow very sick people to get mental health care – especially people suffering psychoses. Families are especially keen to praise the Acts; they see their loved ones refusing treatment when psychotic, or too depressed to get out of bed and talking about ending their lives. Without Mental Health Acts, thousands of patients every year would not receive help. Many would die by suicide. The trick for us all is to ensure our Mental Health Acts balance patient's rights versus the importance of clinicians to intervene when patients have lost the insight and competence to manage their illness.

Finally, it's worth remembering that Mental Health Acts are not the only avenues to ensure someone gets treatment when they are unable to consent themselves. There are other laws that can enforce treatment – judges can make orders, and some countries also have separate Acts to enforce treatment for drug and alcohol problems.

*

This chapter has been a whirlwind tour of how to get the ball rolling regarding treatment for mental illness. There is no single right pathway. There is no 'correct' answer. As we've said so many times in this book, the trick is to try something, anything, and if it helps, persist with it; if it doesn't try something different. If all the advice here seems overwhelming and you're not sure which the right first step is, close your eyes (metaphorically perhaps) and go with your gut instinct. Someone first said this about six thousand years ago:

The journey of a thousand miles begins with one step.

Lao Tzu (circa fourth century BC)

Psychotherapy

Psychotherapy is often looked upon with either mysticism or cynicism. Some people describe it as if some magic happens in the confines of the therapist's room that cannot be understood by an outsider. Others dismiss it as if nothing can be achieved by talking alone. Neither is true.

Psychotherapy really just means 'talking therapy'. It's a clinician trying to help a patient by talking. There are as many types of psychotherapy as there are medications. Each type of has its own way of understanding mental illness and its own techniques. But there are more similarities between them than differences.

Psychotherapy 101

A famous psychiatrist from New York (where else!) called Jerome Frank once did a study where he recorded and studied various types of psychotherapy and healing practices in different settings. In 1993 he and his daughter, Julia, wrote a book called *Persuasion and Healing: A Comparative Study of Psychotherapy* about his findings. They found all forms of successful healing had some core features:

- The therapist is a trained and trusted person who is perceived as wanting to help.
- The therapy takes place in a clearly designated place of healing, usually with all the trappings, like degrees on the wall, books and clinical tools.
- The therapy has a clear rationale, with procedures to help the patient. The patient learns new information about how to address their problems.
- The therapy provides hope and the patient expects to overcome their problems.

The Franks believed these four factors were the keys to success in therapy – not the model or type of therapy, or whether the therapist was a professor, a doctor, a psychologist or a counsellor, and certainly nothing mystical: just these simple factors.

All psychotherapies on offer contain these elements. Their work doesn't necessarily mean *all* therapies with these four factors work – it just means that all successful therapies contain these factors. It's a good starting place to understand why therapy might help – but in order to find out if a specific therapy helps for a specific problem, research into effectiveness is required.

One of the challenges in choosing a type of psychotherapy is evaluating the evidence for its effectiveness. The gold standard for medical evidence is double-blind, placebo-controlled clinical trials. This means every new treatment is studied by giving it to a patient in a research setting, where the patient is either given a placebo or the real treatment (placebo-controlled) and neither the patient nor the clinician knows which treatment they are getting (double-blind).

As you can well imagine, for psychotherapy trials it is almost impossible to find a suitable placebo for psychotherapy, and it is completely impossible to blind the patient and the therapist. So true gold-standard evidence for the effectiveness of psychotherapy is not easy to obtain. But – and this is worth sitting up for – this does not mean psychotherapy isn't effective. It just means our science is not currently good enough to truly evaluate these treatments.

Absence of evidence is not evidence of absence

When evaluating the evidence for psychotherapy, an open mind is required. Why is this important to know? Because many people claim all sorts of arguments for or against psychotherapy, or for or against one sort over another, and you need to take all claims with a grain of salt. Researching psychotherapy is difficult and the evidence base isn't as easy to develop as it is for more simple interventions (like medications) where placebo controlled studies are easier to design. Psychotherapy researchers might be jumping up and down, gritting their teeth at this point (apologies to them all) but this is the state of scientific play.

So how can a patient decide which form of therapy is best for them? Why would one form of psychotherapy be more appropriate for an individual than another? And how do we work out the best fit? We look at the evidence that is available (as meagre as it is), we use clinical judgement, we try to match the therapy to the patient's illness, values and beliefs, and we play clinical trial-and-error. We give it a try, and if it doesn't work we try something else. And we think about Jerome Frank and his core principles.

Who provides psychotherapy?

The term 'psychotherapist' is a general term that can mean almost anything! When choosing one, you need to understand the different sorts of professionals who might call themselves a psychotherapist and decide which is right for you.

Psychotherapy can be done by many types of clinicians: general practitioners, psychologists, psychiatrists, social workers, nurses and counsellors.

Psychologists are specialists in psychotherapy. Their training is anything from six to ten years. Psychology, like medicine, is a regulated profession, so to call yourself a psychologist you must reach certain professional standards and be registered with a national body of some sort. You begin with an undergraduate degree about psychology, then go on to clinical training, which has a number of different pathways. Psychologists can train in any of the types of psychotherapy, and most usually train in a few different types and practise broadly. Psychologists may specialise in a particular form of psychology: for example, neuropsychology, health psychology, sports psychology or forensic psychology.

Psychiatrists train in medicine and then specialise in psychiatry. Specialist training in psychiatry generally takes about five years, and it includes all the medications, diagnoses and types of treatment. The training includes the theoretical aspects of psychotherapy, but not much in the way of actual practical psychotherapy training. Most psychiatrists who practice psychotherapy do extra courses, either during their training or after they have finished. As a consequence, being a psychiatrist does not guarantee the clinician is also an expert psychotherapist.

General practitioners and nurses train in their basic clinical fields, but some develop an interest in psychotherapy and do extra courses in it. Social workers all learn the basics of psychotherapy, mainly various forms of counselling but, like GPs and nurses, only some go on to practise any form of psychotherapy.

A counsellor is the most general term of all. Anyone can call themselves a counsellor. In general, counselling is broader than psychotherapy. Counselling means helping people with a problem – any problem, not just mental health problems.

The key message is that you cannot choose a psychotherapist on title alone.

Choose someone who has training and expertise in the right area and preferably as much clinical experience as possible. But don't be rigid about training – we've met counsellors with minimal training who are naturally gifted as psychotherapists, and we've met psychiatrists and psychologists with over a decade of training that just don't seem to be good with people.

Also, they all charge differently. Before you book anyone, ask about their fees! And, by preference, talk to them first to see if they sound like the sort of person you will feel comfortable with. For the therapy to work, you need to trust them, and you need to feel a rapport. Sometimes you don't find this out for a few sessions. If it's not right, tell them, discuss it, and move on if necessary. Just like medications, there is always some trial and error involved.

But remember, it is okay to question your therapist at any time. You are investing time, money and effort and therapists are providing a service. They are not the same as friends – you must be happy with the service you are receiving.

However, once you have chosen someone and completed the first few sessions, give it a fair go. It's well known that patients start to feel restless and think about quitting therapy just before a major breakthrough. A good rule of thumb is that if you feel like you want to quit, give it another three sessions.

Types of psychotherapy

There are many different kinds of therapy – in this section we look and the main kinds. Some psychotherapists practice one specific type of therapy in its 'pure' form, while others mix and match a little.

Psychodynamic psychotherapy

Psychodynamic psychotherapy is endlessly fascinating and the subject of countless books. It's what most people think of when they imagine psychotherapy. It's psychotherapy as depicted in movies – a middle-aged, slightly odd yet reserved librarian type in a tweed jacket with arm patches; the patient on a couch or comfy chair; the therapist sitting thoughtfully and wisely uncovering deep emotions and exploring past events. This is only partly true! There are many variations and versions of psychodynamic psychotherapy, but all are built on the foundation that there is a dynamic (or moving) flux between things in our conscious awareness and things in our unconscious unawareness – hence the name psychodynamic.

Sigmund Freud was the father of psychodynamic psychotherapy. The basic idea is that our past influences our present in various unconscious ways. Our childhood experiences, our past conflicts, our past relationships and our current circumstances all interact in a part-conscious, part-unconscious cauldron to influence our feelings, our behaviour and our current relationships.

The idea of therapy is to gently gain insight into our unconscious motivations, and so better understand our present – sometimes psychodynamic psychotherapies are also called 'insight-oriented' psychotherapy. A range of techniques are employed to achieve this goal.

Psychodynamic psychotherapy is useful for personality disorders, depression, anorexia nervosa, deliberate self-harm and relationship problems, but can be tried in a range of other conditions as well. The main criterion is that the person wanting the therapy is suitable – it's not for everyone. You need to be 'psychologically minded', meaning you are able to reflect on your past, and can tolerate the sessions, as they can be emotionally distressing as you confront aspects of your past.

The therapy is reflective – the therapist doesn't provide answers as such, but helps the patient uncover their inner feelings. The patient does the vast majority of the talking, with the therapist listening and helping draw links between the past and present.

Psychodynamic psychotherapy is mostly done one-to-one, although group forms have been developed. It begins with a thorough assessment, including building a narrative of the patient's life so far. Sessions usually last an hour, and are usually carried out weekly, although intensive therapy with daily sessions is sometimes used. The patient usually sits in a chair, although some therapists do use a couch, where the patient lies back with the therapist behind them.

Some of the key concepts behind the psychodynamic approach are:

- **the unconscious.** The idea is that our mind has a deep well of invisible material – memories, ways of reacting, ideas and relationships. These can come to the surface (conscious) through various techniques. Even though we are unaware of our unconscious thoughts and motivations, they influence our conscious behaviour, feelings and thoughts. Freud believed that by making the unconscious conscious (gaining insight), cure could be achieved. Some of the techniques to help bring them to the surface include:

  – *interpretation* – the therapist providing an explanatory statement that links some thoughts or feelings or symptoms to their potential unconscious motivations. By their very nature, these are hypotheses based on the therapist's observations. They provide ideas for the patient to reflect upon.

  – *clarification* – questions to clarify things the patient has said to encourage a deeper reflection or to encourage the patient to think about links between their current situation and the past.

- *free association* – asking the patient to talk about whatever comes into their head to observe patterns that might be influenced by unconscious factors.
- *dreams* – sometimes dreams are explored as a rich source of unconscious ideas, feelings and behaviours. Dreams are considered a window to the unconscious.

- **defence mechanisms.** These are unconscious tricks our minds use to deal with stress, anxiety, conflict or any emotions in order to protect us. They are coping mechanisms. They maintain our sense of self-control, our self-esteem and our psychological wellbeing. We all use defences; the pattern or types we use are part of our personality. Some are considered more mature or healthy than others. The therapist's role is to help identify defence mechanisms and bring them to the patient's awareness. This helps the patient acknowledge and tolerate the feelings the defence mechanisms are concealing. Defence mechanisms are not accusations or failures, they are simply everyday ways we deal with stress – we all do them to various degrees. Some examples are:
  - *denial.* Refusing to accept reality, usually because something about it is too stressful to accept. For example, a person who has been diagnosed with cancer may continue as if nothing is wrong, paying no attention to their treatment. Minor levels of denial are extremely common in everyday life.
  - *regression.* Sometimes when faced with stress we regress to an earlier stage of development. For example, a teenager faced with problems at school may become

very clingy and needy with his parents, having
regressed to an earlier stage of development.

- *dissociation*. This is where we split part of our mind
  from conscious awareness. Mostly it is simple
  things like splitting off our awareness of time or
  our surroundings. It is particularly common
  during trauma.
- *projection*. This is where we put our own feelings,
  thoughts or motivations onto another person. For
  example, if a person has feelings of anger that they
  cannot acknowledge, or are unconscious, they may
  accuse someone else of acting in an angry way.
- *intellectualisation*. This is where we strip a subject of
  any uncomfortable emotions and focus purely on the
  detail in a dispassionate manner. For example, a person
  facing a life-threatening illness might focus entirely on
  the biological aspects, studying various treatments in
  detail, but failing to acknowledge their own distress.
- *rationalisation*. This is reframing a situation in a
  different light to minimise distress. For example, a
  person in love who is unexpectedly rejected by their
  partner may declare they always thought it wouldn't
  work because their partner had too many flaws that
  were too hard to tolerate. They might say it was
  for the best.
- *acting out*. This is when we perform some extreme
  behaviour instead of facing our emotions. For
  example, a person facing high levels of anger might
  act physically and throw punches or kick over a table.

Childhood tantrums are a form of acting out. Self-harm is sometimes a form of acting out.

- **transference and counter-transference.** Transference describes the idea that the patient may react to the therapist in ways that reflect past relationships. It refers to the feelings the patient has for their therapist. For example, the patient might respond to the therapist as if they are an authority figure from the patient's past – perhaps a parent. Or maybe they will develop strong feelings for the therapist, reflecting a past emotional relationship. The therapist attempts to understand these responses and use them as clues to the unconscious relationship patterns.

  The idea of transference is one of the reasons it is absolutely essential that the therapist never allows romantic feelings to progress to a real romantic relationship. As well as damaging the therapeutic process, it would be an abuse of the trusting therapeutic relationship.

  Counter-transference refers to the clinician's feelings – both conscious and unconscious – towards the patient. These might result from the clinician's past relationships, or just the way the patient makes the clinician feel. Part of the clinician's training is to recognise their own feelings of counter-transference and hopefully use those feelings to help understand the patient. Virtually all psychodynamic psychotherapists have ongoing supervision with another psychodynamic psychotherapist in order to reflect on issues such as counter-transference and ensure their own unconscious feelings and motivations don't derail the therapy – sort of like ensuring the patient's therapy stays about the patient and the therapist's own issues don't sneak in and corrupt the process.

Obviously there is much more to psychodynamic psychotherapy than described above. It has a rich history not only in medicine but also in philosophy and literature. In particular, there are various different schools of psychodynamic psychotherapy, each with different theoretical underpinnings and techniques.

If you are considering this sort of therapy, take some time to find out about the type being recommended and the practical aspects, such as the time commitment and cost. Unlike most of the other therapies, which are usually relatively short-term (up to three months), psychodynamic psychotherapy is long-term. It's a big investment, personally and financially, but can be enormously worthwhile.

Cognitive behaviour therapy (CBT)

Cognitive behaviour therapy (CBT) has been a revolution in psychotherapy. It partly grew out of frustration with the complexity and challenges of studying psychodynamic psychotherapy in the early 1900s. Psychologists wanted a therapy that was amenable to research, more focused and less time-consuming.

It began as behaviour therapy, and in the 1950s the cognitive element was added. Cognitions are simply thoughts – so instead of focusing entirely on the patient's behaviour, the therapists began to enquire about their thinking as well.

CBT was originally developed for depression, but since then has been adapted to many other disorders, and recently various new forms have developed. It is now the most practised form of psychotherapy around the world. While psychologists remain the key leaders in the field, CBT is also practised by psychiatrists, general practitioners and a range of other clinicians.

CBT is employed in various forms in almost all psychiatric disorders. Its efficacy in depression and anxiety disorders has the largest research base, but CBT also appears to be effective in eating disorders, personality disorders and schizophrenia. CBT can be delivered individually or in groups, and there are even online versions of it. It is a highly flexible and adaptive form of psychotherapy. A typical course of CBT is one session per week for six to twelve weeks.

The basic principle is that thoughts lead to feelings, which lead to behaviours. Each influences the others. If you can identify the thoughts, then you can help modify feelings and behaviours. Similarly, if you can change behaviours, you can alter feelings and thoughts. And so on. CBT therapists work with thoughts, feelings and behaviours.

CBT is very active. The goal is change, not self-understanding. It is best understood by thinking about the two key parts – the cognitive part and the behaviour part.

The cognitive aspect of CBT looks at the way people think and how those thoughts lead to feelings and behaviours. There are many techniques used to recognise and change thinking patterns. For example, the therapist might look for 'automatic thoughts', which are thoughts that immediately pop into our heads in certain situations and influence our behaviour.

A common everyday example is a person facing a social gathering such as a party. They might automatically think: 'I'll hate it. I'll feel uncomfortable. Everyone will be talking and I'll be left alone. I can't socialise well.' The therapist will help break down the thoughts, perhaps explore the evidence for and against this belief, and then challenge the thoughts.

The therapist and patient might set some goals about the next time the person is invited to a party – they might include the patient challenging their thoughts, setting the plan of attending the party, and perhaps some strategies to deal with anxiety leading into the party. This is a very simple example; the actual work is more sophisticated and detailed, of course.

Each of us has different ways of thinking and reacting to particular situations. We often focus on certain aspects – perhaps sometimes the negative aspects. This might be based on our past experiences and the expectations we've developed. The goal of the cognitive aspect of CBT is to recognise these thoughts and develop strategies to change them.

The behavioural aspect of CBT is based on the idea of classical conditioning. The most famous example is Pavlov's dog. Pavlov rang a bell every time he fed his dog. The dog became conditioned to expect food every time he heard a bell, and so began to salivate when the bell sounded, even when there was no food. The same happens with humans. We become conditioned to develop particular emotional responses following certain events.

The simplest example is phobias – irrational fears of certain situations. A child might have been scratched badly by a cat, and thereafter develop a fear of cats. The mere sight of a cat might bring back strong feelings of fear. The child may react by avoiding any contact with cats, reinforcing their fear.

Some of the strategies used in CBT include:

- psychoeducation – education about the psychological processes that underlie the mental health problem the patient is presenting with, such as depression or anxiety
- goal setting – CBT is a focused therapy; goals are set, and tasks are developed to reach those goals
- homework – an integral part of CBT. The therapy sessions are only part of the process. Homework tasks are set to change cognitions and develop new behaviours.
- monitoring – change in CBT is constantly monitored. Often the patient will keep a diary to monitor symptoms: for example, a mood diary including a daily score for depression, notes any significant events and allows the patient to see their progress and find the triggers for low mood
- practical skills – a range of skills may be taught as part of CBT, depending on the problem being treated. Examples include:
  - relaxation training
  - social skills training
  - role play to overcome negative self-talk.
- behavioural hierarchies – most behavioural problems can be broken down into small steps. Take, for example, something simple like a fear of snakes. Various elements of the fear could be noted and built into a hierarchy from least fearful to most fearful. The hierarchy might include looking at pictures of a snake, seeing a movie of a snake, being present in a room with a dead snake, touching a dead snake, being present in a room with a live snake,

and finally touching a live snake. Each step will be approached from the easiest to the hardest, with relaxation skills and negative thoughts being considered along the way. A new step isn't attempted until the previous step is mastered.

CBT is constantly being adapted and developed to treat a wider range of disorders. Various new therapies have been developed based on CBT principles, but with a new element to them. Some examples of these are:

- **Mindfulness-based cognitive therapy (MBCT).** MBCT takes many of the principles of CBT and combines them with mindfulness. Mindfulness borrows ideas from Buddhist philosophies of meditation and awareness. It was originally developed for depression, but is now used widely in other disorders. There are many simple phone and computer apps to aid the practice of mindfulness, which are often used in conjunction with face-to-face therapy

- **Acceptance and commitment therapy (ACT).** ACT also embraces mindfulness, especially the element of accepting and being aware of feelings. The focus is on learning to acknowledge uncomfortable feelings and choosing behaviours (actions) that are not destructive.

- **Dialectical behaviour therapy (DBT).** DBT was developed for personality disorders. It includes elements of CBT, with particular emphasis on life skills training, mindfulness and attention to self-harm and the factors that influence self-harm. DBT is particularly useful for borderline personality disorder.

Supportive psychotherapy

Supportive psychotherapy has different meanings to different therapists. It is a catch-all term to mean any psychotherapy that aims to help and support a person, but without necessarily having a particular theoretical orientation. In a sense, it is what any clinician does when they regularly consult with a patient in difficulty, but without taking them down one of the more formal psychotherapy pathways.

Supportive psychotherapy uses any technique that is seen to be useful for a particular problem. The therapist is willing to chop and change. It is often applied in conjunction with other treatments. For example, a patient being prescribed medications will usually see their clinician regularly for medication review, but will also talk about their problems – how they are coping, their relationships and their current stressors.

Typical techniques might include:

- relaxation training
- problem-solving techniques – these are simple approaches used commonly in various therapies. For example, the clinician might ask the patient to state a problem, list the various options to solve the problem, and then for each examine the pros and cons. Finally, one of the options is chosen, and the pathways to achieve that solution are discussed and planned.
- sleep hygiene – sleep hygiene or sleep training is a simple but very important skill. Inadequate sleep leading to daytime fatigue is one of the most common problems in any mental health disorder. Sleep hygiene helps a person look at their sleep patterns and habits, and find

simple solutions to improve sleep. The basic principles
include:

- learning your sleep body clock and adapting it so you
  sleep when you need to: for example, getting up at the
  same time every day, avoiding daytime naps unless
  they are part of your routine, etc.
- adapting your sleep environment to reduce noise, get
  the right temperature and light (or lack of light), and
  minimise non-sleep activities (other than sex) so
  your body gets trained to sleep in your bedroom
- avoiding drugs that disrupt sleep – no caffeine after
  about 6 pm, minimise alcohol (it makes you sleep, but
  wakes you after about four hours), and avoid nicotine
  at night
- relaxation training for sleep – this may be progressive
  muscle relaxation or hypnosis techniques.

- anger management – teaches people to recognise their
  anger and their triggers, and then develop strategies to
  control anger and its outcomes.
- adherence strategies – because supportive therapy is often
  part of other treatments, helping people to think about
  adherence is a vital part of any therapy. Poor adherence
  is probably the single biggest reason any treatment fails
  from antibiotics to antidepressants. Adherence strategies
  help the patient understand their own views about
  treatment, the challenges faced when on treatment, and
  the various approaches that can make it easier. These
  might include simple problem solving such as an alarm
  reminder for taking tablets, or more complex issues such

as addressing ambivalence about receiving treatments and philosophical angst about taking medications.

Interpersonal psychotherapy

Interpersonal psychotherapy was developed in the United States and borrowed some elements from CBT (time-limited, structured, active) but moved the focus of attention away from thoughts/feelings/actions, towards relationships and their impact on emotions and behaviours.

The basic principle is that there is a strong correlation between the way we function in relationships and our mental health. If we can function better in relationships (of all sorts, not just intimate relationships) then we will improve our mental health.

IP is structured; there is an assessment and then various phases. It typically takes about twelve to sixteen weeks. Each phase has various goals. It was initially developed for depression, but has been adapted for a range of other disorders. There is a strong research base to back up its effectiveness.

IP is particularly useful where there is a strong element of relationship problems that are interacting with the patient's mental health, either as a cause or consequence.

The core elements of therapy are:

- interpersonal inventory – the early phase of treatment examines all significant relationships, their history, and their impact on the patient
- depending on which are present in any given relationship, addressing some or all of the four key problem areas in relationships:
  - grief – a key part of relationships, either in the lead-up

to a loss or in the aftermath. Grief counselling is a core component of IPT.

- interpersonal disputes – examining covert or overt disputes within relationships that are contributing to mental health problems.
- role transitions – relationships go through various changes over time, and these changes may affect mental health. Furthermore, changes in mental health (or other changes, such as job losses) can affect relationships. IPT examines the impact of changing relationships on mental health.
- interpersonal sensitivity – each of us has interpersonal strengths and weaknesses. Examining interpersonal sensitivity is about looking at how we function in relationships and developing strategies to improve our relationship functioning.

Counselling

The term counselling is used very broadly. In fact, anyone can call themselves a counsellor if they wish – it is not regulated, as are terms like doctor, psychologist or psychiatrist. In essence, a counsellor is a person who has trained in helping people in a specific problem area. For example, a relationship counsellor will have training in the skills of providing therapy, plus specific training in relationships – relationship phases, functioning, problems, break-ups and so on. A career counsellor will have training in providing therapy, plus training in all aspects of careers – how to choose a career, suitability for a career, obtaining the skills for a career and entering the job market.

Of course, the counselling field being so broad and so inclusive means there is huge variability in the skills and techniques of different counsellors. Some are highly skilled with years of training: for example, social workers are often called counsellors and many have years of training in all sorts of therapeutic techniques. On the other hand, some counsellors may have only done a six-week course and provide very basic and simple support.

Counselling can be done in groups or individually. It can be based on any of the psychological approaches used in other therapies (psychodynamic, cognitive and so on) or it can be *atheoretical*, meaning it is not based on a psychological theory but rather on a focussed understanding of a particular problem.

The most common sorts of counselling are:

- grief counselling – dealing with loss, in particular after the death of loved ones.
- relationship counselling – sometimes called marriage counselling, aiming to help relationships survive or people cope after they break down
- careers counselling – helping people choose or develop their career.
- drug and alcohol counselling
- counselling for mood and anxiety disorders
- student counselling – focusing on the problems facing students and helping them adapt to their educational environment.
- sex therapy – sex therapists have a broad range of backgrounds. Most are psychologists or counsellors who have trained extensively in human sexuality. The therapy

includes education, exploration of beliefs and practices around sexuality, tips about changing sexual behaviours and homework exercises.

What next?

Choosing the right psychotherapy is a tricky process. It's not as simple as choosing a medication, because all medications are readily available, are of similar cost, have a fairly easy-to-understand evidence base, and you don't necessarily need good rapport with the prescriber or pharmacist for them to work.

Rapport describes your relationship with the therapist. It's whether you trust them, whether you feel they want to help and understand you, and whether you understand them and their approach. In a sense, it's the culmination of the four factors described by Jerome Frank at the start of this chapter. It's hard to research, but most in the field think rapport is an important element of successful therapy. It's hard to work with a therapist unless you feel you have a good rapport.

And finally, psychotherapies are not all equally available – especially in rural areas. The costs vary significantly, as do the skill levels between therapists. Finding the right therapist, offering the right therapy, near you, at a cost you can afford, is a challenge. But a challenge worth taking.

The simplest approach is to see a general clinician, get their opinion on who they recommend and think you will get along with, and what's available near you in your price range. The type of therapy will also depend on your particular problem, and the approach that you believe will best suit your personality and beliefs. And remember, all medicine involves some educated guess work and trial and error, so whatever you end up choosing, give it a fair go. If you have reservations or concerns, don't be shy – discuss them with your therapist. If the doubt is strong, get a second opinion.

Psychotherapy can be enormously rewarding. Many people find it life-changing, and some lifesaving. Both of us (Steve and Dev) have tried it (see our chapters on our own experiences) but in a nutshell, we found it to be both helpful and our preferred type of treatment. We hope you find as much benefit as we did.

Medications

Medications in psychiatry are still controversial. Some people see them as magic pills that can take away life's worries without any significant risks; others as the evil manifestation of 'big pharma' greed, created to medicalise the human condition for the benefit of corporate profit. Many people feel medication for mental issues is an affront to the essence of humanity – they alter the way we experience and react to life's ups and downs and so rob us of the natural experience of life. To a greater or lesser degree, each of these statements is true. Choosing a drug that will alter you – your emotions, your senses, perhaps even your personality – is considerably different to taking a medication to kill an infection, reduce pain or treat a condition like diabetes.

But doctors, when faced with a patient who is suffering, more often than not turn to medications. This is the most natural response. Doctors are not trained to explore the philosophy of prescribing medications. They are trained to recognise syndromes, disorders and diseases, and then recommend the best treatment scientific evidence has to offer. They do this under various constraints – mostly time constraints, sometimes cost constraints and the limits of their own belief systems.

Medications for mental health problems are faster to deliver than psychological approaches and usually cheaper. Therefore, they are the most popular treatments despite scientific evidence suggesting they are not always the most effective. They're easy to prescribe, cheap to buy and simple to take – so it's no wonder that busy doctors and overwhelmed patients reach for tablets ahead of anything else.

In the UK, GPs provide the majority of professional care for psychological problems, and prescribe medications in about 70 per cent of consultations. But it is important to remember that the final decision rests with the patient. A doctor can only recommend what he or she considers the best option – you, the patient, need to agree. Even if you are an involuntary patient, you have some choice – you may be compelled to have treatment, but you can still influence the type of treatment.

Good doctors give the patient information and let them decide. They tell them about the desired effects of the drug, the chances of success and the side effects. If they think the patient is taking the decision too lightly (some patients do), they emphasise some of the risks and encourage discussion. If the patient is struggling to make a decision, good doctors explore their concerns. Sometimes patients ask for the doctor's personal opinion: 'I know you're telling me all the pros and cons, Doc, but if you were in my position, what would you do?' A good doctor will then give their personal opinion, but stress that 'each of us is different'.

Doctors' personal opinions vary widely. Some think medications are the bee's knees and prescribe them for everything. Others think they are a last resort when psychotherapies or other approaches fail or are impractical. It would be nice if it were simple, but it's not!

No decision to use medication in psychiatry should be taken lightly. If you think your doctor is a cowboy with a 'shoot first, ask questions later' approach to prescribing, then slow her or him down with questions. If that doesn't work, seek a second opinion.

All of the medications in this chapter require a prescription from a doctor. Prescribing medications properly requires effort – it's not as simple as just writing the script and handing it over. The doctor and patient should discuss how to use the drug, what to expect, the side effects and what will happen if it doesn't work.

The information in this chapter is general – it is not enough to properly prepare anyone for taking medication. There are lots of rules, tips and tricks for getting the most out of drugs – and just as many exceptions to the rules. Nothing can replace discussion with your doctor.

Medications 101

Every medication in all of medicine has side effects. Every medication has a chance of working and a chance of making you worse (and a chance of doing nothing). Every time you take a drug, for any purpose, it's an experiment – you have no way of knowing whether it will work.

For medications to get approval by government authorities, they have to have been through years of testing, they have to have been proven to be effective (or at least equivalent to current therapies) and they have to be relatively safe, with the benefits outweighing the risks.

All drugs have the potential to interact with each other. Most of the interactions are mild, but the more drugs you're on, the greater the potential for interactions. Your doctor or pharmacist can look up detailed tables and databases that predict all the possible interactions so you can weigh up the risks – but you need to tell your doctor and pharmacist what you are on so they can investigate: don't forget! Take along a list if necessary. This includes over-the-counter supplements, vitamins, herbal remedies and every alternative therapy.

Every medication needs to be taken as recommended or they don't work. Non-adherence is a big problem in health care generally, and psychiatry is no exception. Some studies suggest that about a quarter of all drugs prescribed don't work because they are taken incorrectly. The dosing schedules associated with the medications are well researched. They take into account the metabolism of the drug, the 'therapeutic range' (the dose range that produces the desired effects) and the dose-related side effects.

Most drugs have a minimum effective dose, and if you don't get to that dose you may as well be taking a sugar tablet. Antidepressants are a classic example. Below the minimum recommended dose you get no effect at all.

Your doctor will make dose changes according to your weight, age and any medical illnesses you have. Obviously children and adults with lower weight need lower doses. Also, some medical problems change the drug metabolism, so the dose needs to be adjusted to ensure you get the right amount in your body.

Finally, many drugs have the potential to affect pregnancy.

Some affect the baby and can cause foetal abnormalities. There are huge databases that list all of the risks in pregnancy and give estimated probabilities of problems. If there is any chance you are pregnant, you must discuss it with your doctor and if in doubt they can easily do a pregnancy test before they prescribe anything for you. This also goes for taking drugs during a time when you may become pregnant. Some drugs are so risky we only prescribe them to women on contraception. This does *not* mean you cannot take medications when pregnant (some are very safe); it simply means you must consider the issues, choose the best medication with the least risks, and weigh up the pros and cons. If there is any chance you are pregnant, tell your doctor and pharmacist.

Things to consider when deciding on medications

- There are no objective tests to predict an individual's response.
- It's best to try one drug at a time – single drug therapy is preferable.
- Choice of drug often depends on which side effect profile is most tolerable for the patient.
- Different drugs interact with each other, so always tell your doctor all the drugs you are taking.
- Use medications that are easy to take, e.g. once daily.
- Use medications that the doctor is familiar with; fewer mistakes will be made.
- Don't always leap at the latest medication to hit the market.

Older drugs are tried and tested, and if you've had a previous good response, the chances are it will work again.

Categories of medication

There are four main types of medications in mental health:
- antidepressants
- anti-psychotics
- anti-anxiety medications (also called anxiolytics)
- mood stabilisers.

Even though there are many drugs within each category, they are all pretty similar in how effective they are and how long they take to work. The main difference are between the medications in each group are their side effects.

Each type is used for multiple disorders or problems, so don't be too fixated about the category. For example, antidepressants are not just used for depression – they are also used for anxiety, pain and other problems.

All (except benzodiazepines) are slow to start working, so most people need lots of reassurance and explanation in the early phase so that they don't quit taking the medication before the benefits become tangible. Also, many people get the side effects before the benefits – they need to be warned of this so they don't get disheartened.

Antidepressants

Antidepressants are mainly used to treat depression, anxiety, pain disorders, insomnia and bulimia nervosa. All antidepressants take between two and six weeks to work. You need to take them daily for them to be effective – you can't skip doses based on how you feel. The effectiveness drops off if you miss a dose. When used for depression, all antidepressants are equally effective, with a response rate of about 55 per cent, compared to a placebo response rate of about 35 per cent. Once the person improves, they need to continue taking the medication for between six and twelve months – longer if it is a recurrent disorder or symptoms tend to return.

The choice of antidepressant is based on past response and the side-effect profile. If the first one a person tries hasn't worked after six weeks, then it's best to swap to a different type and try that for six weeks. Just because the first didn't work does not mean the next won't – like all medicine there is an element of trial and error, and there is no way of guessing in advance which will be the right one for a particular person. Most of the side effects are relatively mild and tend to go away after a few weeks. Some antidepressants are dangerous in overdose, but these tend to be the older types, which are less commonly prescribed. The antidepressants released in the last twenty years are mostly safe in overdose, and so they tend to be the ones tried first.

All antidepressants have a dose range – a minimum and a maximum. These are determined by research before the drug is released to the market. The minimum dose is the smallest amount that has been shown to be effective. If you are on less than the minimum dose, the drug is unlikely to work. The maximum dose is the dose that has been shown to be safe, or after which there is no increased chance of the drug working (but probably a higher chance of side effects). The starting dose tends to be even lower than the minimum dose (this reduces the chance of side effects) and is gradually increased until the minimum effective dose is reached. The dose is increased until either the drug works or side effects become a problem. If it doesn't work or the person cannot tolerate the drug, then we swap and try a different antidepressant.

The course of improvement fluctuates. It tends to be three steps forward, one step back. So don't get put off if, after early signs of improvements appear, you slip back – this is normal. After about three months the fluctuations tend to disappear and it's a steadier course of improvement from then on.

Antidepressants are not believed to be addictive, but some people do get withdrawal symptoms. They are mostly mild, and less likely if you gradually reduce the dose before stopping completely. The antidepressants known as SSRIs (Selective Serotin Reuptake Inhibitors) have a specific withdrawal syndrome and abrupt discontinuation has been fatal in some cases.

Common withdrawal symptoms from antidepressant medications

General symptoms: fatigue, headache, sweating and a mild flu-like illness

Sleep: insomnia, vivid dreams

Movement: unsteadiness, abnormal jerky movements, restlessness

Mood: lowered mood, irritability, crying

Others: dizziness, odd physical sensations

The following table lists some of the common antidepressants and gives an indication of common side effects.

Drug	Usual daily dose (mg)	Insomnia	Sedation	Sexual dysfunc- tion[1]	Agitation	Gastro- intestinal[2]	Weight gain
Citalopram	10–40	••	••	•••	•	••	•
Fluoxetine	10–80	••	••	•••	•	••	•
Fluvoxamine	50–200	••	•	•••	••	••	•
Paroxetine	10–50	••	••	•••	•	••	••
Sertraline	25–200	••	••	•••	••	•••	•
Mitrazapine	15–60	•••	•••	•	•	•	•••
Moclobemide	300– 600	••	••	•	•	••	–
Reboxetine	4–10	•••	–	•	•	•	–
Venlafaxine	75–300	••	••	•••	••	•••	•

–   Negligible/absent (<2% chance)

•   Infrequent (>2% chance)

••   Moderately frequent (>10% chance)

••• Frequent (>30% chance)

1. May include decreased libido, anorgasmia and ejaculatory disturbance.

2. May include nausea, anorexia, diarrhoea and abdominal discomfort;
    taking the antidepressant after food may reduce nausea.

Anti-anxiety medications

Anti-anxiety medications refer to a group of drugs that have a variety of effects but are primarily used to treat anxiety. The most common anti-anxiety drugs are the benzodiazepines. Benzodiazepines include drugs like diazepam (Valium), alprazolam (Xanax), oxazepam (Serax) and temazepam (Normison,

Restoril).

As mentioned previously, antidepressants have largely re-placed anti-anxiety drugs for the treatment of anxiety, especially if the anxiety is long-standing or treatment is planned for more than a few months. Nevertheless, anti-anxiety drugs still have a key role to play, especially in acute anxiety that needs to be treated rapidly, or as an addition to other medications.

Benzodiazepines

Benzodiazepines have multiple properties, including muscle relaxation, sedation and psychological relaxation (anti-anxiety). They are also anticonvulsant, meaning they can stop and prevent seizures. As a consequence, they are used for a range of problems other than anxiety, including insomnia, muscle spasm, seizures, and drug and alcohol withdrawal.

The main risk of benzodiazepines, and the reason they have fallen from favour, is addiction.

When benzodiazepines first hit the market in the 1960s they were seen as miracle drugs. Back then, there was almost an epidemic of sedative drugs that caused death in overdose – the barbiturates. These were highly effective at reducing anxiety in a time when there were few, if any, decent alternatives. The benefits of relaxation, exercise, nutrition and psychotherapy were not known at that time. Barbiturate use was widespread and dangerous. So when the benzodiazepines hit the market, they were a huge improvement: they led to less barbiturate use and fewer deaths. By the 1980s benzodiazepines were the largest selling anti-anxiety drugs worldwide.

But in the 1990s the alarm bells started ringing. Some

studies suggested they weren't as effective for long-term anxiety problems as originally thought. Other studies suggested antidepressants were more effective. And the benefits of psychotherapy, particularly cognitive behaviour therapy, started to emerge. Finally, the risks of addiction became better understood, and the benzodiazepines were found to be quite addictive. Addiction means two things – tolerance and withdrawal. Tolerance means you need higher doses the longer you take a drug. Withdrawal means that when you stop you have some sort of syndrome related to your body having a chemical dependence on the drug.

Long-term benzodiazepine use can lead to higher doses. Higher doses mean more side effects – impaired thinking and memory, and excessive sedation during the day. Once this happens, withdrawal becomes a problem. It's very hard to stop benzodiazepines – people feel anxious and crave the drug. Also, the physical effects are prominent – in severe cases of withdrawal people can have seizures, which can be life-threatening. Medical supervision and slow tapering are usually required.

However, like any medication, the difference between a poison and a cure is how the drug is used. If used in appropriate doses with careful supervision and for clear reasons, benzodiazepines are safe and effective.

Here are some tips for safe use:

- Use the benzodiazepines for short periods, unless you have a long-term condition and are under medical supervision.
- If you're using them for sleep, don't take them for more than a few days in a row. By preference, every third night go without (and expect a poor night's sleep) and only for

a few weeks at a time.

- Beware of the maximum dose and never go over. If you find you need more, you are probably addicted and need to think about how to cut back or stop (there are lots of ways: ask your doctor).
- Consider the alternatives – there are many other options: relaxation, cutting back on caffeine, brief psychotherapies, yoga, exercise, antidepressants, melatonin and other supplements available without prescription.
- If you need to stop after being on benzodiazepines for more than about two months, speak to your doctor to get help.

In terms of choosing the right benzodiazepine, there is no evidence that one is superior to another, but different ones tend to be chosen for different problems. The longer-acting benzo-diazepines tend to be used for anxiety, and the shorter-acting ones for sleep. Unfortunately, it's not easy to accurately predict the duration of action in an individual, because it depends on the drug and your body – how you absorb it, your health and other factors. The table overleaf gives a *rough* guide to how long you can expect the effects of the medication to last.

Buspirone

Buspirone is an unusual anti-anxiety medication in that, like antidepressants, it takes up to two weeks to work. Research suggests it is effective in some anxiety disorders (mainly generalised anxiety disorder). The good news is it has relatively little sedation and is not addictive, compared to benzodiazepines. One of the reasons it isn't popular is that it is rapidly metabolised, so you

Drug	Usual dose range	Trade names	Duration of action
Benzodiazepines			
Predominantly anxiolytic			
Alprazolam	0.5–4 mg/day	Xanax	Short
Clonazepam	2–6 mg/day	Rivotril	Long
Diazepam	2–40 mg/day	Valium	Long
Lorazepam	1–10 mg/day	Ativan	Short
Oxazepam	30–90 mg/day	Serax	Short
Predominantly hypnotic			
Nitrazepam	4–10 mg/day	Mogadon	Short
Temazepam	10–30 mg/day	Normison, Restoril	Short
Non-benzodiazepines			
Buspirone	20–30 mg/day	Buspar	Short
Zopiclone	Up to 7.5 mg/day	Zimovane	Short
Zolpidem	5–10 mg/day	Stilnoct	Short

need to take it three times a day. It's worth considering as an alternative to benzodiazepines for anxiety if you're worried about addiction and antidepressants have been tried without success.

Anti-psychotics

The history of anti-psychotic drugs is fascinating and frustrating in equal parts. Prior to 1950, there were no drugs for treating psychoses. Many patients with a psychosis went to hospital and lived there for the rest of their lives. Patients with manic psychosis often died from uncontrollable agitation – they wouldn't sleep or eat or stay still. Sometimes the only way to keep them alive was intermittently holding them down and giving them a mix of high-energy foods such as eggs, milk and nutrients through a tube to their stomach. Many died.

The first anti-psychotic drug (Chlorpromazine) was discovered by chance in 1951. At that time it was considered a wonder drug: for the first time there was a treatment for schizophrenia. It was genuinely a major step forward. Its use spread rapidly throughout the world.

Other drugs with similar properties followed. Unfortunately, problems started to emerge. Some patients didn't respond. Others developed major side effects – the most notorious being involuntary movement disorders. As a result, patients often hated being on the drugs. Clinicians and families were left trying to convince patients the side effects were better than having delusions and hallucinations – but the patients didn't always agree.

A new wave of anti-psychotics began arriving in the 1990s – so called 'atypical' anti-psychotics (sometimes called second-generation anti-psychotics). They were atypical in that they had far fewer movement-related side effects and were easier to take. Unfortunately, other side effects emerged, in particular weight gain, with the risk of diabetes.

Nevertheless, anti-psychotics are still the only effective treatment for psychotic symptoms such as hallucinations and delusions. As problematic as they are, they are life-saving for many.

Benefits

Anti-psychotic drugs are mainly used to treat psychosis from any of its causes – schizophrenia, bipolar disorder, severe depression with psychotic symptoms, and the organic psychoses like delirium. Some are also used in bipolar disorder for the treatment of depression or mania, or for the prevention of further episodes (even in the absence of psychotic symptoms).

Some are also used in other non-psychotic conditions, such as behavioural disturbance in dementia, and occasionally in childhood behavioural disorders, although this is controversial.

Even more controversial, some of the anti-psychotics are used in anxiety disorders, although debate rages as to whether the risk of side effects outweighs the benefits when there are far safer treatments available. The more common view is that medications with this level of risk should be a last resort only after psychotherapies and antidepressants have been unsuccessful.

Important tips for taking anti-psychotics:

- In terms of effectiveness, they are all about equal, with the possible exception of clozapine, which seems to be better for the treatment of chronic schizophrenia where other treatments haven't worked.
- The choice of drug relates to the side effect profile, with the newer agents being favoured because of their lower rate of causing movement disorders.
- Side effects, especially weight gain, diabetes and hypertension, must be closely monitored.
- Clozapine can cause a rare but potentially fatal blood disorder, and as a consequence all patients must be on a blood monitoring program where they have weekly or

monthly blood tests. The drug is not dispensed unless the blood tests are done. With the blood monitoring, it is as safe as the other anti-psychotics. Cardiac monitoring is also required.

- Movement disorders, which are far less common with the newer atypical anti-psychotics, are called extrapyramidal side effects (EPSE). They are mostly treatable by dose reduction, medication change or other drugs added to stop EPSE. They are:
  - acute dystonia (muscle stiffness that can be life-threatening if in the larynx)
  - Parkinsonism (a reversible form of Parkinson's syndrome, consisting of muscle stiffness, tremor and difficulty initiating movements)
  - akathisia (a sort of restlessness)
  - tardive dyskinesia (a delayed-onset movement problem that is very serious because it is sometimes irreversible).

- A rare but potentially fatal side effect to be aware of is neuroleptic malignant syndrome (NMS), which causes fever, muscle stiffness, hypertension and confusion. If this occurs, hospital admission and emergency treatment are required.

Some antipsychotics can be given by injection. The injections can be with a short-acting drug or long-acting drug (up to a month), which are called 'depot' injections. These are useful when adherence is a problem.

The following table lists the main drugs and the key side effects.

Drug	Usual daily dose (mg)	Sedation	Postural hypo-tension[1]	Anti-cholinergic[2]	Extra-pyramidal	Weight gain
Amisupride	100–1000	•	•	–	•	•
Aripiprazole	10–30	–	•	•	•	•
Chlorpromazine	75–500	• • •	• • •	• • •	• •	• • •
Clozapine	200–600	• • •	• • •	• • •	–	• • •
Haloperidol	1–10	•	•	•	• • •	• •
Olanzapine	5–20	• •	•	• •	•	•
Quetiapine	300–750	• • •	• •	•	•	• •
Risperidone	2–6	• • (initially)	• • • (initially)	–	• •	• •
Trifluoperazine	2–6	•	• •	•	• • •	• •
Ziprasidone	80–160	• •	•	•	•	•

–   Negligible/absent (<2% chance)

•   Infrequent (>2% chance)

••   Moderately frequent (>10% chance)

•••   Frequent (>30% chance)

1. A fall in blood pressure (causing dizziness) when going from lying down or sitting to standing.
2. May include blurred vision, dry mouth, constipation, dizziness and, if severe, urinary retention and confusion.

Mood stabilisers

Mood stabilisers are a special group of drugs that are mainly used in bipolar disorder. They are used to treat episodes of mania and depression and as prophylaxis against further episodes. When used effectively in bipolar disorder, they add enormous stability to what might otherwise be a chaotic life. They have saved countless lives through prevention of suicide and death from manic excitement.

In recent years, the use of mood stabilisers has also extended to augmenting treatment in schizophrenia and non-bipolar depression, although the research supporting their role in these disorders is not as strong.

The three main mood stabiliser drugs are lithium, valproate and carbamazepine. All have significant side effects. Lithium has the strongest research behind it, but it requires careful blood monitoring, as the therapeutic window is narrow. This means that if you take too little it is ineffective, but if you take too much it is toxic. However, with good monitoring, lithium can be taken safely for years. In the UK, the NICE quality standard states that women of child-bearing potential should not be prescribed Valproate as it can harm their unborn baby.

All mood stabilisers have problems during pregnancy and breastfeeding. However, the risks are well known, and are mainly a problem in the first three months of pregnancy. With careful planning and monitoring, the risks can be minimised significantly and women with bipolar disorder can safely manage their illness and have children. All psychiatrists and obstetricians are well aware of these risks and can easily give advice to women with bipolar disorder planning a family.

When used for prevention in bipolar disorder, mood stabilisers reduce both the number and the severity of depressive and manic relapses. Knowing when to start a mood stabiliser for prevention is contentious since the drugs need to be taken long-term and usually blood monitoring is required (especially for lithium, but some monitoring is advisable for valproate and carbamazepine as well). Some clinicians recommend starting after a single episode of mania; others wait for at least two episodes of either depression or mania within a two-year period.

Most people taking these drugs are initially reluctant to go on them long-term. When free from mania and depression, they don't feel the need for treatment and they don't want the burden of side effects. Some studies suggest that people with bipolar disorder usually wait about five to seven years before accepting prophylactic treatment.

It's a very difficult decision for a person to make. Until they know how severe their bipolar disorder is, they usually don't want to commit to long-term medications. Yet delaying treatment can result in relapses, which carry high risks. The risks from mania include long periods off work, damage to reputation, financial loss, and periods in hospital, often as an involuntary patient. The risks in depression are similar, and include the risk of suicide.

If a person with bipolar disorder chooses not to go on medication for prevention, they should have a robust plan in place to recognise relapses early so treatment can commence quickly before the episodes progress too far.

*

The last seventy or so years have truly seen a revolution in mental health care on the back of the four classes of drugs described above. Quite literally, millions of lives have been saved and countless more have been improved.

Despite this, many people (especially those unaware of the history of mental illness prior to 1950) are still suspicious of medications or at least wary of their use. Some of this is well justified – overuse has led to unnecessary treatment and unnecessary side effects. The influences of those who have profited from the sale of medications has also, at times, damaged the progress of psychopharmacology.

The key to determining if these medications are right for you is to strip away the rhetoric and focus on the evidence. What illness do you have? What medications are recommended? How strong is the evidence base for them? What are the pros and cons (side effects)? And are there non-pharmacological alternatives to consider first?

All of this requires careful thought. This means you must speak to doctors who know the answers to these questions – not cowboys who reach for the prescription pad before they understand your problems.

The advice in this chapter is very general and should not take the place of a conversation with your doctor.

20

Physical Treatments

The term 'physical treatments' is an odd one. It describes a broad group of treatments where something 'physical' is done – such as surgery, neurostimulation or electroconvulsive therapy. Many of the most controversial treatments in psychiatry fall into this category.

Physical treatments also feature prominently in the history of psychiatry – treatments that have long since been abandoned but, quite frankly, sometimes crossed the line into shameful and at times probably criminal use. Deep sleep therapy (making the patient unconscious for days or weeks in the mistaken belief it would treat psychosis) falls into this category.

Much of the criticism of psychiatry stems from the past use of various physical treatments, often applied involuntarily to patients, or for scientific purposes without adequate ethical guidelines or worst of all, for political purposes. Even some of the physical treatments that survive today and are quite effective have a history that includes misuse or experimentation, which leaves a dark cloud over them that will never be erased. Electroconvulsive therapy (shock therapy) and psychosurgery (lobotomy) are the most obvious examples. Both were developed and used, not always but at some times in their history, in ways that crossed serious ethical boundaries.

The challenge today is to try to separate evidence from hyperbole. Advocates tend to oversell some of these treatments, perhaps to justify the past. Critics tend to prematurely dismiss these treatments, unable to forgive the past. The goal of this chapter is not to judge the history and not to debate the controversial and extensive scientific evidence base – but rather to describe the treatments and let you as the reader decide (in discussion with your own clinician) whether any are of value.

Electroconvulsive therapy (ECT)

Most people are unaware that electroconvulsive therapy, often called 'shock' therapy, is a common treatment. On any given day, thousands of people around the world have ECT. Most psychiatrists will tell you that it is still the most effective treatment ever discovered for depression, and in severe depression with suicidal ideas and marked agitation or retardation (slowing of all movements) it is often life-saving, and sometimes the *only* treatment that works. They will also say that while it does occur all over the world, it should be used more often – if it were, many more lives would be saved.

Despite this, ECT is by far the most controversial treatment used by psychiatrists. It evokes movie images of patients strapped to tables, screaming, as electrodes are applied and they have a seizure – think *One Flew over the Cuckoo's Nest*. Some people see it as a form of mind control or, worse still, a barbaric torture applied to non-conforming patients. This misunderstanding arose from its early history, but is far from the truth today.

ECT was first developed in 1938 after a long-noted observation that patients who suffered seizures sometimes showed improvement in their mental illness. Various ways to induce seizures were explored, before an Italian neurologist and psychiatrist, Ugo Cerletti, discovered that electricity applied to the brain could produce a reliable and safe seizure. For the first decade or so, it was done without anaesthesia. The patient didn't remember anything because they became unconscious as soon as the electricity was applied. But as with any seizure, the patient thrashed around, creating a dramatic and confronting scene.

Modern ECT is performed in hospitals under anaesthetic. The patient receives a light anaesthetic, has a rubber mouthguard placed between their teeth (in case they bite during the seizure and damage their teeth) and then two small electrodes are placed on their head and a small electrical current is passed between the electrodes. This results in an immediate seizure. The seizure usually lasts a minute or two, but because of the drugs given with the anaesthetic, it is barely noticeable. In fact, the patient usually has special leads (EEG leads) on their head to make sure the seizure occurred. This is called 'modified' ECT – it's modified in that drugs are given to prevent the usual arm and leg movements seen in a seizure. This 'modification' prevents any damage to the limbs from thrashing about.

The patient wakes from the anaesthetic about five minutes later and doesn't remember anything from the procedure. They usually take a few hours to fully recover.

ECT usually results in a small but noticeable improvement in symptoms on the day it is given. ECT is continued every second day, usually for between six and twelve treatments, so a full course takes between two and four weeks to complete. Psychiatric medications are usually given at the same time.

ECT is most effective for depression, but it is also used for severe schizophrenia and bipolar disorder. No one knows how ECT works, despite 80 years of research. People think of it as a circuit breaker or jump start, but it's all just educated guesswork.

ECT is a very safe treatment, probably safer than most drugs. There are some small risks associated with having an anaesthetic, and some patients can injure their teeth and other bones from the seizure if it is not adequately modified. Most patients report some mild cognitive (mostly memory) effects, but they are usually short-lived. Patients sometimes report they continue for much longer, but it is hard to know whether this is due to the depression (which also affects memory) or the actual ECT treatment.

Some patients have 'continuation' ECT – meaning they continue ECT for a longer time but only once every one to eight weeks. They do this if their symptoms keep returning and medication doesn't help at all. Continuation ECT keeps symptoms at bay.

Stigma remains the biggest problem with ECT. Portrayals of the procedure in movies and the media continue to scare people. Many times when offered ECT, patients stare in disbelief and fear. Lots of explanation is required to help people make an informed decision.

Informed consent is another problematic issue with ECT. When people are seriously depressed, they are often suicidal, believe they are beyond help and have trouble concentrating – making informed consent difficult. As a consequence, most countries have laws that allow either a judge or a tribunal to make the decision for the patient (if they are assessed as legally incompetent). Many people find this troubling. For virtually every other treatment in medicine, if the patient cannot consent, the family have the final say – this should be the same for ECT. Many people obviously disagree with this view and most courts are on their side. But if the patient and their next of kin are not convinced that ECT is worthwhile, it's hard to justify giving it against their wishes.

Magnetic seizure therapy

Magnetic seizure therapy (MST) is a new treatment that aims to produce seizures, just like ECT, but without the memory side effects. The procedure is similar to ECT – a general anaesthetic and seizures every second day for a few weeks – but instead of electricity, a magnetic field is used across the brain to cause the seizure. This is said to cause fewer memory side effects, and early research is promising, but it has only been used for about a decade and the evidence is not solid enough yet to be fully accepted into mainstream medicine as an alternative to ECT. MST has only been studied and used in depression so far. Once its use is established, it will no doubt be tried in other illnesses where ECT has been shown to have a role.

It is also hoped that MST can provide a useful alternative to ECT – as a 'seizure' therapy without the stigma of ECT, which may make it more acceptable to patients and families.

Transcranial magnetic stimulation

Transcranial magnetic stimulation (TMS) is also relatively new, but is *not* a seizure therapy, and is completely different to ECT and MST.

TMS uses a metal coil placed over the patient's scalp which induces a small magnetic field that changes the activity of neurons in the brain under the coil. When placed over particular parts of the brain, it has been shown to reduce depression. The treatment is given daily (Monday to Friday) for about four to six weeks. Each treatment takes about 30 to 60 minutes. The patient sits in a chair, with no anaesthetic – it doesn't hurt. In fact, the patient usually reports feeling nothing or just a mild tingling in their skin under the coil.

TMS is being trialled in a number of conditions, including anxiety disorders, but so far is only being widely used for depression. Its efficacy seems to be moderate – not as good as ECT, and probably not quite as good as antidepressants. However, it is well tolerated and seems to have little in the way of side effects – although about 0.5 per cent of patients can have a seizure, especially if it's not performed by experts. Some people also report headaches and mild, transient changes in their hearing. No one has figured out for sure how TMS works, but it seems to alter the function of neurons in areas of the brain that seem to be related to depression. Research in this area is intense and ongoing. For those with depression who respond to TMS, up to a third relapse, so they either need ongoing TMS or another therapy after the TMS course has finished. TMS is particularly useful for patients who have not responded to medications but do not want to try ECT.

Deep brain stimulation (DBS)

DBS is still classed as an experimental procedure, meaning its use is not well established yet – more research is required. As a consequence, it tends to be done only as a last resort when all else has failed, and only after strict review by government authorities.

DBS is a surgical procedure where electrodes are implanted in the brain and connected via wires to a small generator placed under the skin somewhere near the breast. The generator sends pulses to the electrodes, which stimulate neurons and change their function.

DBS is well established as a treatment for Parkinson's disease, and has been trialled with some success in severe, treatment-resistant depression and severe obsessive-compulsive disorder.

There is ongoing research and debate about the best place in the brain to place the electrodes. DBS is only performed at specialist medical centres with combined neurosurgery, neurology and psychiatry services, and only after all other treatments have failed and in-depth assessment has occurred.

Psychosurgery

Psychosurgery (neurosurgery for mental disorders) is the most controversial psychiatric treatment of all. It is the modern name for frontal lobotomy, and is also known as 'ablative neurosurgery'. Its history is long and fraught. Psychosurgery was first developed as far back as 1890, but it became popular after it was developed by a Portuguese neurologist António Egas Moniz in the 1940s (he won a Nobel Prize for his work).

In the 1950s and '60s it was very popular, especially in the United States, where its use was unregulated and led to a range of abuses. It virtually disappeared in the '80s and '90s, but with strict regulations and further research, is now available in some places around the world, including Australia, although its use remains highly regulated and very rare.

In psychosurgery, a small part of the brain is cut, effectively rendering the circuits in that part of the brain non-functional. It cannot be reversed. In the early years, the cut was large and resulted in numerous complications and a range of psychological changes, including changes in the person's personality. Modern psychosurgery uses highly specialised instruments that can make very small cuts with very little chance of bleeding and other complications.

Psychosurgery is considered a treatment of last resort, mainly for severe, intractable obsessive-compulsive disorder, but also for severe treatment-resistant depression.

21

Self-Help (or DIY)

When it comes to mental health, the advice you hear beyond therapy and medication is almost always: exercise, nutrition, sleep, meditate – and they all sound … boring? Bland? Hard? Like the medical professional is simply reading off a 'one size fits all' drop-down menu, which can feel a bit accusatory. It's almost as if they're saying, 'If you were off the fags and the cakes and the pies and the booze and the couch, you wouldn't have any problems.' Psychological first aid is important – there is no doubt about that – but there are a lot of other things that help too. These are all within your personal power and you can get started with them while you work with a professional support team.

There is a catch when it comes to DIY. By definition, there are no experts in the field. There is no degree or training in DIY. And we're certainly not experts. We debated long and hard about including this chapter. The rest of this book is a mix of evidence, expertise and experience. But this chapter is a collection of ideas that people have found helpful. If any were truly evidence-based, they would be part of mainstream health care. However, we wanted to tell you what others say helps them in the hope you might find something that is right for you.

We both believe that it's an equation of factors that leads to being unwell, and it's an equation of factors that will help you feel well again.

We believe that doing *something* always helps, even if the thing you are doing isn't helping. The fact you are making an effort and trying to feel better is what helps. If you are frustrated with how you feel, making an attempt to shift your mood will make you feel a little less crap about yourself. Or at the very least stop you feeling worse. In many cases nothing really helps shift your mood except time. But in an attempt to make the passing of time more bearable while you are under a cloud or frazzled out of your mind, doing something will alleviate some of the stress and hopelessness of being unwell. It will also give you a small sense of control.

So our message is: when you don't know what to do, do anything. Do what you can, where you are, with what you have. Feelings are not facts; emotions change. This is just how it is now.

In the clear skies of your happy and confident times you may understand the many factors that cause and contribute to your ups and downs: biology, genetics, environmental factors, circumstances, seasonal and hormonal shifts and so on. But when we feel out of kilter, we often feel it's our fault even though we know it's not. This chapter is all about things that might help in those 'out of kilter' times.

In this chapter, we share some things – beyond medication and therapy – that have worked for us and others we know. Some things may be right up your street; others you may turn your nose up at. The suggestions in this list are not ones that doctors and shrinks usually recommend. They are suggestions you don't normally read about in books, but they are things that we know from personal experience and listening to others have helped people feel better.

You'll probably notice that most of the things in this chapter are aimed at the milder end of the spectrum of mental illness. Also, they are not meant to be 'instead of' the advice in this book, but rather 'as well as' the rest of the advice.

Change your expectations

Mental illnesses – depression and anxiety, in particular – can trick the sufferer into thinking they aren't trying hard enough. As if there were some willpower or personality trait the sufferer should be able to activate in order to overcome it. Sometimes the best approach is to let yourself off the hook for a while. Change your expectations. Be depressed and anxious. Expect it. Invite it in as though it were a guest you weren't expecting: 'Hello, take a seat. Stay as long as you like. What brings you here?'

Plan something

People need something to do, someone to love and something to look forward to. If the world is a very dark place, plan something you can look forward to. Planning a trip is the first thing that comes to mind but you could also plan an outing, a 'perfect day', a dinner party or anything that would make you feel there is some sunshine around the corner. You don't have to pay or book in these things. Just have a think about what you would love to be able to do and plan.

When Dev's twelve-year-old son was building his first gaming computer he would go on computer parts websites and just fill carts with his dream computer parts. He'd never check out but he enjoyed the pure dreaming.

Listen to music

Doctors often suggest playing music to people in a coma. The music needs to be familiar, have special meaning and be something emotionally significant. That's how powerful music can be: it can literally wake someone out of unconsciousness.

Music can do the same for your emotional state. Try making a playlist from important periods of your past: your favourite music from your teenage years, music you listened to when you travelled or when you fell in love. Music that transports you to a different time can rouse happy memories and warm feelings.

Be proactive and create some personalised musical medicine. Put together your ultimate dance, chill, cleaning, exercise or sleep mix. Music has a powerful emotional effect. Tap into tunes, beats, melodies and song to cajole yourself into a better space.

Play some music

'We don't sing because we're happy, we're happy because we sing.' Do you play an instrument? Dust it off and get out your old music. Join a choir. There are heaps of them about. Consider some music lessons. Have you always wanted to sing or learn an instrument? Find a teacher in your area and book a lesson. Even better, check out YouTube. It's full of music teachers providing free online lessons. Music is an incredible mood shifter – add to that the neurological benefits of playing or learning an instrument and you could have yourself a very effective tool in your mental health self-care tool kit. Do you like singing? Think of a song you love, find a backing track online and be a bedroom rockstar. Perhaps you need some ukulele therapy.

Learn something

Learning changes the brain. No one is sure exactly how, but it shakes it up in a good way. Learning something new can be a powerful form of therapy. Look up local courses in your area. Do a short course, whether for one day or six months. Perhaps something you have never thought of before, like pet grooming, servicing your car, pottery, quilting, music theory, shorthand, dressmaking, life drawing, learning a language, book binding – whatever takes your fancy. Or if you don't like crowds, check out YouTube or pick up a book and be your own teacher.

Garden

Neither of us are very good gardeners, but we have both experienced the unexpected joy of gardening. It has huge emotional benefits and has been documented as a particularly effective therapy for grief. Why is this? Is it about being outside? About doing a bit of honest hard work? Watching things grow? Being close to nature? A sense of achievement? All of the above.

There is something inherently hopeful about planting. It brings alive the sentiment 'do something today your future self will thank you for'.

Dev says: 'Twice over winter I have suffered deep months-long depression. In the last few years I have taken to planting bulbs in the autumn. On one of the last sunny days in March, I poke bulbs into the ground with the thought of the coming winter. The bulbs remind me that even though it may seem cold and bleak as we trudge through winter, there is growth going on under the surface invisible to the eye. Knowing the bulbs are beneath the surface doing their thing reminds me soon there will be green shoots followed by happy flowers. It's a great reminder over the winter (when I am most likely to suffer depression) that it's a cycle that's moving even when I can't see or feel it. I also give pots of bulbs to people suffering depression so they can look at the pot and see it as a metaphor. Things are changing and growing, although it may not feel like it. The thought of blossoms on the way is a comforting balm when winter feels as if it will never end.'

You don't need to plant a huge garden. But if you are into gardening, make sure you are getting out there and doing your thing. If you are not a gardener, perhaps start by taking a trip to the local nursery, buying a few bits and pieces and bunging a few seeds in a pot or some hanging baskets. You could plant a flowering shrub near a spot outdoors where you like to sit.

If you don't already have a lovely place to sit outside, create one so you can enjoy a bit of life beyond your four walls. Move your outdoor furniture around so you are in the sun or the shade, depending on the season. Rustle up a lovely blanket or a few soft cushions to take out with you so you're warm and cosy, or cool and covered.

If you are in an apartment or don't have your own garden space, you can google 'things to grow on your windowsill'. We found tulip bulbs in a vase, avocados in a jar floating in water, carrot tops on cotton wool, and growing herbs in egg shells. There are also community gardens, especially in inner city sub-urbs where space is limited, that you can join and start planting with others in your area. Don't underestimate how a little green shoot can lift your spirits.

Pets

We know not everyone can have a pet, but when you think pets, don't just think cats and dogs. What about a goldfish? Or a lizard? How about some guinea pigs? Perhaps you're a ferret kind of person. Rabbits are cute. Have you considered a worm farm? Chickens! That's what you need! A couple of chickens.

The therapeutic benefit of pets is well known. If some animal contact may help your mood, think laterally about how you could incorporate some creatures into your life temporarily or permanently. Many people love dogs but are unable to commit to keeping a dog themselves. If you are this kind of person, let people know you can take their dogs for a walk, have their pup for a sleepover, give them a bath or a brush, lock then in for a play date or even sign up to something like Borrow My Doggy. You can register yourself as a willing and responsible person and people in the area will contact you when they need a pet sitter. You decide when you would like some canine company. Don't underestimate some four-legged medicine. You can make some extra cash and perhaps even meet some new people.

Walking

If you have read this far, 'walking' being on this list won't surprise you. We all know that putting your trainers on and going for an hour's walk in the park is good for your mental health, but if that feels too hard, there is no reason you can't walk in your house. Stride up and down the backyard, do laps of your dining table. If you're feeling energetic, shuffle around the block. Put on a podcast, listen to some music or go natural and just absorb the neighbourhood sounds.

If you're feeling self-conscious drive your car to somewhere you are unlikely to bump into people you know and have a wander around in a nearby suburb.

Why don't you try walking to a coffee and back? We're big fans of dangling the carrot to get some incidental benefits in. Is there a café a walkable distance away where you could grab a coffee, juice, pie, cake or soup? Either eat in or takeaway? Why don't you set yourself a small goal of walking to and from the café with the lure of something delicious? One of the payoffs of this lure is the unexpected benefits. Sure, you are getting a walk, being outside and eating something yummy and getting a sense of achievement from setting a goal and completing it. The unexpected benefits are that you may bump into someone who makes you feel better, stumble across some beautiful street art, smell something lovely, hear some fabulous music or see a human interaction that may lift your spirits. You'll also get a dose of Vitamin D from being in the sun.

Voices in your head

We love audio books and podcasts. It's fantastic to walk and be read to. Find a great audio book and tell yourself you can only listen to it when you walk. Get into the book, you'll be dying to find out what happens next, which will get you moving and may get you feeling and sleeping better. There is a podcast for everyone in every mood and every situation. Browse around to find something that floats your boat and ask your friends for suggestions.

Volunteering/Help out

I'm sure you're thinking 'they're going to suggest the local school, local hospital or local charity'. We're not. We're suggesting helping out closer to home. Do you know someone elderly, ill, disabled, someone doing it tough or a person with kids? Cook them some food, take their dog for a walk, mind their kids, mow their lawn, clean their car, sort out their pantry, or ask them how you can help.

Helping others and being useful can give you a real lift. Many are helped far more than the people they are helping.

When people are feeling low it's not uncommon for them to miss helping others. To have not only the space in one's heart and brain but the energy to do something for another person is a luxury.

Dancing

Put on some music, close the door and dance. Don't dance like no one is watching. Dance like people are watching and you are fabulous. Dress up, nude up or rock out in your pyjamas.

Recent studies have shown regular light dancing increases muscle mass and cardio better than some of the hardcore boring exercises. If you are feeling a little braver there are plenty of dance alternatives that don't require classes, late nights, huge sums of money or costumes. Check out Zumba, Disco Yoga, and Serok.

Cooking

Some people hate cooking. If that's you, skip to the next suggestion.

If you enjoy cooking, you don't have to just cook meals for yourself, you can cook the things you love for others. How long since you have cooked biscuits, whipped up a batch of jam or chutney, made soup or baked bread? Is a school, nursery or hospital near you holding fete, fair or cake stall soon? Make contact and offer your services. You could also find some recipes on the internet for playdoh, finger paint or bubble-blowing solution and spoil the kids in your life.

The tactile experience of cooking is fun, comforting and has a happy ending. It also has incidental benefits like getting you out of the house to buy ingredients, dropping things off to people, feeling useful, making someone's day and being thanked. You could also have a look around the internet or your local newspaper for cooking classes. Organisations like soup kitchens always need people to lend a hand. Keep your eyes open and make some inquiries.

Visit your past

A journey into your past may help dislodge a little darkness and remind you of happier times that may be around the corner again soon. Make a visit to your old nursery, school, university, the first place you had a job, got drunk or fell in love. Make a journey to a place you used to live or your grandparents' old home.

If you have a bit of energy, time and cash, take a road trip to a place you have fond memories of. Pull out old photos, look up a loved teacher and thank them, or make contact with a friend from the past. This kind of time travel can remind you who you are and reunite you with happier times. It can also put into perspective how far you have come and what you have achieved.

Explore

Most of us gravitate to the same places over and over again. We tend to visit the same areas, take the same routes, shop at the same supermarket.

Shake it up a little.

Change your route to work or school. Take public transport instead of driving. If you are walking regularly, go somewhere you've never been before. Buy your groceries somewhere else. Take a drive to a place you have been meaning to check out, the beach, the countryside or just a different side of town. It may be a welcome break from the monotony of your surroundings and a bit of a holiday from yourself.

Massage, meditate and mindfulness

Book a massage, attend a meditation or yoga class, or see if you can find a mindfulness app. There are heaps of resources online. Massage chairs and the hand-held massagers are a godsend if you are not up to face-to-face contact. Any regular armchair can be turned into a massage chair with the help of massage pad/cushion draped over it. They pay themselves off after a few uses. You can buy them online – even on Ebay.

YouTube has some wonderful yoga sessions available. You don't even need to walk out your front door if you are not up to facing people; prop your laptop somewhere you can see it, make a space and you're good to get bendy. Laughter yoga is also recommended.

Of course you can go out and get a massage. If you a) have the money b) can get yourself out of the house c) are okay with a stranger touching you. The benefit of the home massage devices is that they are cheap, don't require another person and are available straight away. Some people love doing things one on one or in groups, others prefer to be at home and on their own.

Another really simple thing many we know have had unexpected comfort from in the dark depths of winter are electric blankets and electric throw rugs. Electric throw rugs work just like your regular electric blanket but they are colourful fluffy things that you throw over you or under you wherever you are sitting. The added bonus is that they are cheap to run. Perfect for people who are sitting still in rooms that are a bit nippy. The warm electric blanket gives you the feeling of being cuddled. Sometimes when you are not feeling that well you don't want the pressure of having to communicate with another human and it's a great relief being able to self soothe with a little cuddly warmth.

Anxiety blanket

Check out weighted blankets. They're blankets made heavy by being weighted down with rice, micro glass beads or *poly pellets*. These blankets are based on deep touch therapy and are particularly effective for anxiety, insomnia, distress and restless legs. They were originally designed for people on the autism spectrum but are being used by many people and therapists to assist in different ways.

The most common response from people when it's put it on them is 'it feels like I am being hugged'. Again, they are not for everyone, but if you find the feeling of weight on top of you comforting, they may be for you. In the same way babies feel calm and secure when they are swaddled, the pressure from these blankets makes the body produce serotonin and endorphins.

Write

It's fantastic that the medicinal benefits of journaling are now well known and these days are commonly promoted by mental health care professionals. Gratitude diaries were a big thing a few years ago and now scribbling down your thoughts, emotions and feelings on a page is one of the first things people suggest to assist processing. Writing works the same way therapy does. It's a process where we create a narrative that makes sense to us.

Other than the obvious cathartic effect of writing, many have found increased optimism by focusing on gratitude. The liberation of taking control of your own personal narrative by documenting your ups and downs is a valuable resource. It helps you understand your stages and phases, reminds you of what helps and that it doesn't last forever.

If you have a story you need to get out join, a writers group, author talk or attend a masterclass. There are many excellent books, apps and websites on writing too. Some with fabulous exercises and writing prompts. Julia Cameron's book *The Artist's Way* talks about Morning Pages for creative people. Three pages of stream of consciousness scribbled as soon as you wake up.

She suggests it for creativity but many have found it's excellent for anxiety and depression as well.

Me time

Take yourself on a date. Somewhere quiet where you can be alone. There are countless very cheap and sometimes free places you can go. Museums, movies, galleries, libraries, talks, parks, zoos, aquariums etc. Google, ask around and check out the newspapers. Show yourself a good time and just absorb and wander around. No pressure. Take in the magnitude of what life is and surrender for a while.

If you're inspired, take a sketchbook, dictaphone or a notepad so you can draw, write or make some audio notes. Take some snaps and be a photojournalist for the day. You never know what will help you process or find some relief from how you've been feeling.

Do something with your hands

What were the things you enjoyed doing as a child? Sewing, woodwork, macramé, cooking, leather work, knitting, drawing, tying knots, scrapbooking, crochet or fiddling around with electronics? Head off to a hobby shop, hardware store or haberdashery. Having a little project to do can occupy and distract you, connect you with positive associations from your past and give you a sense of achievement and satisfaction. If you can't shift your mood you can distract yourself with a bit of 'making' while you wait for the black cloud to lift.

Solving little puzzles and problems often helps unknot our emotions.

Get your shit together

How about attempting to complete a small doable project where you clean, sort or organise something in your home or office? Choose something small, cleaning out your wardrobe, sorting your tax, cleaning out the pantry, organising under the sink, even sorting out a drawer or a shelf if the thought of your whole chest of drawers or your whole bookcase is too hard. Being the agent of a small sense of order can create a circuit breaker. Focus on making a brick not building a wall.

The Japanese are a clutterless society obsessed with Zen and associate it with a sense of inner calm. Chuck some stuff out. Be ruthless. In the bin, off to a good home or take it to a charity shop. Marie Kondo's book *Spark Joy: An Illustrated Guide to the Japanese Art of Tidying* has been a massive best-seller. Her take is to hold each of your items in your hand. If it doesn't 'spark joy' thank the item for its service and move it on.

Water therapy

Have a bath. Go for a swim. Visit the pool. Head off to a spa. Try a floatation tank experience. Take a walk on the beach and if you are feeling game have a dip. Find a waterfall, creek, lake or river, sit close and watch. Water is a balm. Think laterally. Dive in. Cold plunge tubs for the win!

Sex toys

Buy some new sex toys or get out your favourite ones. Self-pleasure is such an important part of self-care. Single, dating or in a relationship, sex toys can be pleasure portals for some 'me time' or to enjoy with your partner/s. Often when you are in a funk your libido is far, far away. Many people would prefer to self-pleasure even if they have a partner because there is less expectation. Purchase a lovely new toy and plan a romantic night in with yourself. And don't forget to text yourself in the morning.

Do a digital detox

One of the things that can increase anxiety and depression is the 24-hour news cycle. Try a digital detox and go off all information for a bit. If you can't manage that then just steer clear of news.

Keep a note in your pocket

When you are unwell you should treat yourself like a very kind person would treat a sick child. Early nights, lots of kindness, yummy nutritious food, a cosy bed and lots to drink and plenty of 'hygge'. (Hygge is a Danish word that means cosiness, a complete absence of anything annoying or overwhelming).

Most people who manage mental illness are very good at counselling and supporting. One thing we have found transformative is to write a note and put it in your pocket to be that supportive helpful person to yourself.

So here's what you do. You write a note to yourself. A few lines or so like 'emotions change, feelings are not fact, this is just how it is now' or 'just keep going' or 'close your eyes and breathe'. Put the note in your pocket and take it out a couple of times during the day and read it. You can even rewrite it and put it back in your pocket. When you go to bed, put it in your pillowcase and as soon as you wake in the morning take it out and keep it on you. 'How does this work?' you may ask. It seems to stop the ruminating, the racing mind, and the sense of dread. It acts as a kind of circuit breaker. It's as if your pocket is doing the self-talk for you. Give it a go. A study found a note in the pocket is more effective to help people lose weight than a dieting and exercise program.

Marijuana and alcohol

If medical marijuana is something you'd like to pursue, then talk to your doctor. If they believe it will help you, they will explain the laws and discuss whether you can gain legal access.

While we're on the topic of recreational drugs, small amounts of alcohol can also relieve anxiety – it works like diazepam

(Valium). Sometimes it's great for episodic anxiety, such as anxiety around public speaking – but sometimes this leads to a path of addiction. Steve once saw an 83-year-old woman with severe liver failure from alcohol. She'd been a teetotaller until the age of fifty-two when her husband died suddenly. Her doctor had recommended she have a nip of her husband's leftover whisky each night to calm her nerves and grief. She never stopped. The nips increased, and by the age of eighty-three she was on half a bottle per day and very unwell.

Self-awareness and common sense (check yourself before you wreck yourself) are key.

Remember: most things are harmful in excessive amounts. We die without water, but too much can drown us.

Read

Steve's not a fan of self-help books himself but he loves recommending them to others. Steve is more a fiction guy because it's distracting.

At one point when Dev was depressed, she was so desperate for anything that would help alleviate the pain that she walked into a bookstore and spent $350 on self-help books. Don't knock it!

Here is a list of a few books you may find helpful, but there are millions of potentials. Pop online, head down to a bookshop or visit the library and have a browse. Sometimes even just a line in a book can be a personal turning point of understanding, integration, revelation, liberation or healing. An 'aha' moment. An audible click. A sizeable shift.

- *The Upward Spiral*, Alex Korb
- *The Brain That Changes Itself,* Norman Doidge
- *The Power of Now*, Eckhart Tolle
- *The Consolations of Philosophy*, Alain de Botton
- *The Drama of Being a Child*, Alice Miller
- *Madness: A Memoir*, Kate Richards
- *The Prophet*, Kahlil Gibran
- *The Noonday Demon*, Andrew Solomon
- *Darkness Visible*, William Styron
- *The Happiness Trap*, Russ Harris
- *Too Soon Old, Too Late Smart,* Gordon Livingston
- *I Had a Black Dog*, Matthew Johnstone
- *Oh, the Places You'll Go!* Dr Seuss

*

Hopefully you'll find this list useful. We're sure there will be some things you've tried, some things that appeal to you and others that don't grab you at all. Keep this list handy, because you never know: one day something that doesn't appeal on first read could be just the tonic to help you through.

Final Words

The most urgent task is the showing of gratitude. Thank you so much for buying this book, reading this book, reading bits of this book, or even just picking this book up and thinking, 'I don't need to read another book, I need to see a professional for a chat about feeling happier and healthier,' and then putting the book back down again.

We mean it: from both of us, a heartfelt thank you, and a hug from Dev (Steve's not a hugger: he'll just shake your hand). Simply engaging with this topic shows you are interested in destigmatising mental health issues, informing yourself and trying to find ways to create greater enjoyment in life for you and the people you love.

We were motivated to write this book to let people know they are not alone and that there is help. We want to show people there are ways to transform pain, grief, trauma and sadness through therapies, medications and education. When you are unwell or someone you know is unwell, it's exhausting and overwhelming. Our hope is that *Mental* manages to make some sense of it all.

As much as we'd love it to, *Mental* doesn't have all the answers.

There is no magic wand, but there is a valuable, satisfying path to a place that makes more sense, and thousands of skilled and experienced people who are enthusiastic to help. This book is the start of a conversation, not the end. We hope it initiates many chats in the pub, at the kitchen table, around the water cooler, in the staff room, and online.

Feeling you have no control over a situation has a crippling effect. We wrote *Mental* to help you feel like you can take control. We were also determined to convey the optimism we feel about mental illness. Mental illness is too often portrayed with a sense of despair, as if it's a life sentence. Nothing could be further from the truth. Virtually everyone improves with help, and most of the help is relatively easy to access.

Humans are funny animals and we are all muddling our way through. We hope this book gives you a few 'aha' moments, some practical help and a feeling of liberation. We hope *Mental* helps you seek help – we've both experienced, and seen in others, the transformative magic of asking for help.

We hope you found *Mental* useful. If there is anything you think is wrong, or not quite right, feel free to contact us.

You can't stop the waves but you can learn to surf.

Jon Kabat-Zinn

See you out in the surf,
Steve and Dev

References

2 WHAT CAUSES MENTAL ILLNESS?

'A large-scale study in 2016': Craig L. Hyde, Michael W. Nagle, Chao Tian, Xing Chen et al., 'Identification of 15 genetic loci associated with risk of major depression in individuals of European descent', *Nature Genetics*, vol. 48, 2016, pp. 1031–6.

6 DEPRESSION

NICE Clinical Guideline: Depression in adults: recognition and management, 2018. NICE guideline CG90

'Potential benefits of sadness': based on J.P. Forgas, 'Don't worry, be sad! On the cognitive, motivational, and interpersonal benefits of negative mood' *Current Directions in Psychological Science*, vol. 22, 2013, pp. 225–32.

'GPs miss depression about half the time': N. Sartorius, T.B. Ustun, Y. Lecrubier & H.V. Wittchen, 'Depression comorbid with anxiety: Results from the WHO study on psychological disorders in primary health care', *British Journal of Psychiatry*, 1996, vol. 168 Suppl. 30, pp. S38–S43.

'Things you need to know if you choose to take an anti-depressant': Adapted from Ellen et al., 'Depression and anxiety: Pharmacological treatment in general practice', *Australian Family Physician*, vol. 36, no. 3, March 2007.

7 ANXIETY

'Over half the people presenting with anxiety present with physical symptoms': D. Goldberg, 'Epidemiology of mental disorders in primary care settings', *Epidemiologic Reviews*, 1995, vol. 17, pp. 182–90.

'The strongest links between anxiety and alcohol abuse are for PTSD, panic and GAD': Joshua P. Smith & Carrie L. Randall, 'Anxiety and Alcohol Use Disorders: Comorbidity and Treatment Considerations', *Current Reviews*, vol. 34, no. 4.

8 PSYCHOSIS

'High potency cannabis and the risk of psychosis': Di Forti M. et al., *British Journal of Psychiatry*, 2009, 195: 488–491.

NICE Clinical Guideline: Psychosis and schizophrenia in adults, 2014. NICE guideline CG178.

'A group in the UK': D. Nutt, L.A. King, W. Saulsbury & C. Blakemore, 'Development of a rational scale to assess the harm of drugs of potential misuse', *Lancet*, 2007, vol. 369, no. 9566, pp. 1047–53.

9 ADDICTION

'Deaths related to drug poisoning: results for England and Wales 1993–2013': Office for National Statistics, *Health Statistics Quarterly*, 2013.

'One new drug a year': Royal College of Psychiatrists 2014: FR/AP/02.

Psychoactive Substances Bill 2015: Home Office of the United Kingdom.

The Misuse of Substances Act 1971: Parliament of the United Kingdom.

Sedatives previously prescribed too often: Trevor R. Norman, Steven R. Ellen & Graham D. Burrows, 'Benzodiazepines in anxiety disorders: Managing therapeutics and dependence', *Medical Journal of Australia*, 1997, vol. 167, pp. 490–5.

Transtheoretical model: J.O. Prochaska, C.C. DiClemente, 'The transtheoretical approach' in J.C. Norcross & M.R. Goldfried (eds), *Handbook of Psychotherapy Integration*, 2nd edn, New York: Oxford University Press, 2005, pp. 147–71.

'Royal Australian and New Zealand College of Psychiatrists clinical practice guidelines for the treatment of schizophrenia and related disorders', *Australian and New Zealand Journal of Psychiatry*, 2005, vol. 39, pp. 1–30.

10 SUICIDE

'Rates and predictors of mental illness in LGB men and women': results from a survey based in England and Wales, *British Journal of Psychiatry*, 2004, 185: 479–85.

World Health Organization suicide estimates: D. Leo, E. Cerin, K. Spathonis & S. Burgis, 'Lifetime risk of suicide ideation and attempts in an Australian community: prevalence, suicidal process, and help-seeking behaviour', *Journal of Affective Disorders*, 2005, June, vol. 86, nos. 2–3, pp. 215–24.

Previous suicide attempt figures: H. Christensen & K. Petrie, 'Suicide prevention: Signposts for a new approach', *Medical Journal of Australia*, 2013, vol. 198, no. 9, pp. 472–4.

14 CHILD AND ADOLESCENT MENTAL HEALTH

NICE Clinical Guideline: Depression in Children and young people: Identification and management in primary, community and secondary care, 2015. NICE guideline CG28.

19 MEDICATIONS

NICE Clinical Guideline: Antenatal and postnatal mental health.NICE Guideline CG192.

Tables adapted from Psychotropic Expert Group, *Therapeutic Guidelines: Psychotropic*, version 7, Melbourne: Therapeutic Guidelines Limited, 2013.

Chlorpromazine: J. Cade, *Mending the Mind: A short history of twentieth-century psychiatry*, Melbourne: Sun Books, 1979.

Resources

NHS Services *www.nhs.uk*
General information about all NHS services.
NHS 111 Online
www.111.nhs.uk (Tel. 111)
To seek immediate medical help for yourself or others call NHS 111. This number is not for emergencies.
999 *(Tel. 999)*
Call 999 in a medical emergency. This is when someone is seriously ill or injured and their life is at risk.
Samaritans *www.samaritans.org (Tel. 116 123)*
A 24-hour free helpline that anyone can call to talk to someone in their own way about whatever is getting to them.
SANEline *www.sane.org.uk (Tel. 0300 304 7000)*
A national out-of-hours mental health helpline offering specialist emotional support, guidance and information to anyone affected by mental illness, including family, friends and carers.

Medical Register
www.gmc-uk.org/ registration-and-licensing
You can search the registration status of all 280,000 doctors practising in the UK online.
General Medical Council
www.gmc-uk.org
A website that helps protect patients and improve UK medical education and practice by supporting students, doctors, educators and healthcare providers.
World Psychiatric Association
www.wpanet.org
An association of national psychiatric societies aimed to increase knowledge and skills necessary for work in the field of mental health and the care for the mentally ill.
British Psychological Society
www.bps.org.uk
Resources to help you learn about psychology, the work that psychologists do and how to find a psychologist if you need support.

Turning Point *www.turning-point.co.uk (Tel. 0207 481 7600)*
A national health and social care provider, with information and advice for friends and family.

Rethink Mental Illness *www.rethink.org (Tel. 0300 5000 927)*
National voluntary organisation that helps people with any severe mental illness, their families and carers.

Support in Mind Scotland
www.supportinmindscotland.org.uk (Tel. 0131 662 4359)
Works to improve the wellbeing and quality of life of people affected by serious mental illness. This includes those who are family members, carers and supporters.

Shine *www.shine.ie*
A service supporting people affected by mental ill health in Ireland.

Mental Health Ireland
www.mentalhealthireland.ie
Provides help to those who are mentally ill and promotes positive mental health in Ireland.

British National Formulary (BNF) *www.bnf.org*
An alphabetical directory of drugs with an entry for every drug with information on dosage and side-effects.

Electronic Medicines Compendium (EMC)
www.medicines.org.uk
This website stores a copy of all approved drug information leaflets.

UK Psychological Trauma Society (formerly UK Trauma Group) *www.ukpts.co.uk*
Clinical network of UK Traumatic Stress Services.

British Association for Behavioural and Cognitive Psychotherapies (BABCP)
www.babcp.com
(Tel. 0161 705 4306)
The lead organisation for CBT in the UK and Ireland. Has a UK register of accredited therapists.

Depression Alliance
www.depressionalliance.org
(Tel. 0845 123 23 20)
Information, support and understanding for people who suffer from depression, and for relatives who want to help. Self-help groups, information, and raising awareness for depression.

Depression UK
www.depressionuk.org
A national mutual support group for people suffering from depression.

Aware *www.aware.ie*
(Tel. 1890 303 302)
Provides information and support to people affected by depression and bipolar disorder in Ireland and Northern Ireland.

Gofal *www.gofal.org.uk*
(Tel. 029 2069 2891)
A Welsh organisation which supports people affected by mental health issues including depression.

Anxiety UK *www.anxietyuk.org. uk (Tel. 08444 775 774)*
A charity for those affected by all anxiety disorders.

No Panic *www.nopanic.org.uk (Tels. 0844 967 4848; Youth Helpline: 01753 840393 – 13 to 20 year olds)*
National Organisation for Phobias, Anxiety, Neurosis, Information and Care. Support for sufferers of Panic Attacks, Phobias, Obsessive Compulsive Disorder, Generalised Anxiety Disorder and Tranquilliser Withdrawal.

Paranoid Thoughts
www.paranoidthoughts.com
This website is all about unfounded paranoid or excessive fears about others.

MDF The Bipolar Organisation
www.mdf.org.uk (Tel. 0207 931 6480)
A user-led charity working to enable people affected by bipolar disorder to take control of their lives.

Bipolar UK *www.bipolaruk.org (Tel. 0333 323 3880)*
Provides support, advice and information for people with bipolar disorder, their friends and carers.

Bipolar Fellowship Scotland
www.bipolarscotland.org.uk (Tel. 0141 560 2050)
Provides information, support and advice for people affected by bipolar disorder and all who care for them. Promotes self-help throughout Scotland, and informs and educates about the illness and the organisation.

Emergence
www.emergenceplus.org.uk
Emergence is a service user-led organisation supporting all people affected by a diagnosis of personality disorder.

Personality disorder
www.personalitydisorder.org.uk
A website that provides information, resources and learning opportunities for those with a personality disorder and their carers.

Alzheimer's Society
www.alzheimers.org.uk (Tel. 0300 222 11 22)
Services, support and information for those suffering from dementia and their carers.

Selfharm UK
www.selfharm.co.uk
A project dedicated to supporting young people who are affected by self-harm.

Self Injury Support
www.selfinjurysupport.org.uk (Tel. 0808 800 8088)
Provides a young women's text and email service, any age helpline for women who self harm, UK-wide listings for self harm support and self help tools.

Alcoholics Anonymous
www.alcoholics-anonymous.org.uk (Tel. 0800 9177 650)
Contact details for all English AA

meetings and general information about AA and alcoholism.

Alcohol Concern
www.alcoholconcern.org.uk
(Tel. 020 7566 9800)
National agency on alcohol misuse which works to reduce the incidence and costs of alcohol-related harm and to increase the range and quality of services available to people with alcohol-related problems.

Drink Aware
www.drinkaware.co.uk
An independent charity working to reduce alcohol misuse and harm in the UK

Drinkline – National Alcohol Helpline *(Tel. 0300 123 1110)*
If you're worried about your own or someone else's drinking, contact Drinkline for a confidential conversation.

Al-Anon *www.al-anonuk.org.uk*
(Tel. 020 7403 0888)
Groups that offer support to anyone whose life is, or has been, affected by someone else's drinking.

Addaction *www.addaction.org.uk*
(Tel. 020 7251 5860)
A specialist drug and alcohol treatment charity. Their addiction services are free and confidential.

Narcotics Anonymous UK
www.ukna.org (Tel. 0300 999 1212)
NA is a non-profit society of men and women for whom drugs had become a major problem.

B-eat (formerly the Eating Disorders Association)
www.b-eat.co.uk (Tels. 0845 634 1414 for adults; 0845 634 7650 – youth helpline for under 25s)
B-eat is the UK's leading charity supporting anyone affected by eating disorders or issues with food, including families and friends.

Bodywhys *www.bodywhys.ie*
(Tel. 1890 200 444)
Support services for eating disorders in Ireland.

DWED (Diabetics with eating disorders website)
www.dwed.org.uk
The only current charity in the UK that supports and advocates for people that struggle with both type 1 diabetes and any kind of eating disorder.

MGEDT (Men get eating disorders too)
www.mengetedstoo.co.uk
A national charity dedicated to representing and supporting the needs of men with eating disorders.

Pandas Foundation
www.pandasfoundation.org.uk
(Tel. 0843 2898401)
An organisation that helps individuals and their families with pre- and postnatal depression advice and support. They also offer support to families in the antenatal period.

Association for Postnatal Depression *www.apni.org*
(Tel. 020 7386 0868)
Provides support to mothers

suffering from post-natal illness including a helpline.

Cry-sis *www.cry-sis.org.uk* *(Tel. 08451 228669)*
Provides self-help and support for families with excessively crying and sleepless and demanding babies.

Home Start *www.home-start.org. uk (Tel. 0800 068 6368)*
Support and practical help for families with at least one child under-five. Help offered to parents finding it hard to cope for many reasons. These include PND or other mental illness, isolation, bereavement, illness of parent or child.

Family Action *www.family-action. org.uk (Tel. 020 7254 6251)*
Support and practical help for families affected by mental illness, including 'Newpin' services offering support to parents of children under-five whose mental health is affecting their ability to provide safe parenting *(Tel. 0808 808 4994)*.

YoungMinds *www.youngminds.org.uk* *(Tel. 0808 802 5544)*
A parents' information service about children and young people's mental health.

Childline *www.childline.org.uk* *(Tel. 0800 1111)*
Free national helpline for young people, free confidential advice on all sorts of problems.

Get Connected *www.hatw.co.uk/ helpline/get-connected* *(Tel. 0808 808 4994)*
A helpline for people under 25 who self-harm.

Papyrus *www.papyrus.org.uk* *(Tel. 0800 068 41 41)*
A charity for the prevention of young suicide with a professionally staffed helpline providing support, practical advice and information to young people worried about themselves, and to anyone concerned that a young person may harm themselves.

Index